Lecture Notes in Economics and Mathematical Systems

Operations Research, Computer Science, Social Science

Edited by M. Beckmann, Providence and H. P. Künzi, Zürich

66

F. Bauer · P. Garabedian
D. Korn

A Theory of Supercritical Wing Sections, with Computer Programs and Examples

Springer-Verlag
Berlin · Heidelberg · New York 1972

Dr. Frances Bauer

Prof. Paul Garabedian

Dr. David Korn

Courant Institute
of Mathematical Sciences

251 Mercer Street
New York, N. Y. 10012 / USA

Work supported by NASA under Grant NGR-33-016-167.
Computations performed at the AEC Computing and
Applied Mathematics Center, New York University,
under Contract AT(30-1)-1480. Reproduction in whole
or in part is permitted for any purpose of the
United States Government.

AMS Subject Classifikations (1970): 76H05, 76G05, 76Jxx, 76N05, 65M05, 35M05, 30A88

ISBN 3-540-05807-9 Springer-Verlag Berlin · Heidelberg · New York
ISBN 0-387-05807-9 Springer-Verlag New York · Heidelberg · Berlin

Preface

At present, there is considerable interest in supercritical wing
technology for the development of aircraft designed to fly near the
speed of sound. The basic principle is the suppression of boundary
layer separation by shifting the shock waves that occur on the wing
toward the trailing edge and making them as weak as possible. The
purpose of this report is to make available to the engineering public
mathematical methods for the design of supercritical wings. These
methods depend on the numerical solution of the partial differential
equations of two-dimensional gas dynamics. The main contribution is
a computer program for the design of shockless transonic airfoils
using the hodograph transformation and analytic continuation into the
complex domain. Another contribution is a program for the analysis
of transonic flow with shocks past an airfoil at off-design conditions.
In our design work we include a turbulent boundary layer correction.

Part I of the paper is devoted to a description of the mathematical theory and need not be studied by those primarily concerned with
running the programs. Part II is a manual for users of our programs
which is independent of the theoretical part. In Part III and in
Appendices II and III we give numerical examples and discuss computational results. The main substance of the report, however, is
contained in the listing of the computer programs themselves in
Appendix IV. We have used the Fortran language throughout and we
have included numerous comment cards in the listing.

This work has been supported by NASA under Grant NGR-33-016-167
and the AEC under Contract AT(30-1)-1480 with NYU. We should like to

express our appreciation to Richard Whitcomb, Anthony Jameson and Donald MacKenzie for helpful suggestions. Norman Kashdan assisted with coding and programming, Frances Beard patiently prepared the first draft, and Connie Engle carefully did the final typescript.

New York, N. Y.

January 1972

Contents

I. THEORY

1. <u>Introduction</u>.

In this paper we investigate a technique of computing airfoil sections that permit shock-free transonic flow around them at a specific Mach number and angle of attack. By transonic we mean that the speed of the aircraft is less than the speed of sound, but close enough to it so that on top of the wing, where the airflow is fastest, the Mach number becomes greater than one. For air the Reynolds number is extremely high, and hence the viscous effects will be confined chiefly to a thin boundary layer provided separation effects can be suppressed. Therefore we take for our equations of motion the equations of potential flow.

The fundamental problem is to find smooth, transonic, steady solutions to the equations of irrotational motion of an inviscid, compressible fluid about an airfoil section in two dimensions. Two main difficulties arise in analyzing this problem. First of all, the partial differential equations of motion are nonlinear. This difficulty can be avoided by using characteristic coordinates in the hodograph plane, where the equations become linear. The second difficulty arises when the speed becomes supersonic, since the equations change from elliptic to hyperbolic type. It has been shown by Morawetz [18] that smooth transonic solutions to the equations of motion do not exist for all airfoil shapes. It follows that the problem of computing shock-free transonic flow past a given profile is not well posed. We overcome the latter difficulty by solving an inverse problem. We compute a smooth transonic flow and then find the body which generates it. To calculate smooth solutions we extend all the variables into the complex domain, a procedure that has been used successfully on the detached shock problem (cf. [10,14,27]). Then we solve a characteristic initial value problem along the complex characteristics. This procedure can be carried out well on an electronic computer.

The problem has gained new impetus because of the recent experimental success (cf. [13,22,25,29]) in achieving virtually shock-free flow in wind tunnel tests. The most recent work employing the hodograph method has been done at the National Aerospace Laboratory (NLR) in Amsterdam. Nieuwland [21] has expanded on the work of Lighthill [17] and has developed a technique of computing thin quasi-elliptical airfoil sections. He pieces together series solutions for the stream function found by separation of variables. A catalogue of flows arrived at by this method is presented by Boerstoel [2]. Experiments in a wind tunnel by Spee and Uijlenhoet [25] show agreement with the theory, thus proving the validity of these solutions. In addition they show that the solutions have a certain amount of stability to fluctuations in speed and angle of attack.

The method used in this paper is similar to the above techniques in that they all use an inverse method based on the hodograph transformation. However, the methods differ widely in other ways. Our method uses finite differences to solve a characteristic initial value problem in complex space as opposed to computing series. We will see that the whole supersonic region can be computed by choosing one set of initial paths. The characteristics of the flow are readily obtained by our procedure and thus the occurrence and location of limiting lines is easily detected. The single-valuedness of the solution in the physical plane is assured by the manner of construction of a singular solution. We are able to compute solutions for any set of initial data in about one minute of CDC 6600 machine time.

In Section 2 we discuss the inverse problem, write the equations of motion in matrix form, and examine their type. All of the variables are extended into the complex domain in Section 3, and the concept of conjugate coordinates is discussed. Characteristic

coordinates are introduced in Section 4 and the equations of motion
are rewritten in characteristic form. Section 5 is a digression on
incompressible flow and the choice of initial data. In Section 6
we show how to find a compressible flow by combining a regular
solution with a singular solution that is related to the fundamental
solution in the hodograph plane. A particular choice of characteristic coordinates is made in analogy with the formulation in Section 5.
A closed form solution of the characteristic transformation is
presented. Simplifications which result from neglecting circulation
are discussed. Section 7 contains a description of the finite difference scheme used to compute solutions of the equations numerically.
We show how to choose paths of initial data which yield the solution
in the subsonic portion of the flow. We introduce the so-called sonic
locus (cf. [27]) in Section 8 and explain how it is used to continue
the solution into the supersonic zone by means of a special set of
initial characteristic paths which yield the whole supersonic zone
outside the body. A brief discussion of the singularities that can
arise in the hodograph transformation appears in Section 9. In
Section 10 we explain how we can prescribe certain arcs of the profile
in the hodograph plane and how we impose the Kutta-Joukowski condition.
In Section 11 we describe briefly how the boundary layer correction
in the design program is made and in Section 12 analysis calculations
are discussed for assessing the behavior of the flow at off-design
conditions.

2. The Inverse Problem of Design.

The approach to a physical problem is quite often simplified by
considering an inverse problem. Determination of the flow around an
airfoil flying at fixed speed is considered a direct problem because
the flow produced is determined by the body. From physical considera-
tions alone it is expected that for any body there is always some flow

produced, although the flow need not be steady or laminar. The
inverse problem consists in calculating a fluid flow and then determining the body which produces it. In practice this means solving a
suitable set of flow equations rather than finding an actual fluid
flow. It cannot be argued that for every solution there must exist
a body which would generate such a flow.

The word flow has been used rather generally in the above
description. Here we will consider two-dimensional, steady,
isentropic, irrotational flow of an inviscid, polytropic gas. The
equations of motion of such a flow are standard in the literature
[3,23]. We let x and y be Cartesian coordinates and let u and v be
the velocity components in the corresponding directions. The density
will be denoted by ρ and the pressure by p. The equation of state
for a polytropic gas is

$$(2.1) \qquad\qquad p = A\rho^\gamma$$

where A and γ are constants. For air $\gamma = 1.4$. The local sound speed
is defined to be $(dp/d\rho)^{1/2}$ and is denoted by c. With this notation
the equations of motion are

$$(2.2A) \qquad\qquad (c^2-u^2)u_x - uv(u_y+v_x) + (c^2-v^2)v_y = 0$$

$$(2.2B) \qquad\qquad v_x - u_y = 0$$

We also have Bernoulli's equation

$$(2.3) \qquad\qquad q^2 + \frac{2}{\gamma-1} c^2 = \hat{q}^2 ; \qquad q^2 = u^2 + v^2$$

where $\hat{q}$ is the limit speed, so c and p are functions of q only.

The fact that mass is conserved is expressed by the continuity
equation

(2.4) $$(\rho u)_x + (\rho v)_y = 0$$

which has been used in the derivation of (2.2A). This equation implies the existence of a stream function ψ such that

(2.5) $$\rho_0 \psi_x = \rho v \; ; \qquad \rho_0 \psi_y = - \rho u$$

where ρ_0 is the stagnation density.

In order for $u(x,y)$, $v(x,y)$ to be a solution to the direct problem of flow around a given airfoil flying at velocity $u = u_\infty$, $v = 0$, we require that u and v have the following properties:

A. $u(x,y)$, $v(x,y)$ is a solution of (2.2A-B).

B. $\psi = \psi_0$ along the airfoil, where ψ_0 is the value of the stream function at stagnation. We shall take $\psi_0 = 0$.

C. As the distance from the airfoil becomes infinite, u approaches u_∞ and v approaches 0.

D. The speed q remains finite.

E. $u(x,y)$, $v(x,y)$ are continuous.

Morawetz [18] has shown that in the transonic case such a solution does not exist for every given profile. Thus the problem is not well posed. It is expected that an existence and uniqueness theorem could be established if requirement E were modified to include discontinuous solutions which satisfy the jump conditions for a shock, subject to a suitable entropy inequality. If the airfoil has a cusped tail, condition D, implying the Kutta-Joukowski condition, presumably ensures uniqueness.

For the inverse problem we calculate an arbitrary solution $u(x,y)$, $v(x,y)$ of (2.2A-B) which also satisfies properties C and E, and we examine the streamline $\psi = \psi_0$. If this streamline encloses some bounded region and condition D is satisfied outside that region, then the region can be interpreted as an airfoil for which $u(x,y)$, $v(x,y)$

is the solution of the direct problem.

To use this method for generating solutions to the inverse problem we must prescribe the speed at infinity and a parameter related to the lift. An arbitrary analytic function is chosen and by use of the method outlined in this paper we associate with it a solution to (2.2A-B) which satisfies property C. The solution obtained is locally analytic but may have certain singularities. In practice the arbitrary function is assigned by specifying a set of parameters, such as the coefficients of a power series. Some of these parameters may be fixed by requiring the solution to satisfy various constraints. For example we may specify the curvature at the nose and the velocity at the trailing edge, in which case the parameters necessary to satisfy these requirements are to be found automatically. If $\psi = \psi_0$ encloses a bounded region and there are no singularities of the solution outside this region, then the solution represents flow around an airfoil.

It is convenient to represent equations (2.2A-B) in the matrix notation

$$(2.6) \qquad \begin{pmatrix} c^2-u^2 & -uv \\ 0 & 1 \end{pmatrix} \begin{pmatrix} u \\ v \end{pmatrix}_x + \begin{pmatrix} -uv & c^2-v^2 \\ -1 & 0 \end{pmatrix} \begin{pmatrix} u \\ v \end{pmatrix}_y = \begin{pmatrix} 0 \\ 0 \end{pmatrix}$$

which is of the form

$$(2.7) \qquad\qquad SU_x + TU_y = 0$$

The type of such a first order system is determined by examining the two roots λ_+ and λ_- of the equation

$$(2.8) \qquad\qquad \text{Det} (S\lambda + T) = 0$$

from which we find that

$$(2.9) \qquad \lambda_{\pm} = \frac{uv \pm c\sqrt{q^2-c^2}}{c^2-u^2}$$

When both roots are real and unequal the system is hyperbolic, while
if the two roots are complex conjugates the system is elliptic. We
call the dimensionless quantity $\frac{q}{c}$ the Mach number and denote it by M.
Clearly both roots of (2.9) are real and unequal when $M > 1$, while
for $M < 1$ the two roots are complex conjugates. For $M = 1$ the roots
are real and equal. From Bernoulli's equation (2.3) we see that the
locus of points in the hodograph plane where $M = 1$ is a circle
$q = $ constant. We call this constant the critical speed and denote it
by c_*. The critical speed is related to the limit speed by the
equation

$$(2.10) \qquad c_* = \mu\hat{q} \; ; \qquad \mu^2 = \frac{\gamma-1}{\gamma+1}$$

For $q > c_*$, $M > 1$ and the flow is supersonic, while for $q < c_*$,
$M < 1$ and it is subsonic.

For supersonic flow λ_+ and λ_- are real and the equations are
hyperbolic. In this case the initial value problem (x and y assigned
along any noncharacteristic curve) and the characteristic initial
value problem (x or y assigned along one characteristic of each
family) are well posed. For subsonic flow λ_+ and λ_- are complex
conjugates and the equations are elliptic. The initial value problem
and the characteristic initial value problem are no longer well posed
in the real domain in this case, and we generally assign boundary
values to formulate a correctly set problem. We are concerned here
with transonic flow, that is, with flow that is partly subsonic and
partly supersonic. We shall be primarily interested in studying the
inverse problem of designing airfoils for shockless flow by constructing solutions of (2.7) that satisfy a characteristic initial value

problem in the complex domain.

3. Complex Extension and the Schwarz Reflection Principle.

In constructing solutions of (2.7) use can be made of the fact
that all the functions in the coefficient matrices S and T are analytic in all of their arguments. This property enables us to extend
the domain of definition of these equations from the real (x,y)-plane
to a four-dimensional domain $x = x_1 + ix_2$, $y = y_1 + iy_2$, where
x_1, x_2, y_1 and y_2 are real. In other words we allow x and y to take on
complex values. In this procedure of complex extension all of the
functions occurring in the coefficient matrices are defined over the
complex domain by analytic continuation. The solutions u and v must
be analytic and will also take on complex values.

We introduce new independent variables z, z^* in the complex
domain by setting

(3.1) $z = x + iy$, $z^* = x - iy$

so that

(3.2) $x = \dfrac{z + z^*}{2}$, $y = \dfrac{z - z^*}{2i}$

In this substitution both x and y are real, i.e. $x_2 = y_2 = 0$, if and
only if $z^* = \bar{z}$ is the complex conjugate of z. We call any pair of
complex coordinates ξ, η with the property that x and y are real when
$\xi = \bar{\eta}$ conjugate coordinates. In particular if we let F be a complex
analytic function which is real on the real axis, then $\xi = F(z)$,
$\eta = F(z^*)$ are conjugate coordinates because by the Schwarz reflection
principle we have $F(z) = \overline{F(\bar{z})}$.

Let ξ and η be conjugate coordinates and assume that $G(\xi, \eta)$ is
analytic in each of its arguments. Then we can express $G(\xi, \eta)$ in
the form

(3.3) $$G(\xi,\eta) = R(\xi,\eta) + iI(\xi,\eta)$$

where

(3.4A) $$R(\xi,\eta) = \frac{1}{2}[G(\xi,\eta) + \overline{G(\overline{\eta},\overline{\xi})}]$$

(3.4B) $$I(\xi,\eta) = \frac{1}{2i}[G(\xi,\eta) - \overline{G(\overline{\eta},\overline{\xi})}]$$

On the real (x,y)-plane $\overline{\eta} = \xi$ because ξ and η are conjugate coordinates, and therefore R and I are real. Moreover, R and I are analytic in each of their arguments. Thus if $G(\xi,\eta)$ is real on the real (x,y)-plane, then $I(\xi,\eta)$ must vanish identically because it is zero on the real (x,y)-plane. We call a complex analytic function G of the two complex variables ξ and η which is real on the real (x,y)-plane a real function, and from (3.4B) we see that

(3.5) $$G(\xi,\eta) = \overline{G(\overline{\eta},\overline{\xi})}$$

for such a function.

In order to form a conceptual picture of this result we examine the relationship between the points ξ,η and $\overline{\eta},\overline{\xi}$. For any complex constants ξ_0,η_0 the locus of points where $\xi = \xi_0$ and the locus of points where $\eta = \eta_0$ are each two-dimensional surfaces in the four-dimensional complex domain. These two surfaces intersect at a point in the complex domain which we designate as ξ_0,η_0. The surface $\xi = \xi_0$ intersects the real (x,y)-plane when $\eta = \overline{\xi}_0$, which means at the point $\xi_0,\overline{\xi}_0$, since ξ and η are conjugate coordinates. Similarly the surface $\eta = \eta_0$ intersects the real domain at $\xi = \overline{\eta}_0$, which is the point $\overline{\eta}_0,\eta_0$. Let us consider the point $\overline{\eta}_0,\overline{\xi}_0$. From relation (3.5) we find that $x(\overline{\eta}_0,\overline{\xi}_0) = \overline{x(\xi_0,\eta_0)}$ and $y(\overline{\eta}_0,\overline{\xi}_0) = \overline{y(\xi_0,\eta_0)}$, since x and y are real functions. Thus the point $\overline{\eta}_0,\overline{\xi}_0$ is the reflection of the point ξ_0,η_0 with respect to the real (x,y)-plane. Figure 1 is a three-dimensional illustration of this elementary result. The real (x,y)-plane is the (x_1,y_1)-plane. The surfaces $\xi = \xi_0$, $\xi = \overline{\eta}_0$, $\eta = \eta_0$, $\eta = \overline{\xi}_0$ are illustrated as lines in the figure. Relation (3.5) is a statement of the fact that a real function takes on complex conjugate values at reflected points in the (x,y)-plane. Using relation (3.5) on the difference quotient $[G(\xi_0+h,\eta_0) - G(\xi_0,\eta_0)]/h$ we can easily prove that

$$(3.6) \qquad G_\xi(\xi_0,\eta_0) = \overline{G_\eta(\overline{\eta}_0,\overline{\xi}_0)}$$

if G is a real function. We will use these results, which comprise our formulation of the Schwarz reflection principle, later.

We return now to our original system of equations (2.6). If $u(\xi,\eta)$, $v(\xi,\eta)$ is an analytic solution, where ξ and η are any pair of conjugate coordinates, then $u(\xi,\overline{\xi})$, $v(\xi,\overline{\xi})$ is a solution over the real domain. If $u(\xi,\overline{\xi})$, $v(\xi,\overline{\xi})$ are real then relations (3.5) and (3.6) must hold for $u(\xi,\eta)$ and $v(\xi,\eta)$. If the equations of motion were linear then $Re\ \{u(\xi,\eta)\}$, $Re\ \{v(\xi,\eta)\}$ would be real solutions of the original equations, too.

4. Characteristic Coordinates.

In Section 2 we wrote our system of equations (2.6) in the matrix notation (2.7). We assume that x,y,u and v have been extended into the complex domain by analytic continuation. Now let X be a non-zero row vector and λ a scalar with the property that

$$(4.1) \qquad X(S\lambda + T) = 0$$

and hence

$$(4.2) \qquad XS\lambda = - XT$$

Clearly a nontrivial X exists only if $S\lambda + T$ is singular, i.e.

(4.3) $$\text{Det } (S\lambda + T) = 0$$

which we have shown has the two roots

(4.4) $$\lambda_\pm = \frac{uv \pm c\sqrt{q^2 - c^2}}{c^2 - u^2}$$

In the real domain the type of differential equation (2.7) is determined by examining the two roots λ_+ and λ_-. In complex space the notion of type loses its meaning. However, we note from equation (4.4) that the roots are distinct provided $q \neq c_*$. The locus of points where $q = c_*$ consists of a two-dimensional surface in the four-dimensional (u,v)-space which we shall call the complex sonic line. We shall see in Section 8 that the complex sonic line plays an important role in the continuation of our flow into the supersonic region.

To each characteristic root λ_+ or λ_- of (4.3) there corresponds a characteristic row vector X_+ or X_-. Multiplying (2.7) on the left by each of these row vectors and applying (4.2), we arrive at ·

(4.5) $$X_+ S (U_x - \lambda_+ U_y) = 0$$

(4.6) $$X_- S (U_x - \lambda_- U_y) = 0$$

which yield two scalar equations each involving differentiation in only one direction with the characteristic slope $dy/dx = -\lambda_\pm$. Carrying out the calculations we discover that

(4.7) $$X_\pm S = (1, -\lambda_\mp)$$

The characteristic directions define two families of integral curves which have the representations

(4.8A) $\qquad \xi(x,y) = \text{const.}$

(4.8B) $\qquad \eta(x,y) = \text{const.}$

in terms of certain analytic functions $\xi(x,y)$ and $\eta(x,y)$. Thus
x and y satisfy

(4.9A) $\qquad y_\xi + \lambda_+ x_\xi = 0$

(4.9B) $\qquad y_\eta + \lambda_- x_\eta = 0$

as functions of the new coordinates ξ and η. Moreover, we can reduce
the system (4.5-6) by means of (4.7) to a pair of canonical equations

(4.10A) $\qquad u_\xi = \lambda_- v_\xi$

(4.10B) $\qquad u_\eta = \lambda_+ v_\eta$

for u and v in terms of ξ and η. The new independent variables ξ and
η are called <u>characteristic coordinates</u>, and equations (4.9A-B),
(4.10A-B) are the equations of motion written in characteristic form.
Clearly ξ and η are not unique, for any function of ξ and any function
of η are again characteristic coordinates.

Equations (4.10A-B) do not contain x and y, so that ξ and η must
be functions of u and v only. Explicit expressions for them can be
found, and in Section 6 we will show how we may choose characteristic
coordinates ξ and η to obtain singular solutions with appropriate
infinities.

In the case that the flow is subsonic in the real domain it is
always possible to find complex analytic characteristic coordinates
ξ and η which are also conjugate coordinates. To show this we let
$w = u - iv$ and $w^* = u + iv$. Clearly w and w^* are conjugate

coordinates in (u,v)-space. We assume that $\xi(w,w^*)$ is a characteristic coordinate and we prove that $\eta(w,w^*) = \overline{\xi(\overline{w}^*,\overline{w})}$ is then a conjugate characteristic coordinate. To do this we note that according to (4.4)

$$(4.11A) \qquad \lambda_+(w,w^*) = \lambda_1(w,w^*) + i\lambda_2(w,w^*)$$

$$(4.11B) \qquad \lambda_-(w,w^*) = \lambda_1(w,w^*) - i\lambda_2(w,w^*)$$

where λ_1 and λ_2 are real functions, so we have

$$(4.12) \qquad \lambda_+(w,w^*) = \overline{\lambda_-(\overline{w}^*,\overline{w})}$$

From equation (4.10A)

$$(4.13) \qquad u_\xi(\overline{w}^*,\overline{w}) = \lambda_-(\overline{w}^*,\overline{w})\; v_\xi(\overline{w}^*,\overline{w})$$

and because u and v are real functions we obtain

$$(4.14) \qquad \overline{\frac{\partial u(w,w^*)}{\partial \xi}} = \overline{\lambda_+(w,w^*)}\;\overline{\frac{\partial v(w,w^*)}{\partial \xi}}$$

or

$$(4.15) \qquad \frac{\partial u}{\partial \overline{\xi}} = \lambda_+(w,w^*)\;\frac{\partial v}{\partial \overline{\xi}}$$

which shows from equation (4.10B) that $\eta = \overline{\xi}$ is indeed a characteristic coordinate.

For the characteristic initial value problem we assign

$$(4.16) \qquad x(\xi,\eta_0) = f(\xi) + g(\eta_0)$$

on $\eta = \eta_0$ and

$$(4.17) \qquad x(\xi_0,\eta) = g(\eta) + f(\xi_0)$$

on $\xi = \xi_0$, where f and g are analytic. We find y along the characteristics by integrating (4.9A-B). If we choose $\xi_0 = \bar{\eta}_0$ the point
$u(\xi_0,\eta_0)$, $v(\xi_0,\eta_0)$ will come out in the real domain, since ξ and η
are conjugate coordinates over the complex (u,v)-space. The solution
$x(\xi,\eta)$, $y(\xi,\eta)$ can be found numerically by the procedure described
in Section 7.

To obtain a real solution there are two options that we use in
practice. Since u and v depend only on ξ and η, equations (4.9A-B)
are linear in (ξ,η)-space and (u,v)-space. Therefore the real part of
x and the real part of y will comprise a solution to these equations
in the real domain $\xi = \bar{\eta}$. Alternately we may try to pick the initial
functions $f(\xi)$ and $g(\eta)$ so that the resulting solution $x(\xi,\eta)$, $y(\xi,\eta)$
is a real function, i.e. real in the real domain. To do this we
assume that $x(\xi,\eta)$, $y(\xi,\eta)$ is a real solution of (4.9A-B). Since
$\xi_0 = \bar{\eta}_0$, we have

$$(4.18) \qquad \overline{g(\bar{\xi})} + \overline{f(\bar{\eta}_0)} = \overline{x(\bar{\eta}_0,\bar{\xi})} = x(\xi,\eta_0) = f(\xi) + g(\eta_0)$$

by the Schwarz principle of reflection (3.5). Thus x is a real
function if

$$(4.19) \qquad\qquad\qquad f(\xi) = \overline{g(\bar{\xi})}$$

and then y must also be a real function. More careful examination
shows that taking the first alternative is equivalent to choosing

$$(4.20A) \qquad x(\xi,\eta_0) = \frac{f(\xi) + \overline{g(\bar{\xi})}}{2} + \frac{\overline{f(\bar{\eta}_0)} + g(\eta_0)}{2}$$

$$(4.20B) \qquad x(\xi_0,\eta) = \frac{\overline{f(\bar{\eta})} + g(\eta)}{2} + \frac{f(\xi_0) + \overline{g(\bar{\xi}_0)}}{2}$$

and using the second alternative.

5. Initial Data.

We assume that the reader is already familiar with many of the aspects of incompressible flow around an airfoil. The purpose of this section is to make some remarks about the problem of incompressible flow that are helpful in the compressible case. Since many incompressible solutions are already known, it is possible to learn the relationship between the initial data we assign on the characteristics and the resulting airfoil. This knowledge motivates our choice of data on the initial characteristics for compressible flow.

We turn to the classical theory of incompressible flow about a body with uniform velocity $u = 1$ at infinity and circulation Γ. Here u, v, x and y are real. Any such flow can be represented by a complex potential $\chi(z) = \phi + i\psi$ which is an analytic function of the complex variable $z = x + iy$.

Let us confine our attention to the case of a circular cylinder, so that

$$(5.1) \qquad \chi(z) = z + \frac{1}{z} + 2ik \log z \ , \qquad k = \frac{\Gamma}{4\pi}$$

Then the formula for the velocity

$$(5.2) \qquad \frac{d\chi}{dz} = w = 1 - \frac{1}{z^2} + \frac{2ik}{z}$$

can be inverted explicitly and yields

$$(5.3) \qquad z(w) = [(1-w-k^2)^{1/2} + ik]^{-1}$$

from which we conclude that there is a branch point at $w = 1-k^2$ as well as a pole on one branch of z in the w-plane at $w = 1$. In more general cases the inverse function $z = z(w)$ can be even more complicated. However, for a wide range of airfoils it will have at most one branch point of first order outside the body, and a simple pole on one branch at w = 1. Therefore we introduce the new variable η defined by

(5.4)
$$\eta(w) = \left[1 - w + B^2\right]^{1/2} - B$$

where B = 0 if k = 0. For the circular cylinder we have

(5.5)
$$z = \frac{1}{\eta}$$

with B = -ik.

Consider now the class of airfoils which have the representation

(5.6)
$$z = \frac{\alpha}{\eta} + g(\eta)$$

where α is a constant and g is an arbitrary analytic function of η. As a function of w, z has a first order branch point at $w = 1 + B^2$ and has a pole at w = 1 for all solutions in this class. Included in the class is the family of symmetric elliptic cylinders defined by

(5.7A)
$$\chi = \hat{z} + \frac{1}{\hat{z}}$$

(5.7B)
$$z = \hat{z} + \frac{E}{\hat{z}}$$

where E is an ellipse parameter ranging between 0 and 1. For E = 0 the ellipse is a circle and for E = 1 it is a straight line segment. Taking the derivative of χ with respect to z we find that

(5.8)
$$\hat{z} = \frac{1}{\eta} (E\eta^2 + \beta^2)^{1/2} \; ; \qquad \beta^2 = 1 - E \, , \qquad B = 0$$

and hence

(5.9)
$$z = \frac{1}{\eta} (E\eta^2 + \beta^2)^{1/2} + \frac{E\eta}{(E\eta^2 + \beta^2)^{1/2}}$$

Clearly (5.9) can be written in the form (5.6) with α = β.

We next apply the technique of the previous sections. Incompressible flow can be viewed as the limiting case of compressible flow where the Mach number vanishes. The equations of motion (2.2) reduce to the familiar Cauchy-Riemann equations

(5.10A) $$u_x + v_y = 0$$

(5.10B) $$v_x - u_y = 0$$

Let us extend u,v,x and y into the complex domain as in Section 3. We compute the characteristic directions and obtain

(5.11) $$\lambda_\pm = \pm i$$

Introducing characteristic coordinates ξ and η in the complex domain as in Section 4, we find that equations (4.9A-B) also hold.

For convenience we rewrite the equations of motion in the form

(5.12A) $$u_\xi = iv_\xi , \qquad u_\eta = -iv_\eta$$

(5.12B) $$y_\xi - ix_\xi = 0, \qquad y_\eta + ix_\eta = 0$$

Because of (5.11) it is possible to show that $w = u - iv$ and $w^* = u+iv$ are characteristic coordinates. We point out that the w described here becomes the analytic continuation of the w used in the first part of this section after u and v have been extended into the complex domain. However, w and w^* are also conjugate coordinates in (u,v)-space, since both u and v are real when $w = \overline{w}^*$. In the real domain $w = \overline{w}^*$, w is the complex velocity introduced in the earlier part of the section. Now since any analytic function of a characteristic coordinate is itself a characteristic coordinate, the complex variables ξ and η defined by

(5.13A) $$\eta(w) = \sqrt{1 + B^2} - w - B$$

(5.13B) $$\xi(w^*) = \sqrt{1 + \bar{B}^2} - w^* - \bar{B}$$

are characteristic coordinates for any complex constant B. Moreover, when $\xi = \bar{\eta}$ we have $w = \bar{w}^*$ so that ξ and η are also conjugate coordinates. For any pair of complex numbers ξ_0, η_0 we can obtain the corresponding complex velocities $u(\xi_0, \eta_0)$, $v(\xi_0, \eta_0)$. Thus by inverting (5.13A-B) we obtain a particular solution of (5.12A). Our problem then reduces to solving (5.12B) for x and y as functions of the characteristic coordinates ξ and η.

If initial values of the type

(5.14A) $$x(\xi, \eta_0) = \overline{g(\bar{\xi})} + g(\eta_0)$$

(5.14B) $$x(\xi_0, \eta) = g(\eta) + \overline{g(\bar{\xi}_0)}$$

are assigned, then in the present case of incompressible flow one sees by inspection that the solution is

(5.15A) $$x(\xi, \eta) = \overline{g(\bar{\xi})} + g(\eta)$$

(5.15B) $$y(\xi, \eta) = \overline{ig(\bar{\xi})} - ig(\eta)$$

In particular we have

(5.16) $$x(\bar{\eta}, \eta) = 2 \, Re \, \{g(\eta)\} \, , \qquad y(\bar{\eta}, \eta) = 2 \, Im \, \{g(\eta)\}$$

in the real domain $\xi = \bar{\eta}$. Comparing this result with (5.6) and (5.9) and eliminating a pole at the origin, we conclude that to obtain the incompressible flow past an elliptic cylinder by our inverse method we should set the arbitrary function $g(\eta)$ equal to

$$(5.17) \qquad g(\eta) = \frac{(E\eta^2 + \beta^2)^{1/2}}{\eta} + \frac{E\eta}{(E\eta^2 + \beta^2)^{1/2}} - \frac{\beta}{\eta}$$

where $\beta = \alpha$.

Even in the compressible case a choice of the initial data g of the kind we have just described generates flow past a reasonable symmetrical airfoil. However, to achieve lift and camber a more complicated expression is required. We have found that it is a good idea to add polynomial terms as well as logarithms that act as sources or sinks controlling the shape of the profile. Therefore in practice we have put

$$(5.18) \quad g(\eta) = E_M E \left[\frac{\eta - E_C}{Z + \sqrt{1-E}} + \frac{\eta - E_C}{Z} \right] + E_T \eta + E_{TSQ} \eta^2$$

$$+ E_{TCU} \eta^3 + \sum_{j=1}^{4} (T_{j1} + iT_{j2}) \log (\eta - T_{j3} - iT_{j4})$$

$$+ \sum_{j=1}^{4} (N_{j1} + iN_{j2}) \log (\eta - N_{j3} - iN_{j4})$$

$$+ \sum_{j=1}^{4} (S_{j1} + iS_{j2}) \log (\eta - S_{j3} - iS_{j4})$$

where

$$Z = \sqrt{E(\eta - E_C)^2 + 1-E}$$

The constants that appear play a role that will be described more fully in Section 5 of Part II of this paper.

6. The Singular Solution.

In Section 5 we saw how characteristic coordinates lead to a particularly simple form of the equations for compressible flow. Interesting flows are obtained by finding regular solutions to the equations of motion and adding them to an appropriate singular solution. Here we find the correct form of the singularity for flow around an airfoil. Since the equtions are linear in the hodograph plane, we may add a regular solution, found by solving a characteristic initial value problem, to the singular solution. In analogy with the previous section we require that the leading term of the singular solution be a pole in the appropriate characteristic coordinate η. To complete the solution we need to add a logarithmic term and a regular term. Thus, we expect the general complex-valued solution to have the form

$$
(6.1A) \qquad\qquad x = \frac{X^1}{\eta} + X^2 \log \eta + X^3
$$

$$
(6.1B) \qquad\qquad y = \frac{Y^1}{\eta} + Y^2 \log \eta + Y^3
$$

where X^i, Y^i are regular functions near $\xi = \eta = 0$. We shall investigate conditions to impose on X^1, Y^1 and X^2, Y^2 in order that X^3, Y^3 become the solution to a nonsingular differential equation. We shall see that X^1 need only depend on ξ. For flow with circulation, X^2 is closely related to the fundamental solution and, in fact, satisfies equations similar to those defining the Riemann function. For flows without circulation, X^2 and Y^2 vanish.

As we indicated in Section 5, incompressible flow can be considered as the limit as $c \to \infty$ of compressible flow. Thus, there exists a characteristic coordinate s with the property that $s \to w$ as $c \to \infty$. We shall endeavor to find s and the corresponding η in this section. We introduce the polar coordinate θ in the hodograph plane given by

(6.2)
$$\theta = \tan^{-1} \frac{v}{u}$$

A solution of (4.10A-B) can be found in terms of q and θ as illustrated by Sears [23]. In particular, he shows that the formulas

(6.3A)
$$\xi = f(q) - \theta$$

(6.3B)
$$\eta = f(q) + \theta$$

define characteristic coordinates ξ and η when

(6.3C)
$$f(q) = \frac{1}{2\mu} \sin^{-1}\left[(\gamma-1) \frac{q^2}{c_*^2} - \gamma\right] + \frac{1}{2} \sin^{-1}\left[(\gamma+1) \frac{c_*^2}{q^2} - \gamma\right]$$

Since any function of a characteristic coordinate is itself a characteristic coordinate, it is clear from (6.3A-B) that for any functions F and G

(6.4A)
$$s = F[f(q) + \theta]$$

(6.4B)
$$t = G[f(q) - \theta]$$

are characteristic coordinates, too. We choose the functions F and G in such a way that s and t will be analogous to w and w^* in the incompressible case. We require that

(6.5A)
$$\lim_{c \to \infty} F[f(q) + \theta] = w = q\, e^{-i\theta}$$

(6.5B)
$$\lim_{c \to \infty} G[f(q) - \theta] = w^* = q\, e^{i\theta}$$

We will show that the functions

(6.6)
$$F(r) = G(r) = C\, e^{-ir}$$

have the desired property, where C is an appropriate constant. With
this choice of F and G, s and t assume the form

(6.7) $\qquad s = C\ e^{-if(q)}\ e^{-i\theta}\ ; \qquad t = C\ e^{-if(q)}\ e^{i\theta}$

The function f can be expressed in the more convenient form

(6.8) $\qquad f(q) = i\ \log\left[h(q)/C\right]$

where

(6.9A) $\qquad h(q) = Cq\left[\left(\sqrt{\Phi_1^2 - 1}\ -\Phi_1\right)^{1/\mu}\ \left(\sqrt{\Phi_2^2 - q^4}\ +\Phi_2\right)\right]^{-1/2}$

(6.9B) $\qquad \Phi_1 = \gamma - \dfrac{\gamma-1}{c_*^2}\ q^2\ ; \qquad\qquad \Phi_2 = (\gamma+1)c_*^2 - q^2\gamma$

Writing s and t in terms of the function h, we have

(6.10) $\qquad s = h(q)\ e^{-i\theta}\ ; \qquad\qquad t = h(q)\ e^{i\theta}$

Finally, by choosing the constant C so that $h(1) = 1$, we have the
desired result. For subsonic flow $q < c_*$ and from (6.9A-B) it
follows that $h(q)$ is real. Thus s and t are conjugate coordinates
when $q < c_*$.

Continuing our analogy with the previous section, we introduce
the new conjugate characteristic coordinates

(6.11A) $\qquad \eta = (1 - s + B^2)^{1/2} - B$

(6.11B) $\qquad \xi = (1 - t + \overline{B}^2)^{1/2} - \overline{B}$

and seek a solution to our problem of the form

(6.12A) $x = Re \ [\dfrac{X^1(\xi,\eta)}{\eta} + X^2(\xi,\eta) \ \log \eta + X^3(\xi,\eta)]$

(6.12B) $y = Re \ [\dfrac{Y^1(\xi,\eta)}{\eta} + Y^2(\xi,\eta) \ \log \eta + Y^3(\xi,\eta)]$

where X^i, Y^i are regular at $\xi = \eta = 0$. Assuming the expressions
inside square brackets to be solutions of the equations of motion
(4.9A-B), too, we find that

(6.13A) $Y_\xi^3 + \lambda_+ X_\xi^3 = - \dfrac{Y_\xi^1 + \lambda_+ X_\xi^1}{\eta} - (Y_\xi^2 + \lambda_+ X_\xi^2) \ \log \eta$

(6.13B) $Y_\eta^3 + \lambda_- X_\eta^3 = \dfrac{Y^1 + \lambda_- X^1}{\eta^2} - \dfrac{Y_\eta^1 + \lambda_- X_\eta^1 + Y^2 + \lambda_- X^2}{\eta} - (Y_\eta^2 + \lambda_- X_\eta^2) \ \log \eta$

In order to be able to compute the answer we require that the right-
hand side of these formulas be regular. Thus we impose the following
conditions on the characteristic $\eta = 0$:

(6.14A) $Y_\xi^1 + \lambda_+ X_\xi^1 = 0 \ ; \qquad Y^1 + \lambda_- X^1 = 0$

(6.14B) $Y^2 + \lambda_- X^2 = (\lambda_-)_\eta X^1$

and we ask that

(6.14C) $Y_\xi^2 + \lambda_+ X_\xi^2 = 0 \ ; \qquad Y_\eta^2 + \lambda_- X_\eta^2 = 0$

everywhere.

In addition we want X^2 and Y^2 to be real when q and θ are real so
that the solution is single-valued in the real physical plane.
Finally, we set $X^1(0,0) = \alpha$ so that it corresponds to the solution
(5.6) for the case of incompressible flow.

Conditions (6.14A) along with the requirement $X^1(0,0) = \alpha$ yield
a linear, first order, ordinary differential equation for X^1 whose

solution can be written in the closed form

$$(6.15) \qquad X^1(\xi,0) = \alpha \exp \{ \int_0^\xi a(r,0) \, dr \} ; \qquad a(\xi,\eta) = \frac{(\lambda_-)_\xi}{\lambda_+ - \lambda_-}$$

Any X^1 satisfying (6.15), together with the corresponding Y^1, can be used in constructing the solution. In particular, we may choose X^1 as a function of ξ only. From (6.14C) we see that X^2 and Y^2 must satisfy the equations of motion (4.9A-B) plus the condition (6.14B) on $\eta = 0$, along with the requirement that they be real at real points of the hodograph plane. This means that we can find X^2 and Y^2 by solving a characteristic initial value problem for the equations of motion with characteristic initial values satisfying the linear equation (6.14B) on $\eta = 0$. Because X^2 and Y^2 must be real functions, we impose corresponding initial data on $\xi = 0$ by reflection. Note that X^2 and Y^2 are essentially the Riemann function of the equations. Having found X^1, Y^1, X^2 and Y^2, we calculate X^3 and Y^3 by solving another characteristic initial value problem. In order to avoid computational difficulties that arise in the neighborhood of $\eta = 0$, we assign the data for the latter problem along characteristics ξ_0, η_0 away from $\eta = 0$.

The stream function ψ can easily be found by integrating (2.5) once x and y are known. We find that

$$(6.16) \qquad \psi = \frac{1}{\rho_0} \int (\rho v \, dx - \rho u \, dy)$$

where we choose the constant of integration so that $\psi = 0$ at q = 0. In this way the body is defined by the streamline $\psi = 0$.

In order for the solution to represent flow around a closed body, it is necessary that ψ return to the same value when we integrate over a closed path around the point at infinity. However, we do not wish to impose this single-valuedness requirement because we need to allow for a sink at infinity that leads to a thin wake trailing behind the airfoil. Such a wake will be necessary for the boundary layer correction discussed later on in Section 11. Now for arbitrary cases including circulation and a wake the integral in question can be evaluated over a curve around $\eta = 0$ in the real hodograph plane $\xi = \bar{\eta}$. Because the integral is independent of path we can use the expansion (6.12) for x and y to show that

$$(6.17) \quad \frac{1}{\rho_0} \oint (\rho v \, dx - \rho u \, dy) = - \frac{2\pi}{\rho_0} Im \, [X_1(0,0)(\rho v)_\eta - Y_1(0,0)(\rho u)_\eta]$$

Using (6.10) and (6.11A), we can express the right-hand side in terms of quantities at $\eta = \bar{\xi} = 0$. We find

$$(6.18) \quad \frac{1}{\rho_0} \oint (\rho v \, dx - \rho u \, dy) = 4\pi \frac{\rho_\infty}{\rho_0} Re \, [B\alpha]$$

where $\alpha = X_1(0,0)$, from which we see that $Re \, [B\alpha]$ must vanish if ψ is single-valued. Similarly we can evaluate the circulation

$$(6.19) \quad \Gamma = \oint (u \, dx + v \, dy)$$

Since this integral is also independent of path, we proceed as above and take it around $\eta = 0$ in the real plane $\xi = \bar{\eta}$. After some manipulation we discover that

$$(6.20) \quad \Gamma = - \frac{4\pi}{\sqrt{1-M_\infty^2}} Im \, [B\alpha]$$

so for a fixed α and B the circulation increases with Mach number by the Prandtl-Glauert factor $(1-M_\infty^2)^{-1/2}$.

For the symmetric non-circulatory case there are simplifications because s becomes an even function of η. From (6.11A) we have

$$(6.21) \quad (\lambda_-)_\eta = (\lambda_-)_s \frac{ds}{d\eta} = 0$$

at $\eta = 0$, so that $X^2 = Y^2 \equiv 0$ satisfies (6.14B-C). Thus a solution of our problem can be found simply by solving a characteristic initial value problem for the nonhomogeneous system of equations (6.13A-B) with X^1 defined by (6.15) and $X^2 = Y^2 \equiv 0$. Since the choice of characteristic initial data is arbitrary, interesting symmetric airfoils can be found by this procedure (cf. [15]).

7. Finite Difference Scheme.

As we discovered in Section 6, we can arrive at a solution of the equations of motion for flow around an airfoil by solving linear ordinary differential equations for X^1, Y^1 and systems of nonhomogeneous linear partial differential equations for X^2, Y^2, X^3 and Y^3. Because the solution to the ordinary differential equations is known in the closed form (6.15), the first part of the numerical procedure can be effected by a quadrature formula. After that X^2 and Y^2 are found by solving characteristic initial value problems with data assigned at $\xi = 0$ and $\eta = 0$. Having determined X^1, Y^1, X^2 and Y^2, we proceed to solve a characteristic initial value problem for the equations

$$(7.1A) \qquad Y^3_\xi + \lambda_+ X^3_\xi = g^1(\xi,\eta) \; ; \qquad g^1(\xi,\eta) = -\frac{Y^1_\xi + \lambda_+ X^1_\xi}{\eta}$$

$$(7.1B) \quad Y^3_\eta + \lambda_- X^3_\eta = g^2(\xi,\eta) \; ; \quad g^2(\xi,\eta) = \frac{Y^1 + \lambda_- X^1}{\eta^2} - \frac{Y^1_\eta + \lambda_- X^1_\eta + Y^2 + \lambda_- X^2}{\eta}$$

with data assigned on another pair of characteristics $\xi = \xi_0$ and $\eta = \eta_0$, to calculate X^3 and Y^3. A very simple finite difference method for integrating these equations has been developed by Massau and is described in Forsythe and Wasow [5]. As we shall see, the method is second order accurate and will always work away from the sonic line, where $\lambda_+ = \lambda_-$.

Suppose $P_1(\xi_1,\eta_1)$ and $P_2(\xi_2,\eta_2)$ are two nearby points in the complex domain at which the solution is known. The point $P_3(\xi_2, \eta_1)$ where the complex characteristics $\xi = \xi_2$ and $\eta = \eta_1$ intersect, as well as the solution at this point, can be found to second order in the distance δ between P_1 and P_2. To do this we first write the difference approximations

(7.2A) $u(P_3) - u(P_1) = \frac{1}{2} [\lambda_-(P_3) + \lambda_-(P_1)][v(P_3) - v(P_1)]$

(7.2B) $u(P_3) - u(P_2) = \frac{1}{2} [\lambda_+(P_3) + \lambda_+(P_2)][v(P_3) - v(P_2)]$

for equations (4.10A-B), which are two algebraic equations for the two unknowns $u(P_3)$ and $v(P_3)$. Then we find X^3 and Y^3 to second order in δ by solving the two simultaneous linear algebraic equations

(7.3A) $Y^3(P_3) - Y^3(P_1) + \tilde{\lambda}_+[X^3(P_3) - X^3(P_1)] = (\xi_2 - \xi_1)\tilde{g}^1$

(7.3B) $Y^3(P_3) - Y^3(P_2) + \tilde{\lambda}_-[X^3(P_3) - X^3(P_2)] = (\eta_1 - \eta_2)\tilde{g}^2$

where

(7.3C) $\tilde{\lambda}_+ = \frac{1}{2} [\lambda_+(P_3) + \lambda_+(P_1)] ; \quad \tilde{\lambda}_- = \frac{1}{2} [\lambda_-(P_3) + \lambda_-(P_2)]$

(7.3D) $\tilde{g}^1 = \frac{1}{2} [g^1(P_3) + g^1(P_1)] ; \quad \tilde{g}^2 = \frac{1}{2} [g^2(P_3) + g^2(P_2)]$

and where it is understood that X^2 and Y^2 have been obtained from similar finite difference equations.

It is important to note that these systems of equations involve complex quantities and must be solved in the complex domain. Thus we use complex arithmetic. The equations can always be solved provided that they are nonsingular. By inspection we see that they coincide only if $\lambda_+ = \lambda_-$, i.e., if we are on the complex sonic line.

Near the complex sonic line λ_+ is nearly equal to λ_- and the equations become ill-conditioned. Thus we can expect less accuracy in the vicinity of the sonic line.

For the characteristic initial value problem defining X^3 and Y^3, analytic data are prescribed on the two characteristic surfaces $\xi = \xi_0$ and $\eta = \eta_0$. On the two-dimensional surface $\xi = \xi_0$ we pick a one-dimensional path of integration $\eta = \eta(\tau)$ starting from $\eta = \eta_0$ and put down grid points $\eta_0, \eta_1, \ldots, \eta_N$. The values of u and v at these points can be found explicitly because the transformation from the character-istic coordinates to the hodograph variables is known in closed form (cf. Section 6). The function X^3 is prescribed on this characteristic surface and Y^3 is found by integrating equation (7.1B). Similarly we lay off a grid of points $\xi_0, \xi_1, \ldots, \xi_N$ on a path $\xi = \xi(\sigma)$ on the char-acteristic $\eta = \eta_0$ emanating from $\xi = \xi_0$ and proceed as before in obtaining u, v, X^3 and Y^3, except that equation (7.1A) is used in place of (7.1B). The arc length parameters σ and τ are real so that the region of solution can easily be visualized in the (σ, τ)-plane. We see that the domain of the solution is a rectangle bounded by four charac-teristics through ξ_0, η_0, ξ_N and η_N. It is clear that the method of Massau can be applied to successive points in each row starting from the first row and working up (cf. Figure 2).

We note here that the difference equations (7.2A-B) for the deter-mination of u and v are used only to facilitate computation. It is of course possible to find u and v directly from the explicit transforma-tion constructed in the previous section. In solving the difference equations (7.2A-B), λ_+ and λ_- are computed at midpoints and stored for later use in the difference equations (7.3A-B). However, along the initial characteristics it is necessary to find u and v directly from the transformation.

Physically we are only interested in the solution for real values of u and v, so we would like to choose paths on the initial characteristic surfaces that yield as many real points of the solution as possible. By examining the equations (6.10) of the transformation to hodograph variables, we find that if s and t are complex conjugates the point u(s,t), v(s,t) is in the real hodograph plane provided

$$(7.4) \qquad st = |s|^2 = |t|^2 \le [h(c_*)]^2$$

From equations (6.11A-B) we see that ξ and η are complex conjugates when s and t are. Thus by choosing initial paths $\xi(\sigma)$, $\eta(\tau)$ which are complex conjugates, we can arrange that the diagonal points of our rectangular two-dimensional grid where $\xi = \bar{\eta}$ will be in the real hodograph plane provided

$$(7.5) \qquad |1 - 2B\eta - \eta^2| \le h(c_*)$$

For these conjugate initial paths, we obtain the solution along a path in the real hodograph plane starting at $\xi_0 = \bar{\eta}_0$ and remaining in the subsonic region.

For reasons of symmetry the calculation has to be done only below the real diagonal, which enables us to eliminate half the computation. If symmetry is not exploited, then the real parts of x and y become the desired solution along the diagonal. By choosing different paths at $\xi = \xi_0$ and $\eta = \eta_0$ we find the solution along corresponding paths in the real hodograph plane. We see that any complex conjugate pair of paths can be continued only until $|1 - 2B\eta - \eta^2| = h(c_*)$, since $\lambda_+ = \lambda_-$ there. However, by choosing conjugate paths which sweep over the whole initial characteristics $\xi = \xi_0$ and $\eta = \eta_0$, we can find the complete subsonic portion of the solution. The choice of paths of integration to find the solution in the supersonic region will be discussed in the next section.

The stream function ψ can be found by using the second order difference scheme

(7.6A) $\psi(P_2) = \psi(P_1) + \rho(P_*)v(P_*)[x(P_2) - x(P_1)]/\rho_0$

$- \rho(P_*)u(P_*)[y(P_2) - y(P_1)]/\rho_0$

(7.6B) $P_* = \dfrac{P_2 + P_1}{2}$

This integration need only be carried out along the path in the real hodograph plane where the solution is sought. The body can be identified by determining points where ψ vanishes along such a path by interpolation. The sonic line can be determined, but with less accuracy, by taking conjugate paths which terminate when $\lambda_+ = \lambda_-$.

8. The Sonic Locus.

In the previous section we showed how the subsonic portion of the flow could be found by our method. At the sonic line λ_+ becomes equal to λ_- and our method breaks down. The lead coefficient of the ordinary differential equation needed for the singular solution becomes infinite, and the linear difference equations approximating the partial differential equations of motion have a determinant that vanishes. These are, however, singularities of the characteristic transformation rather than singularities of the flow, and hence we can expect in general to continue our solution into the supersonic region. If the problem were purely supersonic in nature, we could solve it in the real domain as a characteristic initial value problem directly, and λ_+ and λ_- would be real so that only real arithmetic would be necessary. However, the problem of transonic flow is by no means that simple.

For conjugage paths along conjugate initial characteristics we showed that we could continue our solution until

$$(8.1) \qquad |1 - 2B\eta - \eta^2| = |1 - 2\overline{B}\xi - \xi^2| = h(c_*)$$

We shall call the set of points ξ on $\eta = \eta_0$ and the set of points η on $\xi = \xi_0$ which satisfy relation (8.1) the <u>sonic locus</u>. For convenience we refer to a point ξ on $\eta = \eta_0$ as belonging to the upper sonic locus, while corresponding points η on $\xi = \xi_0$ are said to belong to the lower sonic locus. Note that for each ξ on the upper sonic locus there exists a point η on the lower sonic locus such that $\eta = \overline{\xi}$. The solution found by choosing any two paths terminating at these two conjugate points will always end at a real point on the sonic line. For the detached shock problem a more detailed discussion of the sonic locus is presented in the basic paper by Swenson [27]. In our case the sonic locus can be determined explicitly without knowledge of any solution because the problem is linear in the hodograph plane.

Let us for a moment consider characteristics in the supersonic zone of the real hodograph plane, where q and θ are real and $\hat{q} \geq q \geq c_*$. From equation (6.3C) we see that $f(q)$ is real, so that from (6.7) we have

$$(8.2) \qquad |s| = |t| = C$$

Thus any point in the supersonic region is the intersection of two characteristics on which s and t each have the magnitude C. As a corollary, we can conclude that for every point in the supersonic region, which is determined of course by the two characteristics s and t passing through it, the corresponding ξ and η defined by (6.11A-B) belong to the upper and lower sonic loci, respectively, where (8.1) is satisfied.

We can see the same thing in another way that does not rely on our explicit knowledge of the characteristic transformation. Through

each supersonic point in the hodograph plane pass two characteristics
which can be traced back to the sonic line. From the sonic line we
can trace them further back through the complex domain until they
reach the initial ξ_0 characteristic and the initial η_0 characteristic.
On the other hand, the point of intersection with the ξ_0 characteristic must belong to the lower sonic locus, while the point of intersection with the η_0 characteristic must be on the upper sonic locus,
because the characteristics we have been tracing pass through the
sonic line.

Consider a path on $\xi = \xi_0$ terminating at (ξ_0, η_1), where η_1 belongs
to the lower sonic locus, and consider a path on $\eta = \eta_0$ terminating at
(ξ_1, η_0), where ξ_1 belongs to the upper sonic locus. Assume that for
all other ξ and all other η on these paths $\lambda_+ \neq \lambda_-$. With these
conditions imposed, the solution can be found numerically by the
computational procedure described in the previous section. The
furthest point of the solution will occur at the intersection of the
characteristics through ξ_1 and η_1. The corresponding s and t must
have magnitude C and may, in fact, represent a point in the supersonic
zone. However, we cannot always conclude that the point (ξ_1, η_1) is in
the supersonic zone because the characteristic transformation is not
single-valued. By choosing the paths connecting ξ_0, ξ_1 and η_0, η_1
properly, it is possible to end up on a branch of this transformation
such that the point (ξ_1, η_1) does belong to the real supersonic zone.

Several questions of importance arise. First of all, how can
paths be found connecting ξ_0, ξ_1 and η_0, η_1 and having the required
properties. A heuristic justification for the existence of such paths
is that the set of points for which $\lambda_+ = \lambda_-$ is a two-dimensional
surface, while the solution corresponding to any two initial paths is
also two-dimensional. From the topology of the complex four-space
we expect that we should be able to twist the two-dimensional solution
surface around the two-dimensional complex sonic line. In fact,

paths similar to those used by Swenson [27] for the detached shock problem work here. In order to describe such a path, we consider the point ξ_N on the upper sonic locus which is the complex conjugate of η_1. We assume that ξ_N is to the right of ξ_1 and that η_N, the complex conjugate of ξ_1 on the lower sonic locus, is to the left of η_1. To solve at the point (ξ_1, η_1) in the supersonic region we choose a path of integration on the η_0 characteristic starting from ξ_0 and terminating at ξ_1. The point ξ_N should remain to the left of this path. On the characteristic ξ_0 we integrate from η_0 and terminate at η_1 keeping η_N to the right of our path. If we extend the path ξ_0, ξ_1 by adding new points $\xi_2, \ldots, \xi_N$ on the upper sonic locus, then the points (ξ_2, η_1), (ξ_3, η_1), $\ldots$, (ξ_N, η_1) will also be in the supersonic zone and will lie on the real characteristic η_1. Thus we determine the solution along a characteristic η_1 in the supersonic zone starting at (ξ_1, η_1) and ending on the sonic line at (ξ_N, η_1). If we now go back and extend the path η_0, η_1 to the point η_2 on the lower sonic locus we can repeat the process and find the solution along the characteristic η_2. Continuing in this fashion, we obtain the solution in a region of the supersonic zone bounded by the sonic line together with the two characteristics ξ_1 and η_1. The domain of the solution is the same as it would be if we had solved a real initial value problem with initial data assigned along the sonic line. In Figures 3, 4 and 6 we have illustrated the type of paths involved and the corresponding region of solution in the hodograph plane.

Finally we ask whether the solution is independent of path. This question can be answered affirmatively only if all the data are analytic and there is no singularity of the solution within the region of integration. We may end up on different branches of the solution by taking different initial paths when there is a singularity in the data. Moreover, in the global solution branch points of the flow can be discovered. Section 9 is devoted to a discussion of the various singularities which may be found by this method.

Continuation of the solution into the supersonic region is achieved with one set of initial paths. Moreover, the solution is obtained along characteristics, so the characteristics are easily plotted. The value of the stream function is not known a priori anywhere inside the supersonic region. Hence we must integrate ψ in complex space starting from a point where $\psi = 0$.

9. Branch Points and Limiting Lines.

Our method enables us to find airfoils which have smooth transonic flow around them. The only types of singularity of the flow that can appear unexpectedly are limiting lines and branch points. In this section we explain how the occurrence and location of limiting lines affects the behavior of the flow. We will show how to approximate a solution with a weak shock by making a limiting line appear outside the body in the decelerating portion of the flow.

First consider what singularities may occur. We are primarily concerned with points where the Jacobian of the hodograph transformation is zero,

$$(9.1) \qquad\qquad J = x_u y_v - x_v y_u = 0$$

In the subsonic region J never vanishes unless $x_u = y_v = x_v = y_u = 0$. This can be deduced from the relation

$$(9.2) \qquad (c^2-u^2)x_v^2 + 2uvx_u x_v + (c^2-v^2)x_u^2 = - (c^2-u^2)J$$

based on equation (2.2A). Moreover, when $u^2+v^2 < c^2$ the Jacobian can vanish only at isolated points and hence the only singularities possible in the subsonic portion of the flow are branch points.

Branch points of the solution may result in forking of the streamline $\psi = 0$ so that it does not represent a closed profile. However, it is necessary to impose such a branch point at the location of the tail in the hodograph plane, which, at least for highly cambered airfoils, we place near the locus

(9.3)
$$C_p = \frac{p - p_\infty}{\frac{1}{2} \rho_\infty u_\infty^2} = 0$$

not at q = 0. If we require that x or ψ have a simple critical point at the tail, then there will be two branches of the curve $\psi = 0$ passing through it. If we impose a multiple critical point, which is done by making higher order derivatives of x vanish, then even more forks of the streamline $\psi = 0$ meet at the tail.

For supersonic flow the Jacobian J can change sign without all the derivatives x_u, x_v, y_u, y_v vanishing. This gives rise to limiting lines, which are discussed in some detail by Courant and Friedrichs [3]. They show that J vanishes along a curve in the hodograph plane whose image in the physical plane is a fold called the limiting line. They show further that the fold is an envelope of one of the families of characteristics, while the other family of characteristics forms cusps along it.

It becomes evident that our method makes it easy to identify limiting lines without actually computing the Jacobian J. This can be done simply by plotting the characteristics of the flow in the super-sonic region of the physical plane. In the previous section we showed how the characteristics were obtained in our method of solution. A limiting line is easily recognized by examining the plot because one family of characteristics has cusps there. The effect of a limiting line just inside the body can be shown by considering the speed of the flow along the body. As the limiting line approaches the body there is a more rapid variation of speed. We illustrate this effect by studying the pressure coefficient C_p as a function of the abscissa x. Let us consider the case where the limiting line is inside the body, but in the accelerating portion of the flow. As it approaches the body, sharp increases or peaks are observed in the speed distribution. This type of peaky distribution has been described by Pearcey [22] as being good for the design of shock-free transonic airfoil sections. If we increase the thickness-chord ratio too much, the limiting line appears inside the flow, and it becomes impossible to realize it physically.

The effect of limiting lines in the declerating portion of the flow is reversed. As the limiting line approaches the body, the speed decreases rapidly. However, it may be possible to find a solution with a second order accurate weak shock by piecing the solution together where it has a double fold in the physical plane and emerges on three sheets joined along the folds. We simply join the first sheet of the solution to the third sheet along a shock curve on which Prandtl's relation

$$(9.4) \qquad\qquad q_0 q_1 = c_*^2$$

is satisfied, where q_0 is the speed on the first sheet and q_1 is the corresponding speed on the third sheet.

10. Automatic Selection of Parameters.

Once the method of complex characteristics has been implemented to solve the partial differential equations of gas dynamics (4.9) in the hodograph plane, it remains to formulate auxiliary conditions that will ensure that the solution defines a closed profile with desirable properties in the physical plane. The principal difficulty is to choose in a reasonable way the many parameters that occur in the formula (5.18) for the analytic function specifying the characteristic initial data used in the construction of the solution. In this section we shall show how the parameters that appear linearly in (5.18) can be selected automatically as part of the basic design program.

The real and imaginary parts of the coefficients of the ellipse term, the polynomial terms and the logarithms occurring in (5.18) are determined so that the stream function ψ satisfies an appropriate set of conditions in the hodograph plane. At the nose we prescribe the gradient of x, which also fixes the gradient of y because of the differential equation (4.9). In the initial complex characterstic η-plane we pick a point which will correspond to the tail of the air-foil in the physical plane and impose there the requirements that ψ vanish together with its first and second derivatives. This is our formulation of the Kutta-Joukowski condition in the hodograph plane. Finally, we ask that ψ vanish, at least in the sense of a least squares approximation, at specified points through which it seems reasonable that the profile $\psi = 0$ should pass.

To implement these ideas, let ψ_0 stand for the flow computed with all the coefficients referred to above set equal to zero, and let ψ_j denote the solution associated with zero values of all the coeffici-ents except one, which we conceive of as the jth and which can be either the real or imaginary part of a complex coefficient. Then consider the flow

(10.1) $$\psi = \sum c_j \psi_j$$

with undetermined real coefficients c_j normalized so that

(10.2) $$\sum c_j = 1$$

Denoting the vector with components c_j by C and using matrix notation, we can express the normalization (10.2) and the nose and tail require-ments described above as an inhomogeneous system of eight simultaneous linear equations

(10.3) $$BC = F$$

If, in addition, we ask that ψ vanish at N points corresponding to prescribed locations in the η-plane, we obtain a possibly overdetermined system of N more linear homogeneous equations of the form

$$(10.4) \qquad\qquad\qquad AC = 0$$

Since we will have in general more equations to satisfy than we have unknowns at our disposal, we choose C by requiring that it solve the extremal problem

$$(10.5) \qquad\qquad X_R ||AC||^2 + ||C||_0^2 = \text{minimum}$$

subject to the constraint (10.3), where X_R is some non-negative number and $||C||_0^2$ indicates a suitably weighted average of the squares c_j^2.

The solution of the minimum problem (10.5) satisfies the system of linear equations

$$(10.6) \qquad\qquad (X_R A^* A + I_0)C + B^* \lambda = 0$$

$$(10.7) \qquad\qquad\qquad BC = F$$

where λ is a vector of Lagrange multipliers and I_0 is a diagonal matrix associated with the norm $||C||_0^2$. If the locations of the logarithmic singularities in formula (5.18) are chosen appropriately, the simultaneous equations (10.6) and (10.7) will be non-singular and will determine the automated coefficients C uniquely. In a typical case we distribute nine logarithms more or less evenly outside a curve where we want ψ to vanish in the hodograph plane, and we automate two polynomial terms in addition to the ellipse function, so that we end up with a system of 33 equations for 25 real unknowns $c_0, \ldots, c_{24}$ and 8 Lagrange multipliers $\lambda_1, \ldots, \lambda_8$.

The advantage of the prescription we have just given is that it exploits the fact we know the Dirichlet problem is not well posed, whereas the Tricomi problem is, for transonic flow [18]. Thus we ask that ψ vanish at specified points in the subsonic portion of the hodograph plane, but we leave the supersonic region free. Moreover, we do not solve a full-fledged boundary value problem, but prefer instead to use a construction exploiting analytic continuation of the flow across the sonic line. In the selection of the flow much is still left to good judgment and physical intuition. More about that will be said in Section 5 of Part II of the paper. In some of our examples we have not imposed any least squares approximation of the form (10.6), but have found satisfactory profiles with auxiliary nose and tail requirements of the form (10.7) alone.

Since our automation technique comes very close to solving a boundary value problem, it is natural to compare it with more standard procedures. A significant feature of our method is its use of analytic continuation into the complex domain. This leads to calculation of a solution along one-dimensional paths of integration in the real plane. Fairly complicated paths are needed to compute the supersonic part of the flow, but several stems followed by sprays of forks are sufficient to sweep out the subsonic region. For automation the best paths to use are curves terminating in arcs of the prescribed profile. Thus the desired solution requires only a two-dimensional mesh of grid points rather than three-dimensional arrays of the kind actually involved in most iterative schemes for boundary value problems. Our approach is quite economical and can generate a workable solution in as little as one minute of machine time on the CDC 6600 computer.

11. Boundary Layer Correction.

In order to use inviscid flow theory successfully in the design of shockless transonic airfoils, it is imperative to suppress any significant boundary layer separation. If the boundary layer separates before the last few percent of chord on the profile, it introduces a major perturbation in shape caused by a large wake, so that the shockless solution will not be observed physically. It is therefore necessary to calculate a boundary layer correction that will predict separation and indicate where the airfoil must be streamlined so as to moderate the adverse pressure gradient and bring the point of separation back to the last two or three percent of chord. Moreover, for lifting airfoils even the very thin unseparated boundary layer effectively diminishes the angle of attack and causes a loss of circulation because it is thicker on the upper surface than on the lower surface. The loss of circulation slows the flow down along the upper surface so that the supersonic zone there decreases in size and again the shockless regime is lost. Without a boundary layer correction, the only way to recover this loss is to increase the angle of attack and the free stream Mach number a little.

To overcome these difficulties our design program includes a turbulent boundary layer correction. The potential flow we compute is supposed to be the inviscid flow outside the boundary layer of an actual airfoil. As indicated in Section 6, we have allowed for a sink at infinity so that there will be two trailing streamlines $\psi = 0$ that bound a thin wake behind the airfoil. Because we impose the normalizations $u_\infty = \rho_\infty = 1$ at infinity, the displacement thickness between these trailing streamlines is equal to a jump in ψ that we conceive of as a fictitious form drag C_D. What we actually input in the program is the ratio C_D/C_L, which is equal to the ratio of the period of ψ about infinity divided by the total circulation Γ.

To find the true airfoil generating our inviscid flow it is necessary to subtract from the calculated streamline $\psi = 0$ a displacement thickness obtained from an appropriate boundary layer correction. For this purpose we use the method of Nash and Macdonald [20] for the

estimation of turbulent boundary layers at transonic speeds. In
practice the fictitious form drag coefficient C_D is taken sufficiently
larger than the estimated friction drag coefficient so that after the
reversed boundary layer correction is made a tail remains with a
finite thickness equal to about one half of one percent of the chord
length ℓ of the airfoil. The position of the tail is defined to be
the image of a point in the hodograph plane where we have required that
the gradient of ψ vanish, as described in Section 9.

The method of Nash and Macdonald [20] for determining the displacement thickness δ^* and the momentum thickness θ^* of a two-
dimensional turbulent boundary layer is based on numerical integration
of the von Kármán momentum equation

$$(11.1) \qquad \frac{d\theta^*}{ds} + (2+H-M^2) \frac{dq}{ds} \frac{\theta^*}{q} = \frac{\tau}{\rho q^2}$$

where s, M, ρ, q and τ are the arc length, local Mach number, density,
speed and skin friction along the surface of the airfoil, and H is a
shape factor

$$(11.2) \qquad H = \frac{\delta^*}{\theta^*}$$

that is computed by a set of semi-empirical rules. Both M and q are
known functions of s to be found from our inviscid flow computation
along the streamline $\psi = 0$. Nash and Macdonald specify the skin
friction τ through a version of the logarithmic formula

$$(11.3) \qquad \sqrt{\frac{\rho q^2}{\tau}} = \alpha \, \log \frac{q\theta^*}{\nu} + \beta$$

in which the coefficients α and β depend on both the local Mach number
M and the shape factor H. To calculate the kinematic viscosity ν
we use the Sutherland law

$$(11.4) \qquad \frac{\nu}{\nu_\infty} = \frac{\rho_\infty}{\rho}\left(\frac{T}{T_\infty}\right)^{3/2} \frac{T_\infty + ST_\infty}{T + ST_\infty}$$

where T is the temperature, S is a constant we put equal to .3424, and the subscript ∞ indicates quantities evaluated at infinity in the physical plane.

We integrate the ordinary differential equation (11.1) by means of a second order accurate centered finite difference scheme that is based on unequally spaced points along the streamline $\psi = 0$ that have actually been computed by our inviscid flow program. To get started in the integration it is necessary to set up initial data at two points of transition (x_R, y_R) on the upper and lower surfaces of the airfoil. Because the displacement thickness of the laminar boundary layer appearing before transition is extremely small, we neglect it. At transition we simply assign a value to the local Reynolds number

$$(11.5) \qquad R_\theta = \frac{q\theta^*}{\nu} = Rq \frac{\nu_\infty}{\nu} \frac{\theta^*}{\ell}$$

where R stands for the global Reynolds number of the flow based on the chord length ℓ and the free stream speed $u_\infty = 1$. In most cases we have put

$$(11.6) \qquad R_\theta = 320$$

following a customary analysis of transition from laminar to turbulent flow. This shifts the difficulty to selecting a reasonable abscissa x_R at which transition is supposed to occur. The ratio x_R/ℓ is an arbitrary input parameter of our program for both the upper and lower surfaces of the profile. In practice we usually let it coincide with the value of x/ℓ at the point near the leading edge of the upper surface where the negative of the pressure coefficient

$$(11.7) \qquad C_p = \frac{p - p_\infty}{\frac{1}{2}\rho_\infty u_\infty^2}$$

has its peak. This would seem to be adequate for Reynolds numbers R near 20×10^6. The success of the approach depends on the insensitivity of the results to variations in x_R. The behavior for large R can be simulated at lower R by locating x_R further aft. Finally, separation of the turbulent boundary layer is predicted when the Nash-Macdonald parameter

$$(11.8) \qquad SEP = -\frac{\theta^*}{q}\frac{dq}{ds}$$

exceeds .004.

12. Analysis at Off-Design Conditions.

While the problem of finding shockless transonic flow past a given profile is not well posed, there is every reason to believe that it becomes so if shocks satisfying an appropriate entropy inequality are allowed to appear. For the practical design of shockless airfoils it is important to be able to do off-design calculations including weak shocks in order to assess the variation in the flow when the angle of attack and the free stream Mach number are changed. In particular one wants to avoid designing profiles for which the boundary layer might separate significantly near the design condition. Moreover, one wants to be able to estimate the drag rise Mach number of the airfoil by computing the wave drag associated with the shocks. To handle these questions we have developed a program to perform off-design analysis of the transonic flow past our airfoils by calculating weak solutions of the equations of motion that include one or more shocks satisfying an entropy inequality.

We need an analysis program capable of giving very accurate results at the shockless design condition which we can compare with our hodograph computation. The analysis should also yield a reliable description of weak shocks at off-design conditions without using excessive computer time. It should be able to handle several shocks occurring simultaneously, since that is the situation expected near design. For this purpose we have developed a method that implements a rapidly convergent transonic finite difference scheme due to Murman and his collaborators [16,19] in a coordinate system tried out successfully by Sells [24] which involves mapping the interior of the unit circle conformally onto the exterior of the airfoil. We shall only describe the method very briefly here, referring to a more detailed presentation elsewhere [9], since the primary object of the present paper is the problem of design, not of analysis.

Let

$$(12.1) \qquad x + iy = F(r\ e^{it}) = \sum_{n=-1}^{\infty} a_n r^n\ e^{int}$$

stand for the analytic function which maps the interior of the unit circle $r < 1$ conformally onto the exterior of an airfoil in the (x,y)-plane so that the origin corresponds to infinity, with $|a_{-1}| = 1$, and so that the point $r = 1$, $t = 0$ corresponds to the cusp at the tail. We calculate the map function F by introducing a finite difference approximation to Laplace's equation for the harmonic function

$$(12.2) \qquad W = \log \frac{r^2 |F'(r\ e^{it})|}{|1 - r\ e^{it}|}$$

that is based on a uniform rectangular grid in the (t,r)-plane. To formulate a boundary condition on W, we at first make a spline fit to the (x,y)-coordinates of the profile, or alternately to our design representation of the tangent angle θ as a function of the arc length s measured from the tail, in order to tabulate the curvature $\kappa = \frac{d\theta}{ds}$ in terms of s. Then we use the Cauchy-Riemann equations to establish the boundary condition

(12.3) $$W_r - 2\kappa\ e^W \sin \frac{t}{2} = \frac{1}{2}$$

at $r = 1$, which can be handled by reflection. At $r = 0$, which corresponds to infinity, W is adjusted so it will satisfy the mean value theorem and therefore will not have an unwanted log r term. The unknown W is determined by a successive overrelaxation procedure in which at each cycle the relationship between κ and t at $r = 1$ is updated by considering a numerical evaluation of the formula

(12.4) $$s = \int |F'(e^{it})|\,dt = 2 \int e^W \sin \frac{t}{2}\,dt$$

and using the previously tabulated values of κ as a function of s.

In computing transonic flows with shocks we neglect terms of third order in the shock strength so we can introduce a velocity potential ϕ, which describes isentropic flow. We are therefore restricted to a weak shock approximation in which ϕ and ψ have no jumps. To remove the singularity of ϕ at $r = 0$ we make the substitution

(12.5) $$\phi = \frac{\cos\ (t+\alpha)}{r} + \Phi$$

where α is the angle of attack. In terms of the Sells coordinates t and r, the second order partial differential equation for Φ stemming from (2.2) becomes

(12.6) $$(c^2 - \tilde{u}^2)\Phi_{tt} - 2r\tilde{u}\tilde{v}\Phi_{tr} + r^2(c^2 - \tilde{v}^2)\Phi_{rr} - 2\tilde{u}\tilde{v}\Phi_t$$

$$+ r(c^2 + \tilde{u}^2 - 2\tilde{v}^2)\Phi_r + r^{-1}(\tilde{u}^2 + \tilde{v}^2)(\tilde{u}\omega_t + r\tilde{v}\omega_r) = 0 ,$$

where

(12.7) $$\tilde{u} = \omega^{-1}[r\Phi_t - \sin(t+\alpha)], \qquad \tilde{v} = \omega^{-1}[r^2\Phi_r - \cos(t+\alpha)]$$

and

(12.8) $$\omega = r^2 |F'(r\,e^{it})|$$

At $r = 0$ the function Φ satisfies a boundary condition

(12.9) $$\Phi = \frac{\Gamma}{2\pi}\tan^{-1}[\sqrt{1-M_\infty^2}\,\tan(t+\alpha)]$$

involving the circulation Γ, and at $r = 1$ it satisfies the Neumann boundary condition

(12.10) $$\Phi_r = \cos(t+\alpha)$$

which will again be treated by reflection. The circulation, which is simply a period of Φ, will be determined iteratively so as to fulfill the Kutta-Joukowski condition

(12.11) $$\Phi_t = \sin\,\alpha$$

at $t = 0$, $r = 1$. It remains to indicate how we generalize Murman's finite difference scheme so as to solve the equation (12.6) when it is of mixed elliptic-hyperbolic type.

We lay down a uniform grid with mesh sizes Δt and Δr over the rectangle $0 \le t \le 2\pi$, $0 \le r \le 1$ and set

(12.12) $$\Phi_{j,k} = \Phi(j\,\Delta t, k\,\Delta r)$$

Central difference approximations are used for the first derivatives Φ_t and Φ_r everywhere, and at points where (12.6) is of the elliptic type they are used for the second derivatives, too. However, in the hyperbolic case we introduce the approximation

$$(\Delta t)^2 \Phi_{tt} = 2\Phi_{j,k} - 5\Phi_{j-1,k} + 4\Phi_{j-2,k} - \Phi_{j-3,k}$$
(12.13)
$$- \lambda\,\Delta t(\Phi_{j,k} - 3\Phi_{j-1,k} + 3\Phi_{j-2,k} - \Phi_{j-3,k})$$

where λ is an artificial viscosity parameter that is positive over the range $\pi < t < 2\pi$, but negative over the range $0 < t < \pi$. Similarly we put

(12.14)

$$4\Delta t\Delta r\Phi_{tr} = 3\Phi_{j,k+1} - 4\Phi_{j-1,k+1} + \Phi_{j-2,k+1} - 3\Phi_{j,k-1} + 4\Phi_{j-1,k-1} - \Phi_{j-2,k-1}$$

$$- \lambda\Delta t(\Psi_{j,k+1} - 2\Psi_{j-1,k+1} + \Psi_{j-2,k+1} - \Psi_{j,k-1} + 2\Psi_{j-1,k-1} - \Psi_{j-2,k-1})$$

(12.15) $$(\Delta r)^2\Phi_{rr} = \Phi_{j,k+1} - 2\Phi_{j,k} + \Phi_{j,k-1}$$

Making these substitutions in (12.6), we obtain a system of difference equations for $\Phi_{j,k}$ linear in the contributions originating from
second derivatives. The linearity enables us to establish an iterative
scheme for updating successive rows of values $\Phi_{j,k}$ with the contribution from first derivatives frozen at each cycle. We march forward in
j when $t > \pi$, but backward in j when $t < \pi$. As we sweep repeatedly
over the flow region this procedure for determining $\Phi_{j,k}$ converges
because we always advance in the direction of flow with an artificial
viscosity coefficient $\lambda(\Delta t)^2$ of the same sign that physical viscosity
would have. At each cycle the circulation Γ is readjusted by means of
a finite difference analogue of (12.11). Shock waves develop natural-
ly during the course of the process, but they rarely spread over more
than two mesh intervals. Moreover, the method is second order accurate
in both Δt and Δr for any fixed choice of the artificial viscosity
parameter λ.

Observe that our analysis routine applies to airfoils that have a
trailing edge of finite thickness as well as to cusped profiles. A
thick tail merely generates an imaginary period in the complex analytic map function F which in turn produces a physically realistic wake
in the flow behind the airfoil. However, this model of the wake is not
quite the same as that used for the boundary layer correction in Section 11. Therefore in the analysis program we extend any thick tail
smoothly by an amount proportional to the thickness. This results in a
better approximation to the pressure distribution outside the boundary
layer.

II. USERS MANUAL

1. Introduction.

This part of the report is a users manual for our transonic airfoil programs and is essentially independent of the theory presented
in Part I. By studying this manual it should be possible to learn how
to operate the design and analysis programs even with only a limited
understanding of the mathematical content. We intend to make the
basic method available to those interested in designing transonic airfoils but unwilling to spend the time required to understand the
complicated numerical analysis needed to solve the partial differential
equations of gas dynamics.

The design problem can be run on the computer either as a batch
job or at the teletype (TTY) using a time sharing system. All
programs require at most a field length of 60,000 octal words on the
CDC 6600.

The main programs are described below. Program B calculates the
flow given the free stream Mach number and other parameters chosen to
describe the airfoil. The actual shape of the airfoil resulting from
the parameters is also computed. Program D converts the results into
Calcomp plots of the airfoil and its hodograph and prints the (x,y)-
coordinates of the streamline $\psi = 0$. It also prepares the data
necessary for a turbulent boundary layer correction and for an
analysis of the flow past the airfoil. Program F computes a turbulent
boundary layer correction and Program G, which is our second major
contribution to the transonic airfoil problem, analyzes at off-design
conditions the flow past the profile obtained by Program B.

In order to initiate the main programs, the data describing the
airfoil and the desired flow characteristics must be supplied. These
are stored on a file labelled Tape 7 and used as input to Program B.
Paths of integration used by Program B must also be prescribed.

These are stored on a file labelled Tape 6. When the design problem is run as a batch job the data for Tape 6 and Tape 7 can be prepared on punched cards and used as input for Program B. All programs are written in standard ANSI Fortran IV for the CDC 6600 except where noted and were also checked on an IBM 360-75 by D. MacKenzie of the Grumman Aerospace Corporation.

The efficiency of operation may be greatly increased by the use of a remote time sharing system. Since design is a trial and error procedure the convenience with which the initial parameters can be modified and the speed with which the resulting profile can be seen at the teletype make the use of the teletype time sharing system ideal for this problem. In order to use time sharing several other programs have been developed. The original input data (Tape 6 and Tape 7) for Program B are punched on cards and put on the appropriate files. Programs A and E have been written to permit these data to be changed at the teletype. Program A is used to modify Tape 7, Program E is used to modify Tape 6. Program C has been written to display the results of the calculations at the teletype.

Sections 2, 3, 4, 6 and 7 are devoted to the mechanics of operating the airfoil programs. They were written so that the design can be carried out at a teletype. However, it is possible to submit the programs for batch processing, with Programs A, C and E eliminated and cards used for creating the files Tape 6 and Tape 7. In Section 5 we discuss the selection of parameters in order to arrive at a reasonable airfoil shape. This is an art at which the user's success may well depend on his individual skill and ingenuity. The sample data listed in Appendices I-IV should be helpful in studying and understanding the contents of this manual, debugging the programs for a new computer and learning to operate them.

2. Teletype Operation.

2.1 Program A.

This program modifies file Tape 7, which is an input to Program B. Referring to the sample run in Appendix II, note that the execution of A causes the teletypewriter to print out MAKE CHANGES IN THE PARAMETERS and return the carriage. On the CDC 6600 the designer responds by typing sp $P sp followed by the variables to be modified and ending with a $ and a carriage return, where sp stands for a space. The variables are identified by their namelist conventions, e.g., M = .75, CD = .03. A complex number like B = .01 - .1i can be inserted either as B = .01, -.1 or as B(1) = .01, B(2) = -.1. If many parameters are to be changed and more than one line of type is required for insertion of the data, each line is ended with a comma and a carriage return and the new line begins with a space. The final $ sets up the transfer of the typed data to Tape 7. The program responds by causing the new contents of Tape 7 to be typed out as shown in the sample run in Appendix II. The listing can be suppressed by setting the parameter IP = 0. Appendix I contains a complete table and glossary of parameter names and descriptions for Program A.

2.2 Program B.

Program B for transonic airfoil design consists of several routines making extensive use of complex arithmetic. The two input files Tape 6 and Tape 7 are supplied by the user. Tape 7 contains the parameters mentioned in Section 2.1. When the problem is run from the teletype (TTY) Tape 7 must be available as a file at the TTY. If the problem is run as a batch job, Tape 7 is available from a deck of ten or eleven punched cards. Tape 6 consists of the paths of integration, available as a file at the TTY or on a deck of punched cards. Program B generates two files, Tape 1 and Output. Tape 1 contains the solution to the flow problem (the coordinates of the airfoil and other information) and is used as input to Programs C and D. The file called Output contains information which monitors the progress of Program B.

A detailed description of Tape 6 and Tape 7 is given in Appendix I. Initially Tape 6 and Tape 7 are created from cards, but they can be modified at the TTY by means of Programs E and A respectively. Both output files are rewound automatically before their contents are used by Program B. Program B can be run whenever the two files are available in the required form. Appendix II shows the TTY response to the execution of B. Output from B appears on the file Tape 1 ready for use as input to both Programs C and D. The output of B at the TTY is the contents of the file Output. The failure of B to be completed successfully may be due to errors which arise if supersonic paths are drawn so that they pass through singular points. The teletype message for such difficulties is ARITHMETIC ERROR in the CDC 6600 Scope operating system.

2.3 Program C.

Program C requires Tape 1 as input. Executing C results in a triangular plot of the supersonic region of the solution and a plot of the subsonic region at the TTY as shown in Appendix II. Regions of positive and negative values of the stream function ψ are identified by the symbols P and N, respectively. In the supersonic plot the characteristic coordinates are read horizontally and vertically, and the hypotenuse corresponds to the sonic line. More than one sign change in any row or column indicates the presence of a limiting line. In the subsonic plot paths in the complex η-plane are recorded with N's and P's designating the sign of ψ and the axes are marked at equal intervals of $Re\,(\eta)$ and $Im\,(\eta)$. C produces no other output files.

2.4 Program D.

The execution of D requires Tape 1 as input and produces file Tape 4 as its output. Tape 4 is then sent to the printer; a sample of the printed output, which includes a list of the (x,y)-coordinates of the profile $\psi = 0$, is reproduced in Appendix III. A Calcomp plot is also produced by D. The plot shows the airfoil and Mach lines in the physical plane, a graph of the pressure coefficient C_p, and a diagram of the η-plane showing the sonic locus, automated points, points on the subsonic paths of integration where $\psi = 0$, the two supersonic paths of integration, and arrows indicating the location of logarithms. Program D also creates a file Tape 3 which consists of the (x,y)-coordinates of the profile $\psi = 0$ and the associated u, v and C_p values. This file Tape 3 is used as input to Programs F and G.

2.5 Program E.

The input to Program E is the file Tape 6. The purpose of this program is to modify the paths of integration contained on Tape 6. A detailed description of the use of Program E will be presented in Section 3 after the paths of integration have been discussed.

3. Paths of Integration.

3.1 Tape 6.

Tape 6 is required as input to Program B. It prescribes the paths of integration for Program B. Each path is a polygonal line starting from the initial characteristic at $\eta = A$ and passing through specified points in the η-plane. These paths are either subsonic paths composed of a stem and several forks or supersonic paths consisting of two separate polygonal arcs. At the beginning of Tape 6 there are several subsonic paths, including one to the nose and one to the tail of the profile, which are required for the automation of input parameters from Tape 7. These paths can alter the actual flow, whereas the solution is independent of the remaining paths of integration in the η-plane.

The stem of a subsonic path terminates at some point near the profile $\psi = 0$; from there a number of forks branch out and cross the profile at points which serve to define a portion of the profile. Many paths may be needed to define the entire subsonic profile. By contrast only one pair of supersonic paths is needed to determine the complete arc of the body $\psi = 0$ cut out by the sonic line.

For the design computations subsonic paths with relatively few rather long forks should be used so that the streamline $\psi = 0$ can be traced as it varies with changes in the input parameters. Even after a closed profile has been achieved, with a central streamline crossing from the stagnation point through the origin to the tail, erroneous branches of the locus $\psi=0$ may be found outside the flow region, i.e. inside the airfoil in the physical plane. To eliminate such erroneous loci from the computation of the final airfoil, the forks of the subsonic paths must be shaved closer to the body. At this stage it is desirable to increase the total numbers of forks so that more body points are computed.

The paths may be prescribed in the η-plane or in the η'-plane, which is defined so that the relationship between η' and u,v is independent of B. For small B the η'-plane is approximately a translation of the η-plane by B. The value of C_p at the tail and the trailing edge slope do not vary with changes in B when the location of the tail is prescribed in the η'-plane. Similarly, the stagnation point will be fixed at -1 in the η'-plane.

Each path or fork is headed by a card which contains information about the path or fork that follows. The description of this header card can be found in Table 2.

3.2 Program E.

We now describe how to create and modify paths from the teletype. Rules for creating paths by means of punched cards are easy to deduce (cf. Table 2).

The execution of Program E causes the teletype to print how many paths exist on Tape 6 and the total number of data elements on the tape. The paths are numbered so that Path 0 is the path to the nose and Path 1 is the path to the tail. If full automation is being used -NP least squares paths are next, followed by subsonic and supersonic paths. The teletype then types out the word INSTRUCTION, as shown in the sample run in Appendix II. The instructions recognized by Program E are ADd, DElete, REplace, WRite or ENd. Only the first two characters of the instruction are scanned in selecting which instruction will be executed, and any instruction which is not recognized by Program E will be treated as a WR instruction.

If the instruction EN is entered a new Tape 6 is generated and Program E is terminated. For any other instruction the machine will respond by typing out PATH NUMBER. This is a request for the operator to supply the number of the path that is to be edited. The next teletype print out is FORK NUMBER. On a WR instruction the teletype will respond by printing out the contents of the corresponding path/fork if the fork number is non-negative. If the fork number is negative a diagram showing the contents of the header card of each path will be printed. The teletype will then request the next instruction.

For RE, AD, and DE instructions, the machine will type out CARD NUMBER after the fork number has been entered. If only one card is to be edited enter the corresponding card number. The header card, which is number 0, can be modified only with the RE instruction. For a negative card number the whole fork will be edited and if the fork number is zero the whole path will be edited. A zero card number is treated like a negative card number for AD or DE instructions.

On a RE or AD instruction the TTY will request the NUMBER OF POINTS, the TYPE OF PATH, REAL ETA, IMAG ETA, and the REFINEMENT until the information necessary to complete the instruction is entered. If the operator responds properly to each of these requests, the TTY will type out INSTRUCTION again, i.e., ask for the next instruction. Tape 6 is modified only after the instruction EN has been typed.

Information for sequential responses can be entered on one line by the use of the slash as a delimiter. A path can be added or replaced by typing the following:

$$IN/PN/FN/CN/K/KT/\eta_1/\eta_2/LL/\eta_1/\eta_2/LL...$$

where IN = AD or RE, PN = path number, FN = fork number, CN = card number, $|K|$ = number of endpoints, KT = type of path (stem, fork, or supersonic path), η_1 = location of real coordinate of endpoint, η_2 = location of imaginary coordinate of endpoint, LL = refinement. If $K > 0$, η_1 and η_2 represent coordinates in the η'-plane and if $K < 0$, η_1 and η_2 represent coordinates in the η-plane.

For example, to enter Fork 6 of Path 5 ending at $\eta' = .2 + .3i$ one responds to INSTRUCTION by typing

$$AD/5/6/0/1/0/.2/.3/1$$

and a carriage return. The card number 0 must be given. If Tape 6 already contains a Fork 6 in Path 5, the old Fork 6 is relabelled Fork 7, all higher numbered forks are advanced by 1 and the value of KT for the corresponding stem is adjusted to take this addition into account. Corresponding adjustments are made to account for deletions. If Fork 6 is deleted all higher fork numbers are reduced by one and the value of KT for the stem is reduced by one. If there is more than one correction to a path it is simpler to correct the highest numbered fork first, since an addition or deletion affects only higher numbered forks. The same applies to complete paths. To write out the fork added above, type the instruction WR/5/6; the TTY will respond

$$1 \qquad 0$$
$$.200 \qquad .300 \qquad 1$$

As a more important example, consider the path to the tail labelled as Path 1, Fork 0. Here we take $K = 2$ because this path must have two segments in order to pass around the origin with the right orientation. Figure 6 is a sketch of the η-plane showing the sonic locus and a pair of typical supersonic paths. Since $\eta = A$ lies in the second quadrant, the tail may be reached by either passing above or below the origin. In the present integration scheme it is necessary that the path to the tail be drawn above the origin in the η-plane, i.e., in the clockwise direction. For example, that path may be drawn first to $\eta' = .1 + .1i$ and then to $\eta' = .438 - .369i$. The TTY input is

$$AD/1/0/0/2/0/.1/.1/1/.438/-.369/1$$

To check what has been inserted, type WR/1/0; the TTY responds

$$2 \qquad 0$$
$$.100 \qquad .100 \qquad 1$$
$$.438 \qquad -.369 \qquad 1$$

The path to the nose is identified as 0/0. The second segment alone may be modified by setting $CN = 2$.

3.3 Supersonic Paths.

The supersonic part of the flow is computed from paths that
consist of two asymmetrical polygons. Each of these terminates along
a single arc of the sonic locus that should extend just beyond its
points of intersection with the body $\psi = 0$.

The supersonic paths are entered as two distinct paths on Tape 6.
It is convenient for the two supersonic paths to be the last two on
Tape 6. If for some test runs the calculation in Program B is to be
carried out without the supersonic paths and without full automation,
then the number of paths NP can be decreased so that the program will
exit before carrying out the integration for the supersonic paths.
Thus if the nose paths are the first three paths of Tape 6, the
designer can work on improving only the nose of the profile by setting
NP = 3. Integration is then done along three paths and a good deal of
time can be saved in running Program B.

Choosing a supersonic path correctly is rather intricate because
of the singularities that occur at the complex branch points of
$[u^2+v^2-c^2]^{1/2}$. Therefore the following instructions should be read
carefully before attempting a calculation.

A typical supersonic path is shown in Figure 6. It first drops
vertically from $\eta = A$ to a point below the real η-axis but an ample
distance from the sonic locus. The path then goes to the right to some
arbitrary point and angles down just crossing the sonic locus. After
that it heads left at a distance of about .05 units below the sonic
locus until it reaches the vicinity of the point where the flow is
expected to become supersonic. Finally, it goes up to the sonic locus
and returns to the right along this locus until it reaches a point
slightly to the left of the point where it first crossed the sonic
locus, and there it stops. The first segment which ends at the sonic
locus on the left has an LL < 0 in its description. This informs the
code that we are at what is called a shoulder point. The code forces

all segments following this one to lie exactly on the sonic locus;
they are in fact pasted on this locus.

Program D should be used to plot a graph of the sonic locus in
order to be able to estimate the coordinates of points near it. A
better understanding of the above prescription can be obtained by
studying Figure 6 in conjunction with this description. Note that the
path is made just long enough to encompass the entire supersonic zone.

The other supersonic path drops down from η = A to the left and at
some point to the left of the first path's shoulder it crosses the
sonic locus. It should be noted that difficulty with singularities
can arise if one path crosses the sonic locus too near the shoulder of
the other path. After crossing the sonic locus the second path heads
to the right, again keeping a distance of about .05 units below the
sonic locus. It is also pasted onto the sonic locus at precisely the
point where the other supersonic path ended, which becomes its
shoulder and is again indicated by making LL negative. It now
proceeds to the left along the sonic locus tracing out in reverse
order precisely the same points as the previous path. Program B once
more places them exactly on the sonic locus because these points all
follow the shoulder point where LL is negative.

To assist in understanding these rules two supersonic paths from
an actual case are reproduced in the sample TTY run of Appendix II.
If these two paths are switched then the rows and columns of the
characteristic triangle are interchanged. To avoid the singularities
which arise when $[u^2+v^2-c^2]^{1/2}$ = 0, the inner segments of the paths
should be kept appreciably further from the sonic locus than the outer
segments. The CDC 6600 message ARITHMETIC ERROR when Program B is run
usually indicates that singularities have been encountered. A certain
amount of trial and error in choosing the paths may be required to
avoid such trouble. If KT = 2 on one supersonic path, Program D will
plot the singular points which the other supersonic path should not

approach rather than the path itself. Finally, the program allows the use of a second set of supersonic paths to define the lower surface of the airfoil whenever that becomes necessary.

3.4 Mesh Refinement.

For preliminary design calculations where a high degree of accuracy is not required, a mesh refinement parameter MRP = 1 with AA = .08 can be used for the integration along the paths. A typical run without full automation then takes about 20 seconds on the CDC 6600. At later stages of the design when better resolution is required at the nose and tail or near the sonic line we have used MRP = 2, taking a minute or more of machine time. Finally, for preparation of the coordinates for an experimental model or for the analysis program the finer mesh sizes MRP = 4 or MRP = 8, which assure four or five significant figures in the coordinates, should be used. Also, if $|LL| > 1$ the segment where this occurs is subdivided $|LL|$ times as often as for $|LL| = 1$.

4. Automation.

4.1 Conditions at the Nose and Tail.

Tape 7 contains the parameters specifying the initial analytic function (cf. formula (5.18) in Part I)

$$(5.18) \quad g(\eta) = E_M E \left[\frac{\eta - E_C}{Z + \sqrt{1-E}} + \frac{\eta - E_C}{Z} \right] + E_T \eta + E_{TSQ} \eta^2 + E_{TCU} \eta^3$$

$$+ \sum_{j=1}^{4} (T_{j1} + iT_{j2}) \log (\eta - T_{j3} - iT_{j4})$$

$$+ \sum_{j=1}^{4} (N_{j1} + iN_{j2}) \log (\eta - N_{j3} - iN_{j4})$$

$$+ \sum_{j=1}^{4} (S_{j1} + iS_{j2}) \log (\eta - S_{j3} - iS_{j4})$$

which defines the flow to be calculated by Program B, where

$$Z = \sqrt{E(\eta - E_C)^2 + 1 - E}$$

and

$$T_{jk} = TLj(k), \qquad N_{jk} = NLj(k), \qquad S_{jk} = SLj(k)$$

The three kinds of logarithms have different branch cuts (cf. Appendix I). The parameters are updated in Program A and they are listed in Appendix I. The parameters are chosen so as to generate a closed profile $\psi = 0$ with desirable physical properties.

There are 72 parameters which are available to the designer. However, not all 72 parameters can be selected arbitrarily, since there are three constraints which must be satisfied by the profile in order to obtain a meaningful flow. Four other constraints may be imposed using the program. The seven constraints are

(1) $x_u = 0$ at the tail

(2) $y_u = 0$ at the tail

(3) $\psi = 0$ at the tail

(4) x_v prescribed at the nose

(5) x_u prescribed at the nose

(6) $y_{uu} = 0$ at the tail

(7) $x_{uu} = 0$ at the tail

of which the first three are the required ones. Constraints 6 and 7 ensure a multiple critical point at the tail, which helps to make the angle of flow a negative minimum there, so that the top and bottom surfaces of the airfoil have similar curvature and will not overlap. For some of our examples we have found it a good idea to have the machine compute automatically the coefficients of the ellipse function, the polynomial terms η and η^2 in equation (5 18), and a logarithm near the tail. These four complex coefficients E_M, E_T, E_{TSQ}, and $T_{41} + iT_{42}$

are detemrined by a system of linear equations using the constraints
above and minimizing the sum of their squares. The parameters to be
computed are designated on Tape 7 by their LC numbers starting with
TL1(1) as the first. Since we may automate as many as 31 parameters,
31 different LC numbers (cf. Appendix II) can appear on Tape 7. NK is
the total count of such parameters. If NK is negative then the sum of
the automated coefficients is minimized and $|NK|$-1 constraints are
imposed. For NK > 7 the seven constraints are satisfied and the sum
of squares of the automated coefficients is minimized when full automation is not used. In order for minimization to be performed ABS(NK)
must be greater than 3. Minimization results in nearly equal values
for these parameters, which we have found leads to the best profile.
Only coefficients which appear linearly in formula (5.18) should be
automated. These are the parameters that appear in columns 1-10, 11-20,
41-50 and 51-60, starting with card number 3 in Table 1 of Appendix I.

4.2 Conditions for a Prescribed Profile.

A more extensive automation of the parameters may be performed to
determine the magnitudes of the twelve logarithms, the ellipse term
and the coefficients of η, η^2 and η^3. The seven constraints described
above are still imposed, but additional conditions are included by
prescribing points in the hodograph plane at which ψ ought to vanish.
This means that an approximation to the airfoil must be drawn. Then
the locations of some of the logarithms in equation (5.18) are selected. Their coefficients are determined by satisfying in a least squares
sense the equations which result from prescribing points where $\psi = 0$.

For the full automation paths of integration have to be drawn
through the profile at points where ψ should vanish. The paths along
which the integrations are performed for the automation are now
described differently than those in Section 3. Each path of integration is made up of one or two segments from A to the body, followed by

a polygonal arc consisting of segments connecting the points in the
η'-plane or the η-plane where the body has been prescribed. Six or
seven such paths can be used to describe the entire body. The refinement parameter LL is negative for the first point of an automation
path which is on the body and positive for all subsequent segments.
This is similar to the description for the supersonic paths, where the
first segment which ends on the sonic locus (a shoulder point) has
LL < 0. Segments before and after the shoulder point were defined
with a positive LL. Similarly, for the automation paths segments
before and after the first body point of a path have LL positive. The
mesh can be subdivided by increasing the $|LL|$ value as before.
Increasing the $|LL|$ value gives more weight to a particular segment
in the automation.

Tape 6 now consists of the nose and tail paths followed by a
number of paths used for automation and by the paths of integration
described in Section 3 which are used for determining the flow pattern
when all the constants have been set. The NP value on Tape 7, which
must be taken as negative, becomes the number of paths used in automation. NK is the number of coefficients which are being computed by
the automation routine and it is positive. For full automation NK
must be greater than 7, since in addition to the least squares fit the
seven constraints must be satisfied. The paths for automation can be
inserted in the η-plane or in the η'-plane by appropriate choice of
the sign of K.

For full automation XR acts as a weight. A large value of XR
results in little minimization of the magnitudes of the coefficients,
but a sharp fit to the prescribed body points. For XR small the fit
is no longer so good, but the resulting profile becomes smoother.
We have found XR = 1 satisfactory in most cases. The influence of any
of the prescribed body points can be increased by making LL > 1 on the
corresponding card.

If Program B is executed and NP is negative, a complete automation is carried out using the number of automation paths given by $|NP|$, which appear on Tape 6. The number of parameters automated is given by NK and the specific parameters automated are designated by the LC values on Tape 7. As the program is carried out, messages are printed monitoring the progress. The first set of messages tell which auto-mated path is being worked on to obtain the values of ψ at the end-points. After these integrations are performed the number of points used for the least squares fit is printed. The trace of the coeffici-ent matrix and the determinant of the matrix which must be inverted to solve the complete system of linear equations for the parameters are both printed, together with a statement that the automation is complete. Program B then goes on to solve the flow problem as before and uses the remaining set of paths for integration, printing out when the integration along each path is finished. When all remaining paths are used a message OUT OF PATHS is typed. The Calcomp plot of the η-plane shows the final profile marked by crosses and the prescribed body points marked by circles if the run number, NRN, is positive. For a negative run number NRN the plot of prescribed body points is suppressed.

We have found that using eight or nine logarithms may be suffici-ent to obtain a reasonable flow. This means approximately twenty-three real constants are automated (NK $\cong$ 23). It is inconceivable that all thirty-two possible parameters be automated simultaneously. A closed profile is more easily achieved if some care is given to the location of the tail. A typical run with complete automation takes 80 seconds with MRP = 1. Much of the early design can be done with MRP = 1. When the airfoil is nearly finished small changes can be made without the full automation, using a Tape 6 which does not have the paths for automation and a Tape 7 where NP is positive. These runs are much faster and changes which round and polish the airfoil can be made quickly.

5. Guidelines for Choosing the Input Parameters.

5.1 Logarithms.

In this section we give guidelines, based on both theory and practice, which should be helpful in designing a good airfoil. An experienced user can expect to obtain a satisfactory example after several dozen trial runs, each of which would require about one minute of machine time on the CDC 6600 computer. With or without full automation, the following observations are helpful.

The logarithms defining g and therefore ψ act like a distribution of sources, sinks, and vortices that enable one to adjust the stream-line $\psi = 0$ in the η-plane, which is a transformation of the hodograph plane. The coordinates of the logarithmic singularities, such as $N_{13} + iN_{14}$, should be placed outside the region of the flow in the η-plane, and they should be placed where an effect is desired, since they act like δ-functions. The coefficients of the logarithmic terms, such as $N_{11} + iN_{12}$, are found to influence the body $\psi = 0$ in the following way in the η-plane. In front of the nose, that is, to the left of $\eta = -1$, a coefficient $N_{11} = -1$ tends to push the nose in, whereas the coefficient $N_{12} = \pm1$ twists the streamline. For a log on the positive imaginary axes, the coefficient $N_{12} = -1$ creates a similar pushing log, while $N_{11} = \pm1$ has a lesster twisting effect. Because the upper arc of $\psi = 0$ in the η-plane corresponds to the bottom surface of the airfoil, a pushing log here can keep the speed on the bottom of the airfoil subsonic, giving a flat distribution of the pressure coefficient C_p. A log at the tail, near $\eta = +1$, pushes $\psi = 0$ in there if it has coefficient $T_{11} = -1$, and this tends to thicken the tail in the physical plane. Again, imaginary coefficients $T_{12} = \pm1$ for this log have a twisting effect.

On the negative imaginary axis of the η-plane, a log may be placed just below the sonic locus. With the coefficient S_{12} = +1 this log will thin the airfoil, controlling limiting lines and pushing them inside the profile where they belong. The real part S_{11} of the coefficient of this log again twists ψ = 0. The transonic zone corresponding to the nose of the airfoil is found where ψ = 0 crosses the sonic locus in the third quadrant. For optimum profiles several logs may be needed in this region to control the limiting line, and their choice involves more trial and error than elsewhere because the problem of completely eliminating limiting lines or shock waves is not well posed. Pushing coefficients of logs can be thought of as sources, whereas twisting coefficients should be interpreted as vortices.

Tail logs have branch cuts directed to the right, nose logs have branch cuts directed to the left, and side logs have branch cuts directed downwards. The logs must be placed so that these cuts do not cross the flow or intersect any of the paths of integration, such as the supersonic path. The Calcomp plot created by Program D contains arrows which show the location of the logarithms and the direction of their branch cuts.

5.2 Location of Logarithms and Closing Holes.

A test run of the design program typically yields a level curve ψ = 0 in the η-plane that has holes in it and therefore does not represent a closed profile. If we think of the desired curve as a continuous arc asymptotic to the positive coordinate axes at infinity, then the kind of hole we encounter has a behavior analogous to that of the two sections of an equilateral hyperbola $xy = -\,\varepsilon^2$, which fork outward near the origin. What is desired is a perturbation of the input parameters that will switch these two disjoint arcs over into the continuous section of an opposite hyperbola $xy = \varepsilon^2$ located in the first quadrant, which forms a closed arc past the origin joined asymptotically to the positive x-axis and the positive y-axis at infinity.

A pushing log just outside it will often close such a hole in the locus $\psi = 0$. In particular, to close the nose a pushing log near $N_{13} + iN_{14} = -1.4 + .1i$ has been found to be helpful. However, at the early stages of design it is better not to insert too many of these logs. They are actually more effective at later stages in closing relatively small holes or rounding undesirable bumps in the curvature of the profile. At the beginning it is advisable to adjust the more important parameters, such as the tail location, the branch point B, and the ellipse eccentricity E. If one tail log plus the coefficients of η, η^2 and the ellipse function are automated, it may be possible to succeed with just six additional logs, namely, four pushing logs at the nose, tail and two sides placed near the real and imaginary axes, plus two logs in the first and third quadrants that help to control boundary layer separation on the lower surface and limiting line overlap at the front of the upper surface of the airfoil.

A good general principle seems to be that the best airfoils are achieved by keeping the coefficients of the logarithms and other terms as small as possible and by spacing the logarithms well apart. More specifically, the sum of the squares of the absolute values of the coefficients can be minimized, the number of logs used should be kept down, and the logs should be placed far from the profile. The reason for this rule is that critical points of the stream function ψ tend to occur near the body, creating holes where the locus $\psi = 0$ opens outward in two forks. As we indicated before, such a hole can be closed by placing a pushing logarithm in the opening. This is supposed to move the critical point away from the body. However, according to the argument principle for analytic functions, the logarithm generates a new critical point nearby. It is when the coefficient of the logarithm is relatively small that good control can be maintained over these two critical points. Sometimes small pulling

logs at adjacent locations are more effective than pushing logs directly at an area of difficulty.

The rules discussed above and in Section 5.1 apply for full
automation except that the linear coefficients are now determined by
the program. The location of the logarithms must be chosen so that
the simultaneous equations solved for the coefficients are adequately
non-singular. The determinant of the equations is a measure of the
linear independence of the system. The trace is determined by the
prescribed body points and varies with the location of the nose and
tail and with XR. XR = 0 for the case of nose and tail automation
only, except for one example we did with XR = 1.

5.3 Selecting Other Parameters.

The most important parameters in designing an airfoil at a given
Mach number M are the branch point B and the location of the tail in
the η'-plane. The coefficient of lift increases as the magnitude of B
increases. Since usually the real part of B is small, the imaginary
part of B controls the lift. The argument of B controls the camber
near the tail. If the value of Re (B) is too large the tail may
overlap in the physical plane.

The location of the tail in the hodograph plane determines the
value of C_p there and the trailing edge slope. Choosing C_p = 0 at the
tail tends to avoid boundary layer separation. Moving the location of
the tail in the η-plane towards the origin along the locus C_p = 0
lowers the slope at the tail and thins the airfoil.

The ellipse parameter E has an effect on the thickness-chord ratio
T/C. Small values of E give a fat profile, and big values give a thin
profile. Its real part may be taken near .4, and the absolute value
of its imaginary part should be small. However, the thickness-chord
ratio is also controlled by pushing logs on the positive and negative
imaginary axes which thin the airfoil when their coefficients are

large. Also, a tail location far from $\eta = 0$ fattens the profile.

The translation parameters A and E_C play a less serious role and can be set initially at E_C = .5 + .2i and A = -.1 + ai, where a > 0 should be significantly less than the ordinate of the point where the sonic locus crosses the positive imaginary axis in the η-plane.

The ratio x_v/x_u controls the angle of the profile at the stagnation point and should be small to achieve a vertical tangent there. For profiles with higher lift this ratio should be taken somewhat larger. If five or more parameters are automated then we must prescribe x_u and x_v at the nose. The magnitude of x_u controls the curvature at the nose. For thin airfoils where the radius of curvature is small, x_u should be about .05, and for fat airfoils x_u should be about .1.

The effect of the above parameters is less important when full automation is used, since the automated terms may act to cancel their influence. It is possible to prescribe these parameters in such a way that the curve $\psi = 0$ cannot pass through the prescribed least squares points. For example, contradictions can occur if the prescription of x_u and x_v at the nose is inconsistent with the assigned curve. Therefore care must be taken to choose the least squares curve and the parameters in a consistent fashion.

5.4 Boundary Layer Control.

It is important physically that the tail in the η-plane be located near a point where C_p = 0, that is, near a point where the speed is equal to that at infinity in the (x,y)-plane. This tends to avoid boundary layer separation and leads to a reasonable model of the wake because the central streamline beyond the tail will fit closely to the locus C_p = 0 all the way out to infinity. By placing the tail well back from the origin in the η-plane, we generate a bigger closed loop $\psi = 0$ and therefore a fatter profile in the physical plane. This also increases the negative angle of the flow at the tail and enhances the camber of the airfoil, making it look as if a flap had been lowered at the rear. The tail location is set at Path 1, Fork 0 on Tape 6 in Program E.

Because the branch point parameter B is small, varying it essentially has the effect of making a small translation of the sonic locus in the η-plane. Thus, when $- Im$ (B) is increased the lift goes up, while at the same time the sonic locus moves away from the image of the lower surface of the body, but drives into the image of the upper surface in the η-plane, creating a larger supersonic zone. Most of our experience has been with high lift airfoils. Similarly, as the Mach number M is increased, the waist of the sonic locus pinches in around the body near the imaginary axis of the η-plane. This means that only a narrow body can allow smooth supersonic flow for large M. We have maintained subsonic flow along the lower surface of the airfoil to avoid boundary layer separation in the cambered region of the tail. An optimal configuration is obtained when the profile $\psi = 0$ skirts just inside the sonic locus at the positive imaginary axis in the η-plane.

In addition to the constraints that the flow be subsonic on the bottom surface and that no limiting lines emerge in the supersonic zone of the top surface, we impose a requirement that there be no boundary layer separation. To achieve this, we calculate in Program F the turbulent boundary layer momentum thickness θ^* by a standard procedure due to Nash and Macdonald [20]. Then we streamline so as to avoid separation by imposing the inequality $-\theta^* dq/qds < .004$, except perhaps for the last few percent of the chord. Here q is the speed and s is the arc length along the airfoil. For optimal airfoils, the arc of the level curve $\psi = 0$ in the η-plane corresponding to the bottom surface of the airfoil should be made to follow along the sonic locus, fitting it closely from the subsonic side, but not turning away so abruptly as to cause separation far from the tail.

The ratio CD, which is really equal to C_D/C_L, should be small and positive, since it governs a small sink at infinity allowing the tail to terminate with a corresponding small positive thickness. This is done so that a reversed boundary layer correction can be super-imposed on our airfoil through Program F without making it overlap in an unrealistic way. A reasonable value of CD is .03, which has led us to a tail thickness $\Delta y = .5C_D$ that is about .005 of the chord after the boundary layer correction has been subtracted. Observe here that we conceive of the flow computed by Program B as the one that has been corrected for displacement thickness of the boundary layer on the true airfoil. Finally, the parameter TR should lie in the interval between 0 and 1. It determines how far between the trailing streamlines our virtual location of the tail in the η-plane will lie. For TR = 0 the upper surface terminates right at the virtual tail.

6. The Boundary Layer Program.

Program F computes the displacement thickness of the boundary layer of the airfoil and determines whether the boundary layer separates according to the Nash-Macdonald criterion (cf. [20]). Separation occurs when SEP $\geq$ .004 (cf. Section 11, Part I).

Program F can be run at the teletype (TTY) or as a batch job. The file Tape 3 which is the output of Program D provides the input data for this program. At the teletype Program F is executed and produces the output file Tape 4. The program prints out whether separation occurs on either the top or bottom surface, the x-coordinate of the first occurrence of separation, and the maximum SEP and its x-coordinate. The contents of file Tape 4, which can be sent to the printer, are the new (x,y)-coordinates. The y-coordinates have been corrected for the displacement thickness. The corrected data replaces the input data on file Tape 3, which may then be used as input to Program G.

The Reynolds number RN, the separation parameter SEP, and the percent of chord PCH at which the boundary layer correction computation begins can be changed by means of a data statement in Program F. If PCH is negative the calculation is started at the peak of the pressure distribution C_p in the supersonic region.

7. The Analysis Program.

7.1 Program G.

Program G computes the transonic flow with shock waves around a given airfoil at a prescribed Mach number and angle of attack. The program consists of two parts. The first part processes the airfoil coordinates and does a conformal mapping onto the unit circle, while the second part solves the transonic flow equations for a specified Mach number and angle of attack. The first part need only be executed once, and then the second part can be executed repeatedly for various Mach numbers and angles of attack. In both parts of the program parameters and instructions are entered in a namelist statement format, as in Program A, with P the name of the list. After the specified instruction is complete the message READ P is printed, which is the request for the next instruction and set of parameter changes. We refer to this as control mode. The glossary for Program G lists all input and control parameters along with their default values.

7.2 Conformal Mapping.

When the program is initiated, the control parameter ITYP is set to zero and the number of cycles NS is set to 400. The message READ P is printed and the machine then waits for the first set of namelist parameters. ITYP = 0 and NS > 0 cause execution of the mapping part of the program; any parameters used in this part of the program which are not specified take their default values listed in the glossary.

Airfoil coordinates are specified on Tape 3 in one of five possible formats. The selection of the appropriate format is governed by the parameter FSYM. For FSYM = 1.0 coordinates and velocities output by Program D are used, while for FSYM = 2.0 the (x,y)-coordinates output by Program F are used. Other values of FSYM used for card input defining more general profiles are described in the glossary and in Table 3. In any input format where velocities or slopes are not supplied, smoothing may be applied to airfoil coordinates before computing slopes and cuvatures by cubic splines. The number of smoothing iterations is controlled by the parameter IS.

In the event that the tail has finite thickness the airfoil is automatically extended linearly until it closes or exceeds a chord length TE, whichever occurs sooner.

As an initial guess of the conformal mapping a Fourier series of NFC terms is computed at NMP equally spaced points on the unit circle, and then successive overrelaxation is applied for NS cycles. The relaxation parameter at each point in the M × N grid for the solution of Laplace's equation is called XS, and the relaxation parameter for adjusting arc length along the boundary is called XM. If NS = 1 the Fourier series itself is used for the conformal mapping. If the maximum residual for the mapping function and the arc length change is less than some prescribed tolerance ST specifying convergence, the program returns to control mode. Before returning to control mode, Tape 3 is rewound and data necessary to iterate the mapping further are stored on it. The control parameters ITYP = 0, NS < 0 may be used to resume the mapping for -NS cycles.

7.3 Transonic Flow.

After the mapping, or for that matter any other instruction, is completed the program returns automatically to control mode with ITYP= 1. Now parameters may be set and flow computations or control operations may be performed (cf. Table 4). After every operation except termination the program returns to control mode.

To save the current flow on Tape 3, use ITYP = -1, NS = 0. To retrieve the most recently saved solution from Tape 3, use ITYP = 1, NS = 0. The instruction ITYP = 0, NS = 0 causes the program to terminate, producing printed output and a Calcomp plot.

The mapping is done at a fine grid, but it is possible and even advantageous to do much of the flow calculation at a cruder grid. To double the grid sizes use the instruction ITYP = 1, NS = -1. After the solution has converged at the crude mesh size we go back to the finer grid with the instruction ITYP = -1, NS = 1. Finally, to compute the solution for NS cycles, ITYP and NS must both be positive. If the maximum change in the velocity potential and circulation is less than ST at any cycle, the program returns to control mode in fewer than NS cycles. For ITYP = 2 a Mach number diagram is generated at the completion of the NS cycles. For ITYP = 3 the coefficient of pressure C_p and the local Mach number are printed out at each point, and for ITYP = 4 a Calcomp plot is also generated.

The parameters XS, XM and XPHI are used as relaxation parameters. XPHI is the relaxation factor for the circulation Γ determined to satisfy the Kutta-Joukowski condition. If XPHI = 0.0, the Kutta-Joukowski condition will not be satisfied, but the parameter YA will be added to the lift coefficient C_L. XS is the maximum relaxation factor used at each point in the grid where the local Mach number is less than the free stream Mach number EM. XM is the minimum relaxation factor and is used everywhere in the supersonic region. The relaxation factor at intermediate points is a linear function of the square of the local Mach number.

An important role is played by the artificial viscosity parameter $EP = 1 - \lambda \Delta t$, where $\lambda (\Delta t)^2$ is the artificial viscosity and Δt is the mesh size in t. This term imposes an entropy inequality ensuring that the solution will be unique, but it is effective only if λ is large enough, which means that EP is small. The larger the value of EP the less the truncation error will be. In practice we use EP = 0.0 until the solution has almost converged and then increase EP to as large a value as possible while maintaining convergence. For flows with weak nearby shocks it often becomes necessary to use small values of EP to get the right answer, and in any case it is necessary to take EP < 1.

7.4   Teletype versus Batch Mode.

Program G can be executed in batch mode as well as with a time sharing system. When one executes a batch job, a sequence of data cards in namelist convention must be supplied in advance with the appropriate instruction given after each entrance into control mode.

The output, however, is different for TTY operation than for batch mode operation. The parameter IZ is used to control the number of characters as well as the output file selected for each line of output. For TTY operation IZ < 80 is recommended. This causes one line to print after every KP cycles of computation on the mapping or the solution. At all other cycles this line of information is written onto Tape 4. Before a return to control mode two lines of information are printed at the TTY and sent to Tape 4. For ITYP = 2 the Mach number diagram is printed at the teletype, while for ITYP > 2 the output is sent to Tape 4. Upon termination, Tape 4 can be sent to the printer.

For batch mode with $IZ \geq 80$ all the output will be sent to the printer. For $ITYP \geq 2$ and IZ > 120 the quantities x, y and C_p at each point on the body will be sent to Tape 4, which may be used for punched output. For IZ = 130, Tape 4 will not be rewound before writing onto it.

We refer to the teletype example in Appendix II for an illustration showing how Program G operates in practice and how long it takes on the CDC 6600.

III. EXAMPLES

1. Four Lifting Airfoils.

We have developed four principal examples to illustrate how the method of designing shockless transonic airfoils works in practice. They took varying numbers of test runs of the program to produce, with the earliest case requiring hundreds of trials, but the later ones needing less as we gained experience. All models were designed to have a maximum thickness-chord ratio T/C for given free stream Mach number M_∞ and lift coefficient C_L, subject to the constraints that the boundary layer not separate far from the tail, that the flow remain safely subsonic along the lower surface, and that the profile be reasonably smooth and blunt at the nose. In all cases we assumed that these desiderata could be achieved best by locating the tail in the hodograph plane at a point where the pressure coefficient C_p would be as near as possible to zero.

For our first example (cf. Figure 5) we set $M_\infty = .79$ with $T/C = .1$ and achieved the apparently maximum possible lift coefficient $C_L = .68$. At the tail in the hodograph plane a multiple critical point was imposed on the stream function ψ. The lift is evenly distributed along the chord, but it was not easy to eliminate separation of the turbulent boundary layer at about 80% of chord along the lower surface. Also, the supersonic zone above the upper surface is quite large, and limiting lines would penetrate the flow at either end of the sonic line if we attempted to increase the lift more without altering M_∞ or T/C. The camber of the airfoil resulted from making C_p vanish at the tail.

Our next example (cf. Figure 7) is at $M = .83$, $C_L = .6$ and $T/C = .07$. Such a case is perhaps too thin to be of much physical interest, for we had to introduce a rather large fictitious form drag coefficient C_D in order to obtain a tail that would be reasonably thick. There is no tendency whatever toward boundary layer separation on the lower surface, but the supersonic zone is huge, which may cause excessive sensitivity of the flow to changes in the angle of attack. Tape 7 for this model is listed under run number 1 of the teletype exercises carried out in Appendix II. Similarly Tape 7 for the previous profile is listed in the same exercises under run number 2.

The third airfoil (cf. Figure 9) was designed at M = .75 and C_L = .67 to yield a large thickness-chord ratio T/C = .15. In contrast to the two earlier examples this one was obtained using the more complete automation procedure described in Section 4.2 of Part II, which produced results much faster. At the lower Mach number M = .75 it was not feasible to bring the pressure coefficient C_p at the tail all the way down to zero. Moreover, we had some difficulty avoiding boundary layer separation on the lower surface of such a fat profile. The input data as well as a listing of the (x,y)-coordinates of the airfoil are presented in Appendix III.

We worked out a fourth example as part of an attempt to maximize the quantity M^2C_L under the constraints T/C $\geq$ .1, $C_D \leq$ .01. R. T. Jones [11] suggested this extremal problem because of the role it plays in his design of a skewed wing minimizing the drag of asymmetric aircraft operating just above the speed of sound. The profile we obtained has M_∞ = .75 and T/C = .1 combined with the unusually high lift coefficient C_L = 1, so that M^2C_L = .55. It has more camber than any of our other models, but was relatively easy to develop because we again used the full automation of Section 4.2, Part II. The example is readily reconstructed from the data in Figure 12 specifying the locations of logarithms and automation paths for its characteristic initial η-plane. Also, Program A is supposed to simulate this case by default if no file Tape 7 is found.

2. Comparison with Analysis and Experiment.

One of the earliest shockless airfoils we designed (cf. [7]) has
been tested at the two-dimensional high Reynolds number wind tunnel of
the National Aeronautical Establishment in Ottawa. The experimental
measurements have been compared with both design and analysis computations performed using our transonic flow programs, and extensive
tabulations of the results are presented in a National Research
Council of Canada technical report (cf. [12]). The agreement between
theory and experiment was excellent.

We have used the analysis program to study several examples at
off-design conditions. In Figures 13-17 we display some runs made on
our high lift airfoil maximizing $M^2 C_L$, which has a large supersonic
zone on the upper surface and considerable camber of the lower surface.
When the speed is just critical over most of the upper surface it is
seen that a pronounced supercritical peak occurs near the leading edge
of the upper surface that brings to mind the ideas advanced by Pearcey
[22], although it results here merely from the imposition of shockless
flow at a higher speed. At intermediate conditions below design the
flow is found to exhibit several weak shocks bounding separate supersonic zones rather than the single sharp one visualized in naive
models of the transonic problem. These shocks may not be very well
defined when they are extremely weak. At design we obtain reasonable
agreement with our hodograph calculation, and above design our isentropic evaluation of the wave drag coefficient C_D turns out to be
successful enough to predict drag rise reliably.

In Figure 18 we show the result of the analysis program when it
is applied after subtraction of the boundary layer correction from the
airfoil coordinates. This not only describes the effect of the turbulent boundary layer on the flow through a comparison with Figure 16,
but also indicates the true shape the wing section should have.

Finally, in Figure 19 we have adjusted the free stream Mach number M
and the angle of attack ALP in an attempt to achieve nearly shockless
flow with the boundary layer absent. For a highly cambered airfoil
loaded heavily at the tail this adjustment is not very effective,
although it was for the test of one of our earlier wing sections (cf.
[12]) where the supersonic zone was smaller and the trailing edge was
turned down less.

At Langley Research Center a test of the airfoil we designed to be
shockless at M = .79 is planned using a steel model with four inch
chord length. The Reynolds number of the experiment will be approximately R = 3 × 10^6. The same profile will be used for the skewed wing
of a five foot asymmetric model airplane designed by R. T. Jones for
transonic wind tunnel tests at the Ames Research Center in Moffett
Field. It is also for this application that we have developed our
high lift example with M^2C_L = .55. Finally, J. Kacprzynski and
L. Ohman intend to make a test of our 15% thick airfoil in their two-
dimensional high Reynolds number facility at the National Aeronautical
Establishment in Ottawa.

3. Conclusions.

We have developed a series of computer programs that enables one
to design shockless transonic airfoils in a few dozen runs requiring
not more than an hour or two of CDC 6600 machine time. Our analysis
routine can be used to ascertain whether the profiles behave well at
off-design conditions, or to smooth coordinates and obtain a desirable
shape more quickly when perfectly shockless flow is not essential. The
boundary layer correction determined by Program F indicates how to
avoid separation by suppressing adverse pressure gradients, although
the results are restricted to high Reynolds numbers for which the
boundary layer in the rear of the airfoil will be turbulent. The
correction to the coordinates is also important for highly cambered

airfoils because it apparently cannot be simulated by adjustments in
Mach number and angle of attack. There is experimental evidence that
the method provides a successful tool for application to supercritical
wing technology.

A number of examples help establish that shockless airfoils are
appropriate for the design of supercritical wings. In particular they
are preferable to shapes tailored to give constant free streamline
pressure distributions at critical speed, since they exhibit a peaky
distribution of the Pearcey type at comparable off-design conditions.
Analysis supports the contention that shockless flow can be achieved
in practice when boundary layer separation is suppressed, but it also
shows that transonic flow is unusually sensitive to changes in the
angle of attack or free stream Mach number. However, this same sensitivity can be exploited to give high performance in such characteristics as the lift of a transonic airfoil. Thus it seems likely that
shockless wing sections will be used in the construction of the next
generation of aircraft designed to operate near the speed of sound.

In closing we remark that the programs we have described could be
converted to treat the important problem of a cascade of transonic
compressor or turbine blades. In the case of Program B for design it
would only be necessary to replace the pole of x and y that is located
at the origin in the complex η-plane by an appropriate pair of match-
ing logarithmic singularities nearby. A more difficult but still
quite hopeful undertaking would be to extend our analysis method
to calculate genuinely three-dimensional flow past airfoils or through
transonic cascades. The most serious question that could arise in
such an investigation would be how to handle the vortex sheets following the blades.

References

1. Bergman, S., Integral operators in the theory of linear partial differential equations, Springer, Berlin, 1961.

2. Boerstoel, J. W., "A survey of symmetrical transonic potential flows around quasi-elliptical aerofoil sections," N.L.R. Report TR.T.172 (1967).

3. Courant, R. and Friedrichs, K. O., Supersonic flow and shock waves, Interscience, New York, 1948.

4. Filippov, A. F., "On the application of the method of finite differences to the solution of the problem of Tricomi," Izv. Akad. Nauk SSSR Ser. Mat., Vol. 21, pp. 73-88 (1957).

5. Forsythe, G. E. and Wasow, W. R., Finite difference methods for partial differential equations, Wiley, New York, 1960.

6. Garabedian, P. R., Partial differential equations, Wiley, New York, 1964.

7. Garabedian, P. R. and Korn, D. G., "Numerical design of transonic airfoils," Numerical solution of partial differential equations-II, ed. by B. Hubbard, Academic Press, New York, 1971, pp. 253-271.

8. Garabedian, P. R. and Korn, D. G., "Numerical design of shockless transonic airfoils," Actes du Congrès International des Mathémati-ciens, Vol. 3, pp. 95-97 (1971).

9. Garabedian, P. R., and Korn, D. G., "Analysis of transonic airfoils," Comm. Pure Appl. Math., Vol. 24, pp. 841-851 (1971).

10. Garabedian, P. R., and Lieberstein, H. M., "On the numerical calcu-lation of detached bow shock waves in hypersonic flow," J. Aero. Sci., Vol. 25, pp. 109-118 (1958).

11. Jones, R. T., "Reduction of wave drag by antisymmetric arrangement of wings and bodies," A.I.A.A. Journal (to appear).

12. Kacprzynski, J. J., Ohman, L. H., Garabedian, P. R., and Korn, D.G., "Analysis of the flow past a shockless lifting airfoil in design and off-design conditions," N.R.C. of Canada Aeronautical Report

LR-554, Ottawa, 1971.

13. Koppe, E. and Meier, G., "Erfahrungen mit optischen Methoden bei der Untersuchung transsonischer Strömungen," Zeit. Flugwissenschaften, Vol. 13, pp. 143-157 (1965).

14. Korn, D. G., "Computation of hypersonic axially symmetric flow at low Mach numbers," Report NYU-NYO-1480-99 (1968).

15. Korn, D. G., "Computation of shock-free transonic flows for airfoil design," Report NYU-NYO-1480-125 (1969).

16. Krupp, J. A., "The numerical calculation of plane steady transonic flows past thin lifting airfoils," Boeing Sci. Res. Lab. Rep. D180-12958-1, Seattle, 1971.

17. Lighthill, M. J., "The hodograph transformation in transonic flow, II and III," Proc. Roy. Soc. London, Vol. A191, pp. 341-369 (1947).

18. Morawetz, C. S., "On the non-existence of continuous transonic flows past profiles, I, II and III," Comm. Pure Appl. Math., Vol. 9, pp. 45-68 (1956), Vol. 10, pp. 107-131 (1957), Vol. II, pp. 129-144 (1958).

19. Murman, E. M. and Cole, J. D., "Calculation of plane steady transonic flows," A.I.A.A. Journal, Vol. 9, pp. 114-121 (1971).

20. Nash, J. F. and Macdonald, A. G. J., "The calculation of momentum thickness in a turbulent boundary layer at Mach numbers up to unity," Aeronautical Research Council C. P. No. 963, London, 1967.

21. Nieuwland, G. Y., "Transonic potential flow around a family of quasi-elliptical aerofoil sections," N.L.R. Report TR.T172 (1967).

22. Pearcey, H. H., "The aerodynamic design of section shapes for swept wings," Advan. Aero. Sci., Vol. 3 (1962).

23. Sears, W. R., General theory of high-speed aerodynamics, Princeton University Press, Princeton, 1954.

24. Sells, C. C. L., "Plane subcritical flow past a lifting aerofoil," Proc. Roy. Soc. London, Vol. A308, pp. 377-401 (1968).

25. Spee, B. M., and Uijlenhoet, R., "Experimental verification of shock-free transonic flow around quasi-elliptical aerofoil sections," N.L.R. Report MP 68003 U (1969).

26. Steger, J. L., and Lomax, H., "Numerical calculation of transonic flow about two-dimensional airfoils by relaxation procedures," A.I.A.A. 4th Fluid and Plasma Dynamics Conference, Palo Alto, Calif., June 21-23, 1971.

27. Swenson, E. V., "Geometry of the complex characteristics in transonic flow," Comm. Pure Appl. Math., Vol. 21, pp. 175-185 (1968).

28. Tomotika, S., and Tamada, K., "Studies in two-dimensional transonic flows of compressible fluid. Part I," Quart. Appl. Math., Vol. 7, pp. 381-397 (1950).

29. Whitcomb, R. T., and Clark, L. R., "An airfoil shape for efficient flight at supercritical Mach numbers," NASA TM X-1109 (Confidential Report), July 1965.

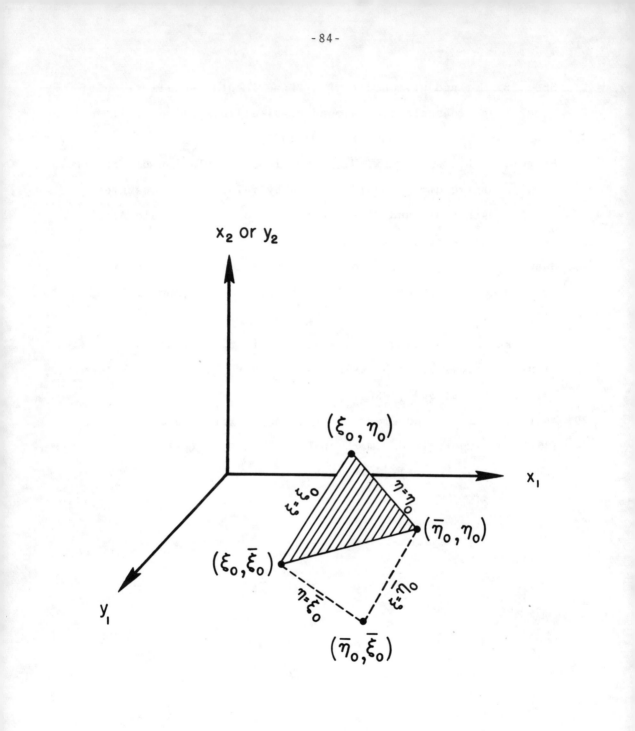

Figure 1   COMPLEX DOMAIN

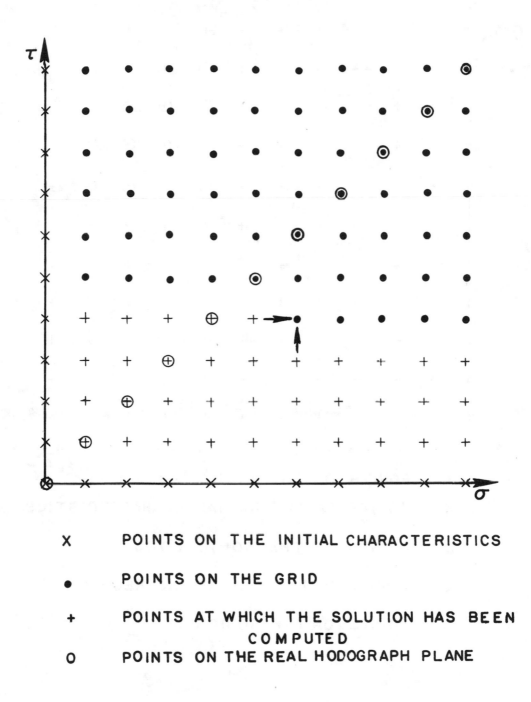

X   POINTS ON THE INITIAL CHARACTERISTICS

•   POINTS ON THE GRID

+   POINTS AT WHICH THE SOLUTION HAS BEEN COMPUTED

O   POINTS ON THE REAL HODOGRAPH PLANE

Figure 2   MESH FOR SUBSONIC PATHS

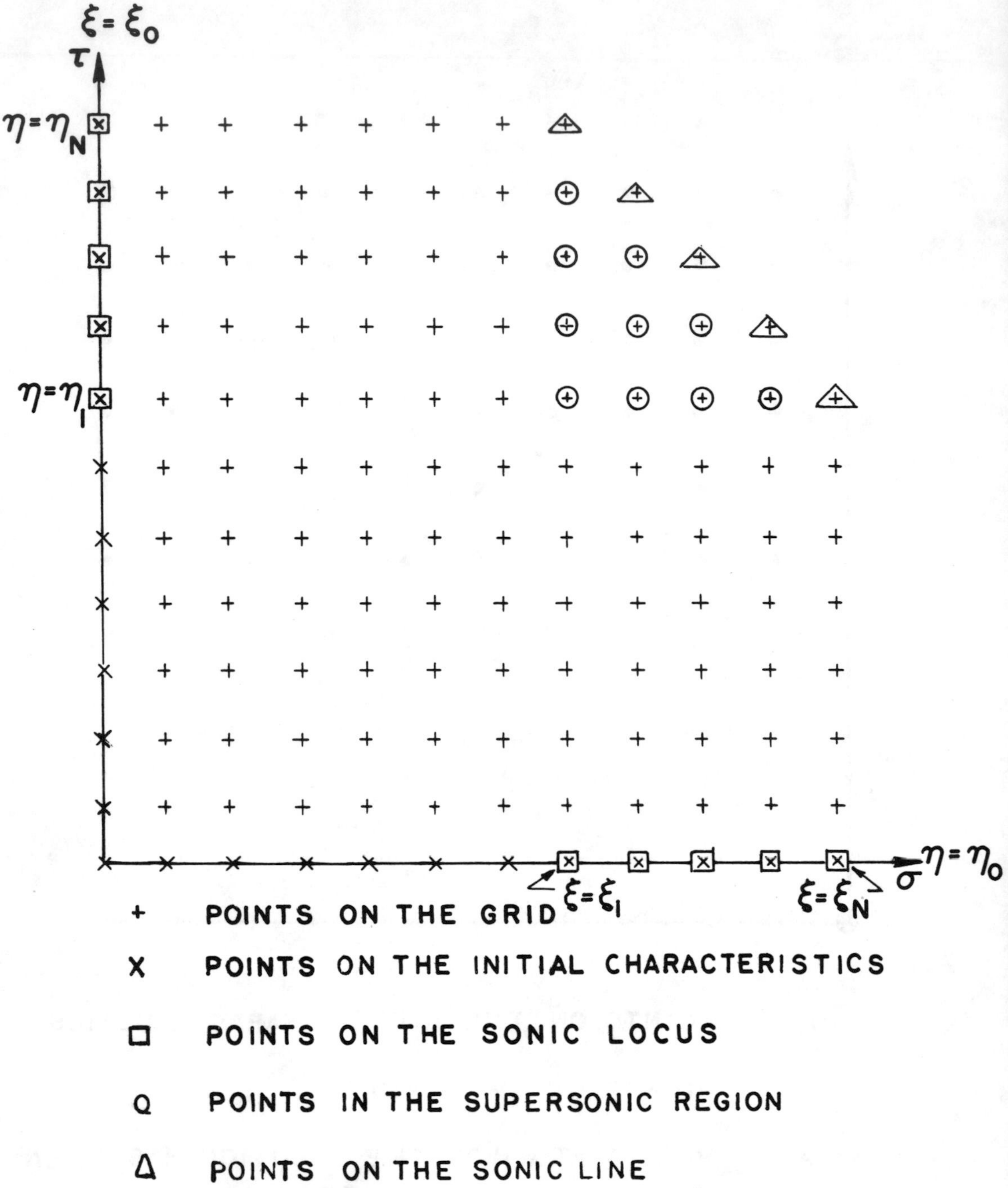

Figure 3   MESH FOR SUPERSONIC PATHS

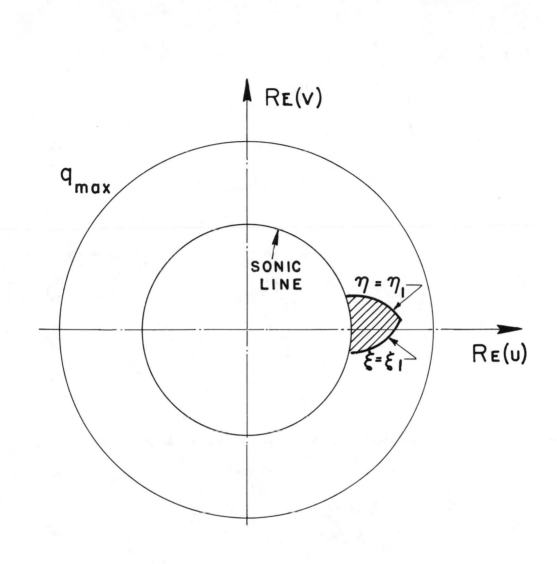

Figure 4 HODOGRAPH PLANE

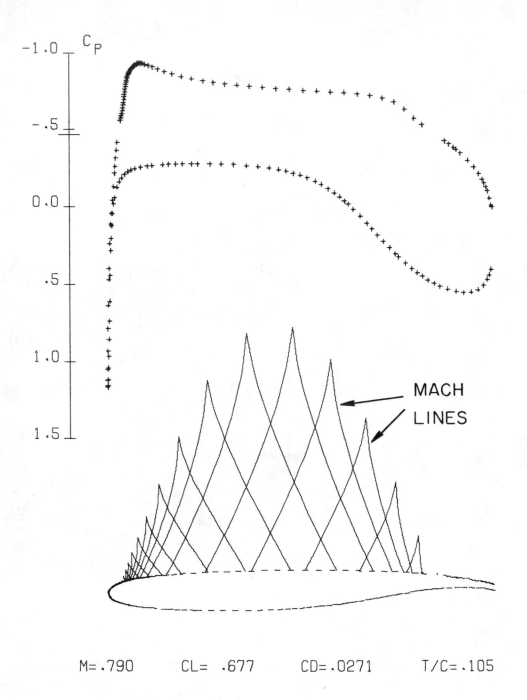

C_P

$M = .790$ $CL = .677$ $CD = .0271$ $T/C = .105$

Figure 5   SUPERCRITICAL WING SECTION

- 89 -

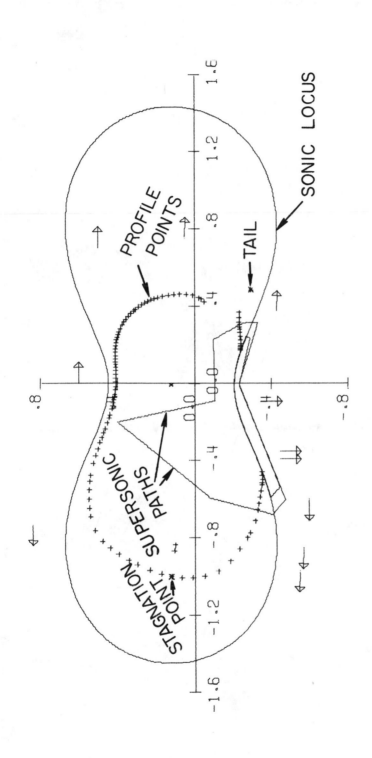

Figure 6   PLANE OF INITIAL DATA FOR FIG. 5

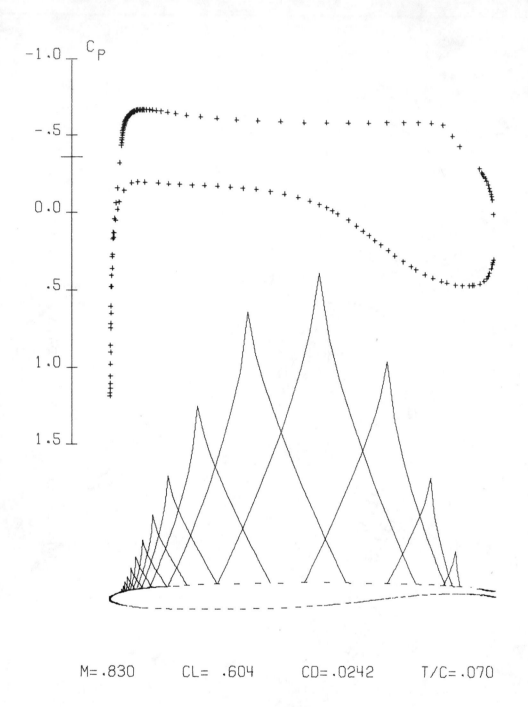

M=.830   CL= .604   CD=.0242   T/C=.070

Figure 7   THIN SHOCKLESS AIRFOIL

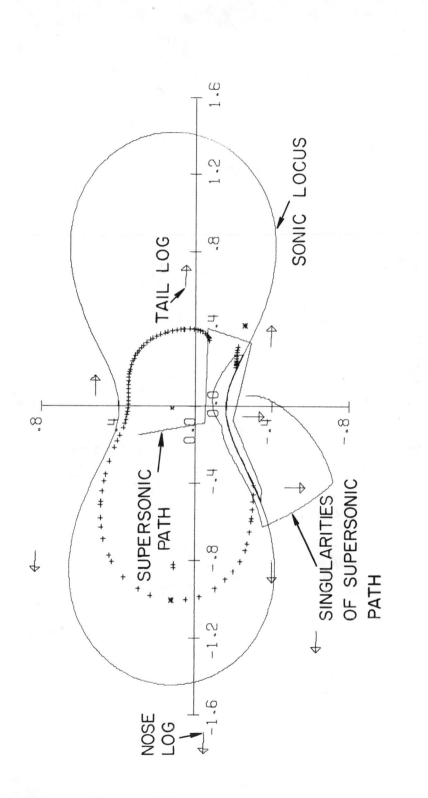

Figure 8 PLANE OF INITIAL DATA FOR FIG. 7

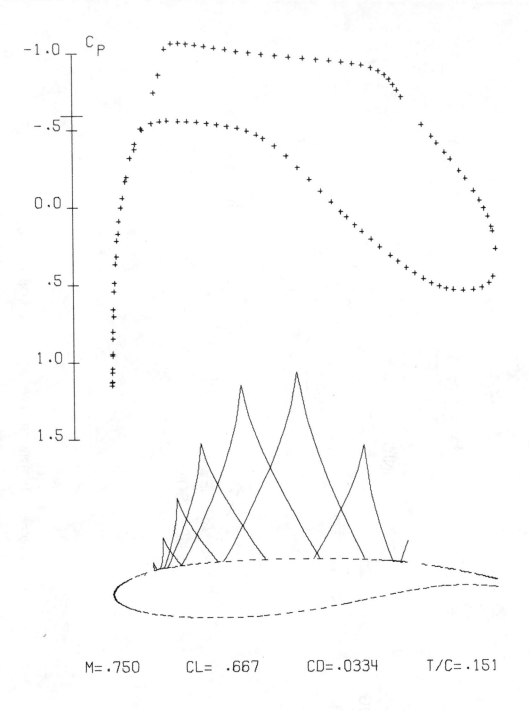

M=.750   CL= .667   CD=.0334   T/C=.151

Figure 9   THICK SHOCKLESS AIRFOIL

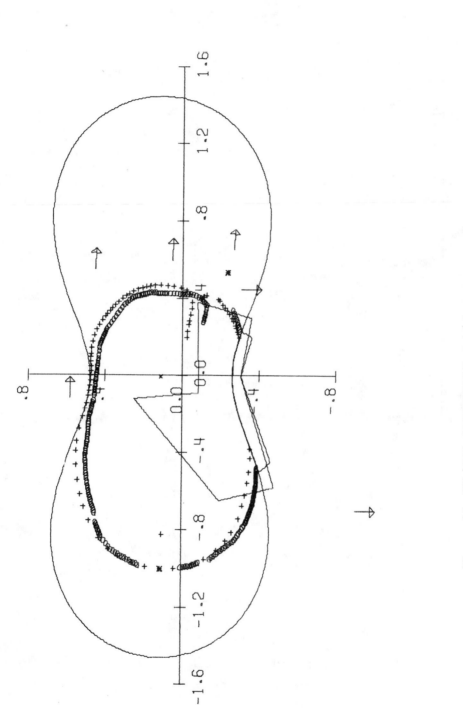

Figure 10   PLANE OF INITIAL DATA FOR FIG. 9

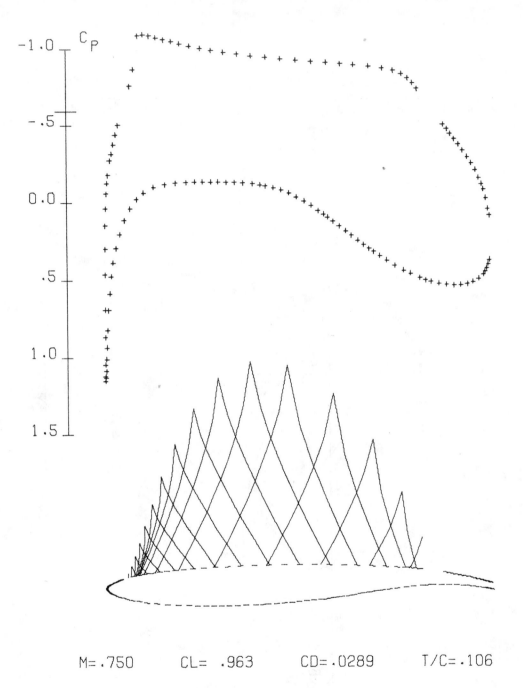

M=.750   CL= .963   CD=.0289   T/C=.106

Figure 11   HIGH LIFT AIRFOIL

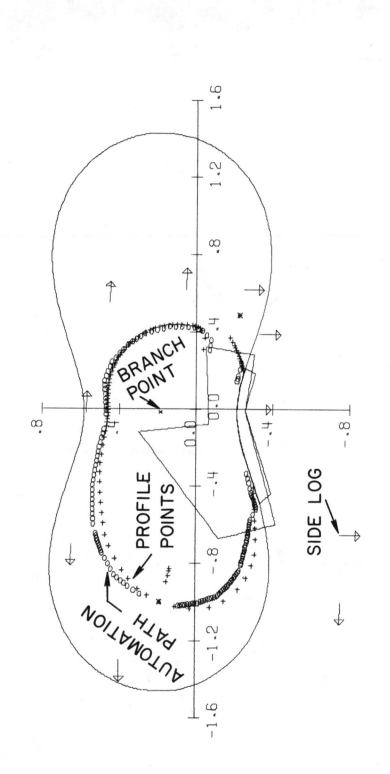

Figure 12   PLANE OF INITIAL DATA FOR FIG. 11

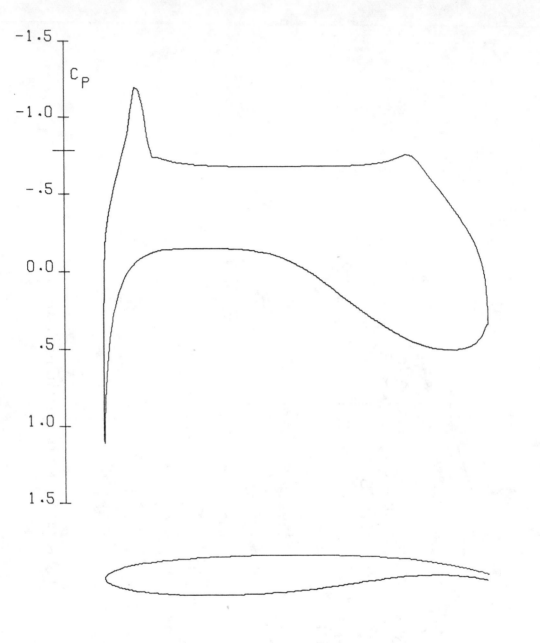

M= .700   T/C= .105   CL= .775   CD= .001   ALP= 0.00

M×N= 160×30   NCY= 600   EP= 0.00

Figure 13   ANALYSIS AT AVERAGE CRITICAL SPEED

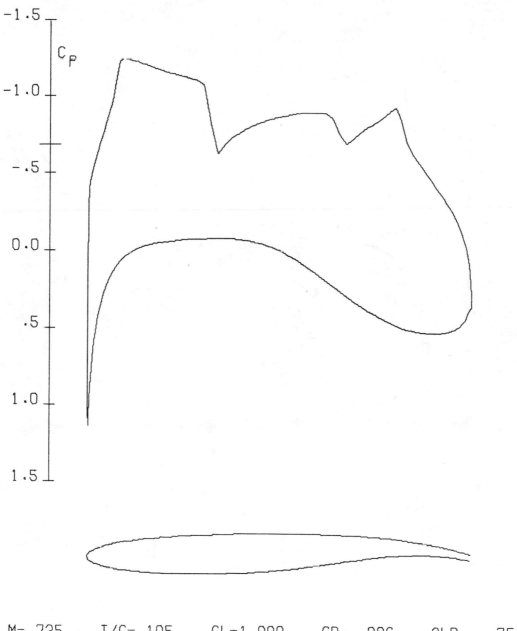

M=.725   T/C=.105   CL=1.000   CD= .006   ALP= .75

MxN= 160x30   NCY= 500   EP= .40

Figure 14   FLOW WITH THREE SHOCKS

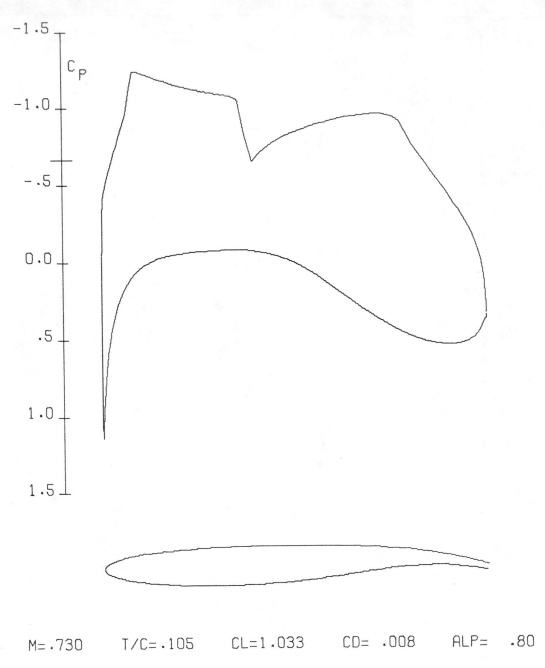

M=.730   T/C=.105   CL=1.033   CD= .008   ALP= .80

M×N= 160×30   NCY= 600   EP= 0.00

Figure 15   CASE WHERE REAR SHOCK DISAPPEARS

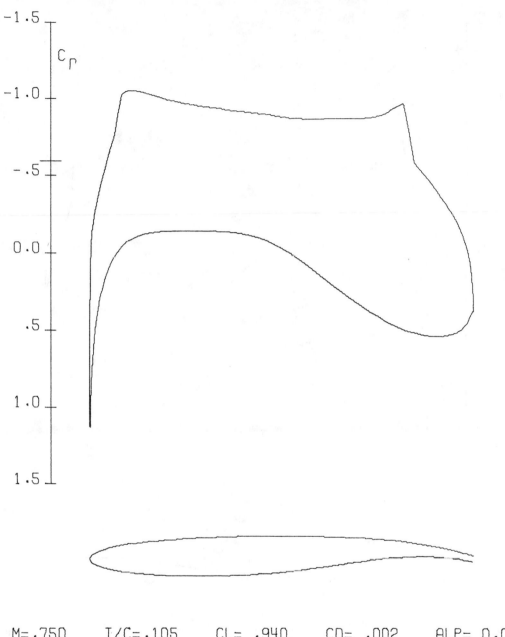

M=.750   T/C=.105   CL= .940   CD= .002   ALP= 0.00

M×N= 160×30   NCY= 800   EP=   .80

Figure 16   ANALYSIS AT DESIGN CONDITIONS

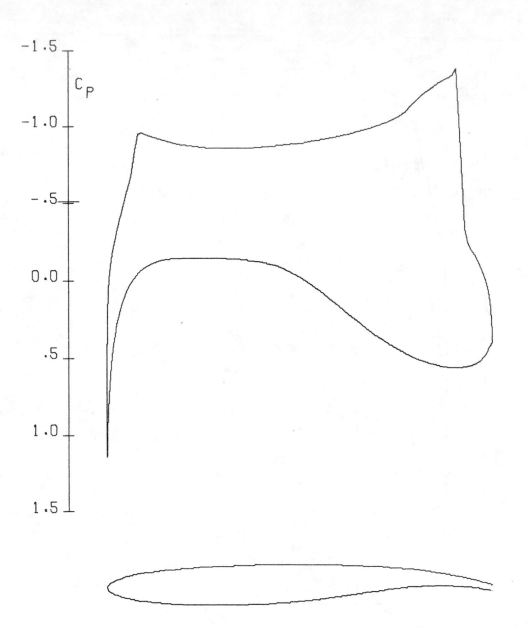

M=.775   T/C=.105   CL=1.017   CD= .022   ALP= 0.00

M×N= 160×30   NCY= 800   EP= 0.00

Figure 17   DRAG RISE

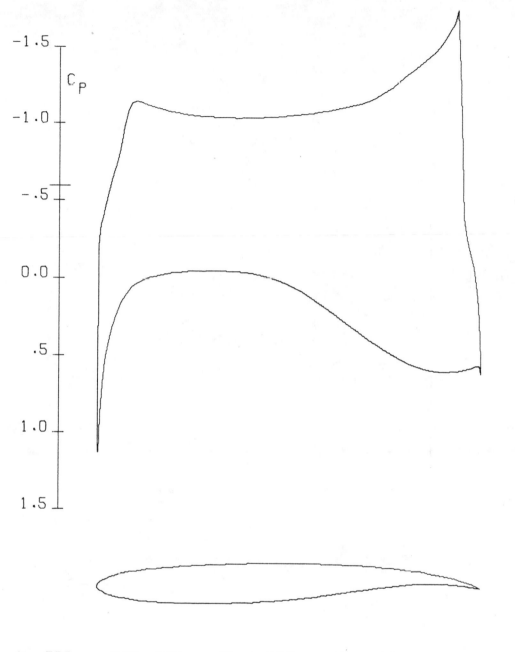

M=.750   T/C=.104   CL=1.306   CD= .032   ALP= 0.00

MxN= 160x30   NCY= 800   EP= 0.00

Figure 18   FLOW AT DESIGN WITHOUT BOUNDARY LAYER

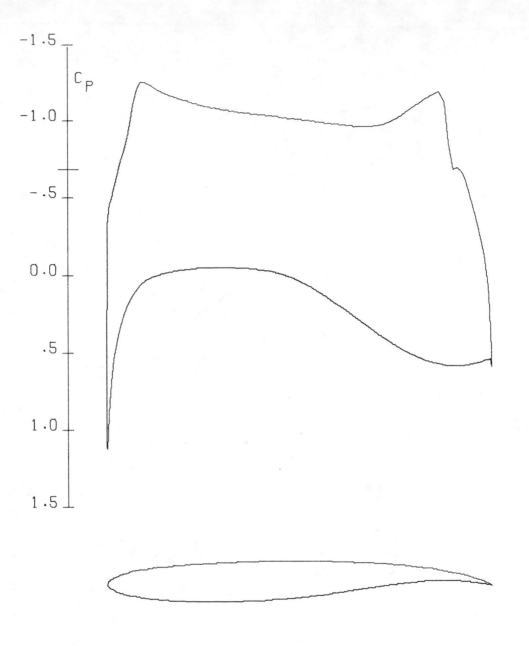

M=.725   T/C=.104   CL=1.187   CD= .008   ALP= 0.00

M×N= 160×30   NCY= 800   EP= -.50

Figure 19   IMPROVED FLOW WITHOUT BOUNDARY LAYER

Appendix I

Glossaries and Tables.

Various flow parameters such as the free stream Mach number and the gas constant are supplied to the program as input from Tape 7. Parameters dealing with the initial function are assigned and automated parameters must be designated as such. General information regarding the run is also supplied from this file. A detailed description of Tape 7 is given in Table 1 and the glossary below.

Tape 6 consists of cards of two types defining the paths of integration. The first type of card tells whether the path is subsonic or supersonic, how many points in the polygon will determine the path, and the number of forks the path will have. Cards of the second type contain an endpoint of a line segment in the complex plane and a number which can be used to further refine the mesh spacing along that segment of the polygonal path. Note that for subsonic paths, only a path in the η'- or η-plane is prescribed. The program obtains a corresponding path in the ξ-plane by reflection. In the glossary of Tape 6 below, columns refer to card input only.

Glossary of Tape 7 Parameters

NP	Integer. The number of paths to be used on Tape 6 if NP > 0, otherwise -NP is the number of automation paths.
NRN	Integer. ABS(NRN) is the run number. If NRN is negative least squares points not plotted.
MRP	Integer. Mesh refinement parameter. Doubling the value of MRP cuts the mesh spacing in half.
A = A(1) +iA(2)	Complex. Locates the initial characteristics η_0 = A and ξ_0 = $\overline{A}$.
AA	Real. Used along with MRP in determining the approximate mesh spacing AA/MRP.
GAM	Real. Gas constant γ. For air GAM = 1.4.
M	Real. The free stream Mach number M, which must be less than 1.
B = B(1) +iB(2)	Complex. The point η = -B corresponds to a branch point in the hodograph plane.
CD	Real. Ratio of drag to lift measured by periods of ψ and ϕ.
TR	Real. Number between 0 and 1 specifying relative location of artificial tail between trailing streamlines ψ = 0.
NK	Integer. NK > 0 is the number of automated parameters. If NK < 0 then $|NK|$-1 is the number of constraints. NK $\leq$ 31.
LC	Vector with components LC(k).
LC(k)	Integer. The number of a parameter to be automated; parameters are counted in succession starting with TL1(1) as number 1.
TLj	Four-dimensional vectors with components TLj(k).
TLj(1) + iTLj(2)	Complex. Coefficient of a logarithmic term with branch cut at 0°.
TLj(3) +iTLj(4)	Complex. Corresponding location of the tail logarithm in the η-plane.
NLj	Four-dimensional vectors with components NLj(k).
NLj(1) +iNLj(2)	Complex. Coefficient of a logarithmic term with branch cut at 180°.

NLj(3) + iNLj(4)	Complex. Corresponding location of the nose logarithm in the η-plane.
SLj	Four-dimensional vectors with components SLj(k).
SLj(1) + iSLj(2)	Complex. Coefficient of logarithmic term with branch cut at -90°.
SLj(3) + iSLj(4)	Complex. Corresponding location of the side logarithm in the η-plane.
E = E(1) + iE(2)	Complex. Ellipse parameter.
EC = EC(1) + iEC(2)	Complex. Centering parameter for ellipse term.
EM = EM(1) + iEM(2)	Complex. Coefficient of ellipse term.
ET = ET(1) + iET(2)	Complex. Coefficient of η term.
ETSQ = ETSQ(1) + iETSQ(2)	Complex. Coefficient of η^2 term.
ETCU = ETCU(1) + iETCU(2)	Complex. Coefficient of η^3 term.
XU	Real. x_u at the nose. Relates to curvature and slope at stagnation point.
XV	Real. x_v at the nose. Relates to curvature and slope at stagnation point.
XR	Real. Controls automation.
IP	Integer. IP = 0 suppresses TTY display of Tape 7.

COLS. CARDS	1-5	6-10	11-15	16-20	21-25	26-30	31-35	36-40	41-45	46-50	51-55	56-60
1	NP	NRN	MRP	A(1)	A(2)	AA	GAM	M	B(1)	B(2)	CD	TR
2	NK	LC(1)	LC(2)	LC(3)	LC(4)	LC(5)	LC(6)	LC(7)	LC(8)	LC(9)	LC(10)	etc.
2A	LC(16)	LC(17)	LC(18)	LC(19)	LC(20)	LC(21)	LC(22)	LC(23)	LC(24)	LC(25)	LC(26)	etc.
3	TL1(1)	TL1(2)	TL1(3)	TL1(4)			TL2(1)	TL2(2)	TL2(3)	TL2(4)		
4	TL3(1)	TL3(2)	TL3(3)	TL3(4)			TL4(1)	TL4(2)	TL4(3)	TL4(4)		
5	NL1(1)	NL1(2)	NL1(3)	NL1(4)			NL2(1)	NL2(2)	NL2(3)	NL2(4)		
6	NL3(1)	NL3(2)	NL3(3)	NL3(4)			NL4(1)	NL4(2)	NL4(3)	NL4(4)		
7	SL1(1)	SL1(2)	SL1(3)	SL1(4)			SL2(1)	SL2(2)	SL2(3)	SL2(4)		
8	SL3(1)	SL3(2)	SL3(3)	SL3(4)			SL4(1)	SL4(2)	SL4(3)	SL4(4)		
9	EM(1)	EM(2)	E(1)	E(2)			ET(1)	ET(2)	EC(1)	EC(2)		
10	ETSQ(1)	ETSQ(2)	XU	XV			ETCU(1)	ETCU(2)	XR			

CARDS COLS.	1-10	11-20	21-30	31-40	41-50	51-60	61-70	71-80

Table 1. Names of Tape 7 parameters in their locations on cards.

Glossary of Tape 6 Parameters

IN	Hollerith, ADd, DElete, REplace, WRite, or ENd.
PN	Integer. Path number.
FN	Integer. Fork number.
CN	Integer. Card number.
K	Integer. ABS(K) is the number of endpoints in the polygon to follow. K>0: η'-plane; K<0: η-plane.
KT	Integer. Columns 4-6. If KT < 0, stem follows and KT = number of forks issuing from it. If KT = 0 fork or bare stem follows. If KT > 0, supersonic path follows; if KT = 1 this path plots; if KT = 2 singularities plot instead; if KT > 2, no plot.
$\eta = \eta_1 + i\eta_2$	Complex. Endpoint in η-plane or η'-plane.
LL	Integer. Columns 41-45. If LL > 0 the mesh in this segment is subdivided into LL times as many parts as for LL = 1. If LL < 0 same subdivision as above, but point and its successors pasted to sonic locus in case of supersonic path. For automation paths, least squares starts at LL < 0 .

COLS. CARDS	1-3	4-6	
TYPE 1	K	KT	
TYPE 2	η_1	η_2	LL
CARDS COLS.	1-20	21-40	41-45

Table 2. Card images of Tape 6 parameters.

Glossary of Parameters for Program G

EM   Real. The free stream Mach number. It must be less than 1. Default .75 or design M.

ALP   Real. Angle of attack in degrees relative to angle 0° at design. Default 0.

M   Integer. Number of intervals in circle plane around the airfoil. Maximum is 160 without changing dimension statements. Default 160.

N   Integer. Number of intervals in the radial direction of circle plane. Maximum is 30 without changing dimension statements. Default 30.

NS   Integer. Used along with ITYP in determining the type of operation and the number of cycles to be performed. Default 400.

ITYP   Integer. Used along with NS in determining the type of operation performed. See description in Table 4. ITYP is always set equal to 1 before returning to control mode. Upon termination ITYP is set equal to 4. Default 0.

NCY   Integer. Total number of cycles since the last change in Mach number, angle of attack, or grid size. Default 0.

XS   Real. Maximum relaxation factor. Used for relaxation factor at every point in computing the mapping function. Used at each point in the solution at which the local Mach number is less than or equal to the free stream Mach number. The relaxation at a point with local Mach number between free stream and 1. is a linear function of XS and XM. Default 1.9.

XM   Real. Minimum relaxation factor. Used at each super-sonic point in the grid and usually set equal to 1.0 although underrelaxation is permitted. Used along with XS in determining the relaxation at each point between free stream Mach number and 1.0 (see above). Default 1.0.

XPHI   Real. Relaxation on the circulation. If XPHI ≠ 0 then XPHI * YA will be the correction applied to the circulation to satisfy the Kutta condition at the tail. XPHI cannot be negative for convergence and has some upper bound. If XPHI = 0 then YA will be the correction to C_L. Default 1.

YA   Real. Correction to circulation. If XPHI = 0 then YA will be the change in circulation at the first cycle and will then be set to zero. If XPHI ≠ 0, YA will be computed in the program as the amount by which the Kutta condition is violated. Default 0.

ST   Real. Tolerance to which residuals should converge. For the mapping part, the program will return to control mode if the maximum of the change in arc length and the change in the mapping modulus at each point is less than ST even if the NS cycles are not complete. In finding the solution the program returns to control mode if the maximum change in the velocity potential and circulation is less than ST. Default 0.

KP   Integer. Print parameter. The output from every KPth cycle will be sent to output and the rest will go onto Tape 4, which may be printed on completion of the run.

IZ   Integer. Width of output line control. Controls the number of characters on a line of output as well as the file to which they will be written. Default 70.

II   Integer. The velocity potential at the point II, JJ is written out at each cycle. Default 130.

JJ   Integer. The velocity potential at the point II, JJ is written out at each cycle. Default 1.

EP   Real. Controls the amount of artificial viscosity $\lambda(\Delta t)^2$ because $\lambda \Delta t = 1 - EP$. See text for full description. EP < 1. Default 0.

FSYM   Selects one of five input formats on airfoil coordinates.

FSYM=1.0 is compatable with Tape 3 produced by Program D.
FSYM=2.0 is compatable with Tape 3 produced by Program F.
FSYM=3.0 uses u,v,x,y from punched cards.
FSYM=4.0 uses x,y from punched cards.
FSYM=5.0 uses x,y,θ from punched cards. Default 1.

IS   Integer. Controls number of iterations smoothing (x,y)-coordinates. Default 10.

NFC   Integer. Number of terms in Fourier series. Default 16.

NMP   Integer. Number of mesh points on unit circle. Default 300.

TE   Real. Extended x-coordinate of tail. Default $1 + .3C_D$, where C_D is fictitious design form drag coefficient, if FSYM < 3, otherwise default 1.

NRN   Integer. Run number. Default design NRN for FSYM < 3, otherwise 1.

FNU   Real. Number of points on upper surface defining airfoil.

FNL   Real. Number of points on lower surface defining airfoil.

EPSIL   Real. Trailing edge angle times π.

Output Parameters

MXP   Maximum row for supersonic region.

RES   Maximum residual for Φ or for mapping function.

IK   Location of maximum residual is IK, JK.

JK   Location of maximum residual is IK, JK.

TIME	Total CP time.
CL	Coefficient of lift.
S	Arc length.
T	Angle in plane of unit circle.
PHI	Velocity potential.
S/L	Ratio of arc lengths.
KP and KPP	Derivatives of curvature K.

COLS. CARDS	1-10	11-20	21-30	31-40	41-50	51-60
1	Title in Hollerith					
2	FNU	FNL	ESPIL			
3	Blank					
4	Coordinates at nose					
⋮	Points on upper surface					
FNU+3	Coordinates at tail					
FNU+4	Blank					
FNU+5	Coordinates at nose					
⋮	Points on lower surface					
FNU+FNL+4	Coordinates at tail					

Deck structure.

COLS. FSYM	1-10	11-20	21-30	31-40
3.0	u	v	x	y
4.0			x	y
5.0	x	y	$\theta°$	

Data Structure.

Table 3. Tape 3 card input to Program G.

	ITYP < 0	ITYP = 0	ITYP > 0
NS < 0	RETURN TO CONTROL MODE	RESTART MAPPING	CRUDER GRID
NS = 0	STORE ON TAPE	TERMINATE PROGRAM	RETRIEVE FROM TAPE
NS > 0	FINER GRID	MAP COMPUTATION	FLOW COMPUTATION

Table 4.   Control of Program G.

Appendix II

Sample Teletype Run.

SAMPLE TTY RUN

** THE FIRST STEP IS TO SET UP TAPE 7 USING PROGRAM A**

A.
MAKE CHANGES IN THE PARAMETERS
  $P NRN=1$

RUN NUMBER   1
THE CURRENT VALUES ARE

  13   1   2 -.150   .300   .080 1.400   .830   .012 -.119   .040 0.000
  -8 49 50 53 54 57 58 13 14

  -.590 -.050   .620   .050   0.000 0.000   .700   .500
  0.000 -.660   .050   .520   0.000 0.000   .308   -.394

  0.000 0.000 -.600   -.600   -.015 -.060   -.750   .830
  -.200   .250 -1.160   -.630   -.280   .250 -1.690   -.050

  -.100   .040 -.420   -.460   .010   .010   -.800   -.400
  0.000   .750 -.050   -.250   0.000 0.000   .900 0.000

  0.000 0.000   .450   .100   0.000 0.000   .500   .350
  0.000 0.000   .040   .005   0.000 0.000 0.000
  EXIT
COMMAND -

THE NEXT STEP IS TO CALCULATE THE FLOW BY MEANS OF PROGRAM B

B.
INITIALIZATION COMPLETE
NOSE AUTOMATION COMPLETE
THERE ARE   0 POINTS USED FOR LEAST SQUARES
AUTOMATION COMPLETE
DETERMINANT =   .26249E+05
PATH 1 IS FINISHED
PATH 2 IS FINISHED
PATH 3 IS FINISHED
PATH 4 IS FINISHED
PATH 5 IS FINISHED
PATH 6 IS FINISHED
PATH 7 IS FINISHED
PATH 8 IS FINISHED
PATH 9 IS FINISHED
PATH 10 IS FINISHED
PATH 11 IS FINISHED
PATH 12 IS FINISHED
PATH 13 IS FINISHED
TOTAL CP TIME IS 59.0 SECONDS
  EXIT
COMMAND -

**THE MAIN PROGRAM IS FINISHED SO WE CAN PROCEED TO GENERATE TTY
  OUTPUT**

C.

```
N N N N N N N N N N N N N N N N N N N N N N N
N N N N N N N N N N N N N N N N N N N N N N N
N N N N N N N N N N N N N N N N N N N N N N
N N N N N N N N N N N N N N N N N N N N N P
N N N N N N N N N N N N N N N N N P P P
N N N N N N N N N N N N N N N P P P
N N N N N N N N N N N N N N N P P P
N N N N N N N N N N N N N N P P P
N N N N N N N N N N N P P P P
N N N N N N N N N P P P P P
N N N N N N N N P P P P P
N N N N N N N N P P P P
N N N N N N N P P P P
N N N N N N N P P P
N N N N N N N P P P
N N N N N N P P P
N N N N N P P
N N N N N P
N N N N P
N N N P
N N N
N N
N
```

```
                P  P  P
              P  PPPPPPPPPP
           PPPPP PPNNP   PPNPPP        PPPP
           PPPPNNNN NNNNNNNNNNNPPNPPPPPPPPPPPPPP
         PPPNNNNN    NNNNNNNNNNNNNNNNNNNNN PNPPPP
      P   NNN          NNNNNNNNNN NNN     NNNNPPPP
       PPNNNNNNNNNNNN  NNNNNN  N    NNN       PP
       NNPPPPN       PNNPNNNN    N    NNN    PPP
   +- NNNN----+-PPPP-PPP+PP----P--+------NNNPPP-------+--------
       NNNNPPPPPPP  PP  PP        PP              PP
        NN NPPP PPP    PP         PPPPPPPPP
         N NNNPPPP   PP            PPNNNPPP
          N NNNNNNNNN
            N  NNN                  +
```

EXIT
COMMAND -

**THE TRIANGULAR PLOT DESCRIBES THE SUPERSONIC PART OF THE FLOW
  AND THE LOWER DIAGRAM DESCRIBES THE SUBSONIC HODOGRAPH**

**NOW WE CHANGE TAPES 6 AND 7 TO GET A NEW FLOW AT ANOTHER MACH
  NUMBER. FIRST WE CALL PROGRAM E TO ADJUST THE TAIL AND SUPER-
  SONIC PATHS**

```
E.
 15 PATHS    699 DATA ELEMENTS

INSTRUCTION
 WR/1/0
 2  0
    .100     .100     1
    .438    -.369     1
INSTRUCTION
 RE/1/0/2/.5/-.405/1/WR/1/0
 2  0
    .100     .100     1
    .500    -.405     1
INSTRUCTION
 WR/14/0/WR/15/0
 9  1
  -.102    -.140     2
   .428    -.176     2
   .348    -.400     2
  -.072    -.295     2
  -.432    -.461     2
  -.492    -.460    -2
  -.242    -.351     2
  -.122    -.306     2
   .288    -.366     2
 9  2
  -.642    -.201     2
  -.600    -.530     2
  -.432    -.461     2
  -.072    -.295     2
   .258    -.381     2
   .288    -.362    -2
  -.122    -.306     2
  -.242    -.351     2
  -.492    -.460     2
INSTRUCTION
 AD/14/0/0/10/1/-.1/-.2/2/.25/-.2/2/.33/-.36/2/.33/-.44/2/0./-.33
REFINEMENT
 2/-.54/-.56/2/-.592/-.515/-2/-.31/-.4/2/0./-.3/2/.26/-.38/2
INSTRUCTION
 DE/15/0/0/RE/15/0/-1/9/1/-.6/-.2/2/-.68/-.53/2/-.6/-.59/2/0./-.33
REFINEMENT
 2/.25/-.4/2/.26/-.38/-2/0./-.3/2/-.31/-.4/2/-.592/-.515/2/END
 EXIT
COMMAND -


**WE UPDATE TAPE 7 BY CALLING PROGRAM A AND CHANGE MANY PARAMETERS**

A.
MAKE CHANGES IN THE PARAMETERS
  $P A=-.2,.4,M=.79,B=.008,-.121,TR=.1,TL1=-.8,-.2,.75,.05,

 TL2(1)=-.2,TL2(2)=-.2,TL3(2)=-.68,0.,.6,TL4(3)=.37,-.43,XR=1.,

 NL1(1)=-.05,.53,NL2=.03,-.07,-.73,.84,NL3=-.15,.24,-.97,-.55,

 NL4=.06,.08,-.85,-.57,SL1=-.05,0.,-.39,-.45,SL2=0.,.2,-.35,-.45,

 SL3=.05,.45,-.09,-.35,E=.4,.2,EC(2)=.3,XU=.079,XV=.031,MRP=4$
```

```
RUN NUMBER    2
THE CURRENT VALUES ARE

 13   2   4  -.200    .400    .080  1.400    .790     .008 -.121    .040    .100
 -8  49  50  53   54   57   58  13   14

 -.800   -.200    .750    .050        -.200   -.200    .700    .500
 0.000   -.680   0.000    .600        0.000   0.000    .370   -.430

 -.050    .530   -.600   -.600         .030   -.070   -.730    .840
 -.150    .240   -.970   -.550         .060    .080   -.850   -.570

 -.050   0.000   -.390   -.450        0.000    .200   -.350   -.450
  .050    .450   -.090   -.350        0.000   0.000    .900   0.000

 0.000   0.000    .400    .200        0.000   0.000    .500    .300
 0.000   0.000    .079    .031        0.000   0.000   1.000
 EXIT
COMMAND - B.
INITIALIZATION COMPLETE
NOSE AUTOMATION COMPLETE
THERE ARE    0 POINTS USED FOR LEAST SQUARES
AUTOMATION COMPLETE
DETERMINANT =  .13391E+05
PATH   1 IS FINISHED
PATH   2 IS FINISHED
PATH   3 IS FINISHED
PATH   4 IS FINISHED
PATH   5 IS FINISHED
PATH   6 IS FINISHED
PATH   7 IS FINISHED
PATH   8 IS FINISHED
PATH   9 IS FINISHED
PATH  10 IS FINISHED
PATH  11 IS FINISHED
PATH  12 IS FINISHED
PATH  13 IS FINISHED
TOTAL CP TIME IS 233.8 SECONDS
 EXIT
COMMAND -

**WE CALL PROGRAM D TO GET A GOOD PLOT OF THIS RUN**

D.
 EXIT
COMMAND - BATCH(TAPE4,PRINT,END)
COMMAND -

**SAVE TAPE 3 FOR LATER USE IN PROGRAM G**

REWIND(TAPE3,T3)
COMMAND - COPYBF(TAPE3,T3)
COMMAND -

**NEXT PROGRAM F IS APPLIED TO TAPE 3 TO SEE IF AND WHERE THE
   TURBULENT BOUNDARY LAYER SEPARATES**
```

```
F.
SEPARATION OCCURS ON TOP
SEPARATION FIRST OCCURS AT X=  .97884
MAXIMUM NASH MACDONALD SEP=  .01716 AT X=  .99609
NO SEPARATION ON BOTTOM
MAXIMUM NASH MACDONALD SEP=  .00377 AT X=  .83180
 EXIT
COMMAND - BATCH(TAPE4,PRINT,END)
COMMAND -

**FINALLY WE DO ANALYSIS OF AIRFOIL BY MEANS OF PROGRAM G**

REWIND(T3,TAPE3)
COMMAND - COPYBF(T3,TAPE3)
COMMAND - G.
READ P
  $P ITYP=0,NS=400,KP=50,ST=.1E-5,TE=1.007$
M=.790    CL= .677    CD=.0271    T/C=.105              RUN    2


        DEL S        RES         S/L         W(0)
        .755E-01   0.          1.00007    -1.30110
        .684E-03    .113E-04    .99990    -1.30108
        .319E-04    .347E-05    .99982    -1.30104
        .960E-05    .879E-06    .99976    -1.30097
        .268E-05    .204E-06    .99970    -1.30090


ANGLE OF ZERO LIFT = -2.78376         OUTER MAPPING RADIUS =    .27230
THE THICKNESS TO CHORD RATIO IS .1040



EM=.790    ALP= 0.00    EP=0.00    M*N=160*30    NCY= 232    NS= 400
XS=1.90    XM=1.00    XPHI=1.00    ST= .1E-05    TIME=   41.58


READ P

**THE MAPPING IS DONE SO WE GO TO THE CRUDER GRID AND COMPUTE THE
   FLOW**

 $P NS=-1$
EM=.790    ALP= 0.00    EP=0.00    M*N= 80*15    NCY=  0    NS=  0
XS=1.90    XM=1.00    XPHI=1.00    ST= .1E-05    TIME=   41.73

READ P
  $P NS=600,KP=100,XS=1.4,ITYP=2$
MXP      RES        YA          CL        PHI     IK  JK
 0    .985E-06   0.          .46135    .72469    0   0
 7    .624E-03   .441E-04    .66065    .87800   45   1
 9    .275E-03   .334E-04    .67690    .89435   46   1
 9    .150E-03   .273E-04    .68639    .89734   47   2
 9    .897E-04   .609E-05    .69037    .89568   46   1
10    .598E-04   .381E-05    .69201    .89303   46   1
EM=.790    ALP= 0.00    EP=0.00    M*N= 80*15    NCY= 600    NS= 600
XS=1.40    XM=1.00    XPHI=1.00    ST= .1E-05    TIME= 124.84


   CD=  .00565       CL=  .69233       CM= -.23198
```

```
XXXXXXXXXXXXXXXXXXXXXXXXXXXXXXXXXXXXXXXXXXXXXXXXXXXXXXXXXXXXXXXXXXXXXXXXX
XXXXXXXXXXXXXXXXXXXXXXXXXXXXXXXXXXXXXXXXXXXXXXYYYYYYYYYYYYYYYYYYXXXXXXXXXXX
XXXXXXXXXXXXXXXXXXXXXXXXXXXXXXXXXXXXXXXXXXYYYYYYYYYYYYYYYYYYYYYXXXXXXXXXX
XXXXXXXXXXXXXXXXXXXXXXXXXXXXXXXXXXXXXXXXXYYYYYYYYYYYYYYYYYYYYYYXXXXXXXXX
XXXXXXXXXXXXXXXXXXXXXXXXXXXXXXXXXXXXXXXXXXYYYYYYYZZZZZZZZZYYYYYYYYYYXXXXXXXXX
XXXXXXXXXXXXXXXXXXXXXXXXXXXXXXXXXXXXXXXXXYYYYYYZZZZZZZZZZZZZYYYYYYYYXXXXXXXXX
XXXXXXXXXXXXXXXXXXXXXXXXXXXXXXXXXXXXXXXXYYYYZZZZZZZ000ZZZZZZYYYYYYXXXXXXXXX
XXXXXXXXXXXXXYYYXXXXXXXXXWWWWWWWXXXXXXXXYYYYZZZZ000000000ZZZZYYYYYXXXXXXX
WXXXXXXXXXXXYYYYYYXXXXXXXWWWWWWWWWXXXXYYZZZZZ0000000000000ZZZYYYYXXXXXXX
WWXXXXXXXXYYYYYYYYXXXXXXWWWWWWWWWWWXXXYYZZZ00000000000000000ZZYYYYYXXXXXX
WWXXXXXXYYYYYYYYYYYYXXXWWWWVVVWWWXXXYYZZ000000000000000000000ZYYYYYXXXXXX
WWXXXXXYYYYYYYYYYYYYYXXXWWWVVVVVWWXXXYYZZ00000000000000000000110ZZYYYYXXXXX
WWXXXXYYYYYYYYYYYYYYYYXXWVUUUUVVWXYZ0000000000000000000000111110ZZYYYXXXW
WWXXXXYYYYYYYYYYYYYYYYYXXWVUTTUVWXYZ0011111111100000001111110ZZZYYYXXXW
WWXXXXYYYYYYYYYYYYYYYYYYYXXWUSSTVWYZ011111111111111111111111111ZZZZYYYXW
WWXXXXYYYYYYYYYYYYYYYYYYYYXXWUSSTVWYZ011111111111111111111111111ZZZZYYYXW
READ P
```

**THIS PLOT SHOWS THE SONIC LINE BECAUSE 1 MEANS M=1.1, 0 MEANS M=1.0,
Z MEANS M=.9, Y MEANS M=.8, AND SO FORTH**

GO BACK TO FINER GRID

```
 $P NS=1,ITYP=-1$
EM=.790   ALP= 0.00    EP=0.00    M*N=160*30    NCY=    0    NS=     1
XS=1.40   XM=1.00   XPHI=1.00    ST= .1E-05   TIME= 125.33

READ P
   $P XS=1.7,NS=300,KP=50$
MXP     RES        YA         CL        PHI    IK  JK
10     .436E-04   .250E-05   .69304    .89049  45   1
19     .102E-03   .257E-04   .69251    .91090 140   1
19     .343E-04   .264E-04   .69756    .91604 140   4
19     .248E-04   .150E-04   .70104    .91832 102   9
19     .808E-04   .822E-05   .70297    .91914 140   1
19     .215E-04   .473E-05   .70404    .91932 101   8
EM=.790   ALP= 0.00    EP=0.00    M*N=160*30   NCY= 300    NS= 300
XS=1.70   XM=1.00   XPHI=1.00    ST= .1E-05   TIME= 288.96
READ P
```

WE NOW DECREASE THE AMOUNT OF ARTIFICIAL VISCOSITY AND CONTINUE

```
 $P EP=.5$
MXP     RES        YA         CL        PHI    IK  JK
19     .197E-04   .302E-05   .70468    .91921 100   6
20     .722E-04   .241E-04   .70702    .93567 139   1
20     .311E-04   .197E-04   .71102    .93901 140   1
20     .207E-04   .114E-04   .71363    .94054 105  11
20     .185E-04   .658E-05   .71512    .94118 103   9
20     .164E-04   .407E-05   .71600    .94139 102   8
EM=.790   ALP= 0.00    EP= .50    M*N=160*30   NCY= 600    NS= 300
XS=1.70   XM=1.00   XPHI=1.00    ST= .1E-05   TIME= 451.98

READ P
  $P NS=0,ITYP=0$
 EXIT
COMMAND - BATCH(TAPE4,PRINT,END)
COMMAND -
```

Appendix III

Sample Output. Listing of (x,y)-Coordinates.

01/13/72

RUN= 25

CIRCULATORY FLOW ABOUT A TRANSONIC AIRFOIL

M= .750   CL= .667   CD= .033   T/C= .151

TAPE 6, PATH 0

```
2  0
  -.800     0.000     2
 -1.000     0.000     1

2  0
   .300     0.000     1
   .550    -.340      1
```


TAPE 7

```
-6   25    4   -.120    .250  .080  1.40  .750     .007  -.110  .050   .500
17   49   50   57   58   53   54    9   14   10   34    1   38    2   37    5
 6   33
```

```
-.150   -.134    .600    .050        -.048   -.174    .550    .450
 .013   -.082    .650   -.270         0.000  -.066   -.120    .580

 0.000   0.000  -1.330   .050         0.000   0.000  -.650    .900
 0.000   0.000  -2.000  0.000         0.000   0.000  -2.000  0.000

-.112   -.017    .450   -.300          .146   -.228   -.700   -.900
 0.000   0.000  -1.100  -.350         0.000   0.000   0.000   -.900

 .707    .117    .460    .100          .305    .053    .500    .050
 .073    .092    .095    .010         0.000   0.000    .500
```

AUTOMATION PATHS

```
6   0
  -.948    -.260    -1
  -.848    -.390     1
  -.763    -.445     1
  -.663    -.480     2
  -.563    -.495     2
  -.478    -.495     2

4   0
  -.800    0.000     2
  -.995    -.110    -1
  -.985    -.160     1
  -.970    -.200     1

6   0
  -.800    0.000     2
  -.980     .110    -1
  -.935     .200     1
  -.900     .250     1
  -.840     .300     1
  -.760     .330     1

7   0
  -.128     .330    -1
  -.213     .355     1
  -.323     .365     1
  -.418     .380     1
  -.523     .375     1
  -.623     .360     1
  -.713     .335     1

15   0
  -.098     .325    -1
  -.003     .315     1
   .102     .305     1
   .182     .300     1
   .261     .270     1
   .390     .183     1
   .427     .140     1
   .450     .060     1
   .447    -.030     1
   .443    -.095     1
   .442    -.150     1
   .420    -.200     1
   .382    -.230     1
   .337    -.220     1
   .297    -.208     1

4   0
  -.093    -.210     1
   .242    -.400    -1
   .292    -.390     1
   .353    -.365     1
```

U	V	X	Y	CP
,74997	=,10746	,99270	,01674	,45212
,72975	=,08695	,98222	,01813	,49042
,71449	=,05514	,96314	,02001	,52066
,70760	=,02694	,94194	,02123	,53452
,70509	,00376	,91535	,02167	,53940
,70728	,03046	,89049	,02107	,53481
,71209	,05039	,87118	,01997	,52515
,71888	,06768	,85374	,01853	,51172
,72961	,08653	,83361	,01638	,49073
,74350	,10420	,81299	,01370	,46378
,76261	,12227	,78905	,01009	,42688
,78106	,13570	,76831	,00662	,39135
,80140	,14748	,74691	,00277	,35219
,82177	,15702	,72636	=,00107	,31291
,85042	,16744	,69860	=,00648	,25757
,87525	,17420	,67541	=,01108	,20950
,90187	,17943	,65141	=,01587	,15782
,92360	,18230	,63247	=,01962	,11556
,94839	,18410	,61156	=,02374	,06729
,96736	,18447	,59603	=,02672	,03032
,99879	,18318	,57109	=,03139	=,03100
1,03437	,17887	,54381	=,03625	=,10046
1,07312	,17061	,51481	=,04107	=,17615
1,11300	,15783	,48495	=,04556	=,25405
1,15103	,14066	,45509	=,04950	=,32827
1,18414	,12011	,42564	=,05278	=,39276
1,21032	,09757	,39647	=,05543	=,44359
1,22193	,08443	,37963	=,05668	=,46604
1,23515	,06500	,35495	=,05818	=,49151
1,24488	,04529	,32935	=,05933	=,51028
1,25188	,02579	,30353	=,06006	=,52396
1,25705	,00641	,27781	=,06040	=,53440
1,26099	=,01359	,25197	=,06033	=,54290
1,26401	=,03560	,22514	=,05980	=,55021
1,26559	=,05868	,19948	=,05885	=,55540
1,26524	=,08181	,17649	=,05758	=,55739
1,26373	=,11702	,14651	=,05523	=,56005
1,25927	=,14429	,12767	=,05329	=,55660
1,24775	=,18614	,10500	=,05035	=,54394
1,21623	=,24973	,08043	=,04606	=,50158
1,15659	=,31257	,06149	=,04160	=,40940
1,09829	=,35715	,04975	=,03804	=,31842
1,00125	=,41238	,03617	=,03308	=,16842
,88653	=,46019	,02512	=,02798	,00230
,76825	=,49372	,01727	=,02347	,16995
,65999	=,51168	,01224	=,01993	,31570
,52857	=,51462	,00798	=,01633	,48575
,35522	=,48305	,00444	=,01233	,70027
,23778	=,42653	,00279	=,00977	,84661
,15316	=,35702	,00178	=,00772	,95535
,06989	=,24434	,00083	=,00505	1,06502
,02278	=,13022	,00028	=,00263	1,12588
,00000	=,00000	0,00000	0,00000	1,14865

,00770	,12335	*,00000	,00243	1,12874
,06123	,28016	,00044	,00561	1,04240
,13010	,37857	,00108	,00789	,94366
,23757	,47006	,00225	,01066	,79904
,34730	,52571	,00380	,01325	,65590
,43877	,55086	,00543	,01549	,54078
,58134	,56262	,00908	,01949	,36262
,69809	,55204	,01381	,02360	,21407
,79218	,53318	,01951	,02774	,08926
,89903	,50296	,02901	,03354	*,06070
,98842	,47149	,04026	,03934	*,19376
1,10314	,42385	,06013	,04783	*,37495
1,18295	,38620	,07762	,05402	*,50751
1,31866	,31454	,11196	,06361	*,74368
1,38165	,28192	,12472	,06644	*,85858
1,47627	,22628	,14041	,06922	-1,03211
1,49754	,19534	,15846	,07176	-1,06642
1,50195	,17295	,17816	,07418	-1,06978
1,50162	,15406	,19884	,07643	-1,06494
1,49933	,13661	,22118	,07860	-1,05681
1,49592	,12014	,24527	,08067	-1,04695
1,49189	,10435	,27121	,08262	-1,03628
1,48756	,08908	,29903	,08443	-1,02534
1,48316	,07417	,32875	,08607	-1,01459
1,47867	,05959	,36033	,08750	-1,00399
1,47436	,04521	,39358	,08868	*,99402
1,47009	,03106	,42823	,08958	*,98443
1,46602	,01704	,46379	,09017	*,97552
1,46204	,00320	,49962	,09042	*,96706
1,45807	*,01041	,53490	,09033	*,95886
1,45398	*,02376	,56871	,08993	*,95068
1,44949	=,03666	,60012	,08928	*,94191
1,44448	#,04906	,62835	,08844	*,93223
1,43862	*,06075	,65285	,08751	*,92094
1,42995	=,07426	,67789	,08633	*,90419
1,41926	%,08696	,69783	,08520	*,88335
1,40628	#,09870	,71326	,08419	*,85779
1,39118	,10979	,72544	,08328	*,82785
1,37405	*,12043	,73581	,08242	*,79371
1,35496	*,13087	,74577	,08149	*,75557
1,33371	*,14127	,75655	,08041	*,71300
1,24242	*,18074	,80969	,07342	*,53107
1,20475	=,19395	,83427	,06965	*,45632
1,18253	=,20087	,84882	,06725	*,41232
1,15184	#,20954	,86898	,06369	*,35172
1,12890	#,21514	,88367	,06095	*,30650
1,09119	#,22276	,90690	,05636	*,23231
1,06467	=,22707	,92240	,05311	*,18032
1,02456	#,23173	,94389	,04837	*,10194
,99319	#,23393	,95873	,04495	*,04091
,96634	#,23486	,96974	,04231	,01104
,93859	=,23464	,97932	,03995	,06458
,90410	=,23262	,98847	,03761	,13082
,89016	*,23032	,99145	,03685	,15796
,77915	*,35838	1,00000	,02547	,27448

A SELECTION OF PATHS FROM TAPE 6

```
1-10
       -.800000000000      0.000000000000    2
1   0
     -1.050000000000      -.090000000000    1
1   0
     -1.050000000000      -.230000000000    1
1   0
     -1.060000000000      -.390000000000    1
1   0
      -.970000000000      -.470000000000    1
1   0
     -1.000000000000       .080000000000    1
1   0
      -.980000000000       .290000000000    1
1   0
      -.920000000000       .330000000000    1
1   0
      -.850000000000       .380000000000    1
1   0
      -.750000000000       .390000000000    1
1   0
     -1.000000000000       .170000000000    1
8   1
      -.650000000000      -.300000000000    2
      -.580000000000      -.585000000000    2
      0.000000000000      -.400000000000    2
       .210000000000      -.460000000000    2
       .240000000000      -.410000000000   -2
      0.000000000000      -.350000000000    1
      -.260000000000      -.400000000000    1
      -.510000000000      -.475000000000    1
9   1
      -.100000000000      -.170000000000    2
       .400000000000      -.180000000000    2
       .310000000000      -.460000000000    2
      0.000000000000      -.400000000000    2
      -.450000000000      -.565000000000    2
      -.510000000000      -.475000000000   -2
      -.260000000000      -.400000000000    1
      0.000000000000      -.350000000000    1
       .240000000000      -.410000000000    1
```

Appendix IV

Listing of Programs A-G.

```
C      PROGRAM A-UPDATES INPUT PARAMETERS, TAPE 7

       PROGRAM A(TAPE7=102,INPUT=102,OUTPUT=102,TAPE2=OUTPUT,TAPE5=INPUT)
C      CHANGES DATA ON TAPE7
       CALL MAIN
       CALL EXIT
       END

       SUBROUTINE MAIN
       REAL M,NL1,NL2,NL3,NL4
       DIMENSION A(2),B(2),LC(31),TL1(4),TL2(4),TL3(4),TL4(4),NL1(4),
      1 NL2(4),NL3(4),NL4(4),SL1(4),SL2(4),SL3(4),SL4(4),EM(2),E(2),
      2 ET(2),EC(2),ETSQ(2),ETCU(2)
C      ****NON-ANSI****
       NAMELIST /P/ NP,NRN,MRP,A,AA,GAMMA,M,B,CD,TR,NK,LC,TL1,TL2,TL3,
      1 TL4,NL1,NL2,NL3,NL4,SL1,SL2,SL3,SL4,EM,E,ET,EC,ETSQ,XU,XV,ETCU,
      2 XR,IP
       DATA NK,LC,TL1,TL2,TL3,TL4,NL1,NL2,NL3,NL4,SL1,SL2,SL3,SL4,EM,
      1 E,ET,EC,ETSQ,XU,XV,ETCU,XR,IP/  3,37,38,33,25,26,34,01,49,50,
      2 05,06,10,17,18,21,22,53,54,57,02,42,58,46,60,00,00,00,00,00,00,
      3 00,-.339,-.099,.62,.05,.014,-.158,.55,.45,0.,-.218,-.02,.57,0.,
      4 0.,.9,0.,-.041,-.037,-1.,-.75,.005,.027, -.7,.65,-.022,-.015,
      5 -1.3,.4,0.,0.,-2.,0.,-.02,-.134,.620,-.240,-.239,-.063,.39,-.33
      6 ,0.,.24,0.,-.28,0.,-.151,-.65,-.75,.44,-.282,.46,.1,.222,-.079
      7 ,.5,.05,.141,-.005,.045,.04,0.,0.,2.,1/
       N2 = 2
       N5 = 5
       N7 = 7
       REWIND N7
C      READ IN OLD TAPE7
       READ (N7,30) NP,NRN,MRP,A,AA,GAMMA,M,B,CD,TR
C      ****CHECK FOR AN END OF FILE****
       IF (EOF(N7).NE.0) GO TO 20
       READ (N7,40) NK,(LC(I),I = 1,15)
       IF (NK.GT.15) READ (N7,40) (LC(I),I = 16,31)
       READ (N7,50) TL1,TL2,TL3,TL4,NL1,NL2,NL3,NL4,SL1,SL2,SL3,SL4,
      1 EM,E,ET,EC,ETSQ,XU,XV,ETCU,XR
       NRN = NRN+1
       IF (NRN.LE.0) NRN = NRN-2
   10  WRITE (N2,60)
C      ****NON-ANSI****
       READ (N5,P)
       REWIND N7
C      WRITE OUT NEW TAPE7
       WRITE (N7,30) NP,NRN,MRP,A,AA,GAMMA,M,B,CD,TR
       WRITE (N7,40) NK,(LC(I),I = 1,15)
       IF (NK.GT.15) WRITE (N7,40) (LC(I),I = 16,31)
       WRITE (N7,50) TL1,TL2,TL3,TL4,NL1,NL2,NL3,NL4,SL1,SL2,SL3,SL4,
      1 EM,E,ET,EC,ETSQ,XU,XV,ETCU,XR
       IF (IP.EQ.0) RETURN
C      WRITE OUT TAPE7 AT TELETYPE
       N = IABS(NRN)
       WRITE (N2,70) N
       WRITE (N2,80) NP,NRN,MRP,A,AA,GAMMA,M,B,CD,TR
```

```
      N = IABS(NK)
      WRITE (N2,90) NK,(LC(I),I = 1,N)
      WRITE (N2,100) TL1,TL2,TL3,TL4
      WRITE (N2,100) NL1,NL2,NL3,NL4
      WRITE (N2,100) SL1,SL2,SL3,SL4
      WRITE (N2,100) EM,E,ET,EC,ETSQ,XU,XV,ETCU,XR
      RETURN
C     NO FILE TAPE 7 EXISTS, USE DEFAULT VALUES
   20 WRITE (N2,110)
      NP = 99
      NRN = 1
      MRP = 4
      A(1) = -.12
      A(2) = .3
      AA = .08
      GAMMA = 1.4
      M = .75
      B(1) = .016
      B(2) = -.185
      CD = .03
      TR = .5
      GO TO 10
   30 FORMAT (3I5,9F5.3)
   40 FORMAT (16I5)
   50 FORMAT(8F10.4)
   60 FORMAT (32H MAKE CHANGES IN THE PARAMETERS /)
   70 FORMAT (/11H RUN NUMBER,I5/23H THE CURRENT VALUES ARE /)
   80 FORMAT (1X,3I3,6F7.3,3F6.3)
   90 FORMAT (16I4/)
  100 FORMAT (/4F7.3,5X,4F7.3/4F7.3,5X,4F7.3)
  110 FORMAT (19H DEFAULT TAPE7 USED )
      END




C     PROGRAM B-CALCULATES TRANSONIC FLOW

      PROGRAM B(TAPE7=102,TAPE6=777,TAPE1,OUTPUT=102,TAPE2=OUTPUT)
      COMPLEX U,X1,X3,TAO,ETA,T,Z,ARG,ARG2,ARG3,BP,A,TEMP
      COMMON /A/ C(40),ARG(5),ARG2(5),ARG3(4)
      COMMON U(4,540),X1(2,360),X3(2,360),TAO(2,360),ETA(360),T(2,360),Z
C     LBM IS THE DIMENSION SIZE
C     **THE SECOND DIMENSION OF U IS 1.5*LBM**
C     U(K,I) IS U,V,Y2,X2 AT ETA(I)
C     X1(K,I) IS Y1,X1 AT S(I)
C     X3(K,I) IS Y3,X3 AT ETA(I)
C     TAO(K,I) IS LAMBDA+,LAMBDA- AT ETA(I)
C     ETA(I) IS ETA AT POINT I
C     T(K,I) IS LAMBDA+,LAMBDA- ON THE INITIAL CHARACTERISTIC
      COMMON /C/ TEMP(20),BB(8,33)
C     TEMP IS USED AS TEMPORARY STORAGE
C     BB IS USED TO STORE THE COEFFICIENT MATRIX FOR AUTOMATION
      COMMON /D/ AA,N,M,MRP,NN,NR,II,JJ,KK,IP,NP,LBM,TIME
C     N IS THE POINT ETA=A ON THE INITIAL CHARACTERISTIC
C     NN IS THE POINT AT THE END OF THE ETA PATH
C     M IS THE NUMBER OF REAL POINTS OF THE SOLUTION ON THE PATH
```

```
C     KK.GT.0 FOR SUPERSONIC PATHS,KK=0 FOR FORKS,KK.LT.0 FOR STEMS
      COMMON /E/ FF(66),NK,NCR,LC(31)
C     FF STORES THE PARAMETERS FOR THE INITIAL FUNCTION
C     NK IS THE NUMBER OF AUTOMATED PARAMETERS
C     NCR IS THE NUMBER OF AUTOMATED CONSTRAINTS
C     LC IS THE LIST OF PARAMETERS TO BE AUTOMATED
      COMMON /F/ XP(36)
      COMMON /G/ N1,N2,N6,N7
      DIMENSION S(1)
      EQUIVALENCE (BP,C(27)), (GAMMA,C(3)), (EM,C(8)), (S(1),T(1,1))
      DATA NO /0/
C     S(I) IS XI AT THE POINT I
C     **THE VALUE OF LBM MUST BE ALTERED WHEN THE DIMENSION SIZE IS**
      LBM = 360
C     **THE NUMBER OF CONSTRAINTS MAY BE LOWERED IF DESIRED**
      NCR = 7
      KK = 0
      N1 = 1
      N2 = 2
      N6 = 6
      N7 = 7
C     ****SECOND GIVES ELAPSED CP TIME IN SECONDS****
      CALL SECOND (TIME)
      REWIND N1
      REWIND N6
      REWIND N7
      READ (N7,50) NP,NRN,MRP,A,AA,GAMMA,EM,BP,CD,TR
C     NP IS THE NUMBER OF PATHS
C     NRN IS THE RUN NUMBER
C     MRP IS A MESH REFINEMENT PARAMETER
C     A IS LOCATION OF THE INITIAL CHARACTERISTIC
C     AA/MRP IS THE MAXIMUM MESH SPACING
C     GAMMA IS A GAS CONSTANT
C     EM IS THE FREE STREAM MACH NUMBER
C     BP IS THE LOCATION OF THE BRANCH POINT CALLED B IN PROGRAM A
C     CD IS THE DRAG TO LIFT RATIO
      N = CABS(A)/AA+.999
      N = 1+MRP*N
C     READ PARAMETERS TO BE AUTOMATED
      READ (N7,60) NK,(LC(LI),LI = 1,15)
      IF (IABS(NK).GT.15) READ (N7,60) (LC(LI),LI = 16,31)
C     READS PARAMETERS NEEDED FOR THE CHARACTERISTIC INITIAL DATA
      READ (N7,70) (FF(I),I = 1,63)
      CALL CONST (CONJG(A)/FLOAT(N-1),CD,TR)
      DO 10 I = 2,5
   10 ARG2(I) = ARG(I)
      II = N
      WRITE (N2,80)
      CALL TAIL (NO)
      WRITE (N2,90)
      NQ = NP
      IF (NP.LE.0) NQ = 99
      DO 40 LI = 1,NQ
      CALL STEP (NO+LI-1)
C     KK IS POSITIVE FOR SUPERSONIC FLOW
C     KK IS NEGATIVE FOR A STEM AND -KK IS THE NUMBER OF FORKS
C     KK IS ZERO FOR A FORK
      IF (KK.GE.0) GO TO 40
      L = -KK
```

```
C     STORE U,V,X,Y AND PSI AT THE END OF THE PATH
      I = NR+M-1
      TEMP(13) = TEMP(19)
      TEMP(14) = X1(1,I)
      TEMP(15) = X1(2,I)
      I = 4*NN+M
      TEMP(16) = CMPLX(S(I),0.)
      DO 20 I = 1,4
 20   ARG3(I) = ARG(I+1)
      DO 30 I = 1,L
      CALL STP2
 30   CONTINUE
 40   WRITE (N2,100) LI
      CALL SECOND (T2)
      TIME = T2-TIME
      WRITE (N2,110) TIME
      CALL EXIT
 50   FORMAT (3I5,9F5.3)
 60   FORMAT (16I5)
 70   FORMAT (8F10.4)
 80   FORMAT (25H INITIALIZATION COMPLETE )
 90   FORMAT (20H AUTOMATION COMPLETE )
100   FORMAT (5H PATH,I3,12H IS FINISHED )
110   FORMAT (17H TOTAL CP TIME IS,F6.1,8H SECONDS)
      END

      SUBROUTINE CONST (H,CD,TR)
C     INITIALIZATION ROUTINE
      COMPLEX U,X1,X3,TAO,ETA,T,Z,ARG,ARG2,H,CMP(10),CE(9),ONE,TEMP,TMP,
     1CSQRT,HSH,HP
      COMMON /A/ C(40),ARG(5),ARG2(5)
      COMMON U(4,540),X1(2,360),X3(2,360),TAO(2,360),ETA(360),T(2,360),Z
      COMMON /C/ TEMP(20),BB(8,33)
      COMMON /D/ AA,N
      COMMON /E/ FF(66),NK,NCR,LC(15)
      COMMON /F/ HP
      DIMENSION SI(5)
      EQUIVALENCE (ONE,CMP(1),C(21)), (CE(1),FF(49)), (SI(1),BB(5,2))
      EXTERNAL CSQRT
C     SET UP COMPLEX CONSTANTS
      CMP(1) = (1.,0.)
      CMP(2) = (0.,3.1415926536)
      CMP(3) = (0.,1.)
C     CMP(4) IS THE BRANCH POINT BP
      CMP(5) = CONJG(CMP(4))
      CMP(6) = CMP(4)+CMP(4)
      CMP(7) = CMP(5)+CMP(5)
      CMP(8) = CMP(4)*CMP(4)
      CMP(9) = CMP(1)+CMP(5)*CMP(5)
      CMP(10) = -CSQRT(ONE+CMP(8),ONE)-CMP(4)
C     SETS UP BRANCHES FOR COMPLEX SQUARE ROOTS
      ARG(1) = CMP(3)
      ARG(2) = ONE
      ARG(3) = ONE
      ARG(4) = ONE
      ARG(5) = CMP(3)
      ARG2(1) = CMP(3)
C     SET UP REAL CONSTANTS USED IN PROGRAM
      C(1) = .5
```

```
      C(2) = 1./3.
C     C(3) = GAS CONSTANT GAMMA
      C(4) = C(1)*(C(3)-1.)
      C(5) = C(1)/C(4)
      GP1 = C(3)+1.
      C(6) = -SQRT(GP1*C(5))
      C(7) = -C(1)*GP1*C(4)
C     C(8) IS THE FREE STREAM MACH NUMBER
      C(8) = AMAX1(C(8),1.E-40)
      C(9) = 1./(C(8)*C(8))+C(4)
      C(10) = C(9)+C(9)
      C(11) = C(4)*(C(8)*C(8))
      C(12) = 1.+C(11)
      C(13) = C(4)*GP1/C(9)
      C(14) = C(1)*C(3)*C(9)
      C(15) = C(6)*C(13)
      C(18) = 1.
      C(18) = 1./REAL(HSH(ONE))
      C(19) = SQRT(C(18))
      C(20) = .999*C(19)
      IF (NK.EQ.0) GO TO 20
C     SET UP AUTOMATION CONDITIONS
      NCR = NCR + 1
      NRP = IABS(NK)+1
      IF (LC(2).EQ.LC(1)) GO TO 20
      JJ = NRP-1
      NK = ISIGN(NRP,NK)
      NRP = NRP+1
   10 LC(JJ+1) = LC(JJ)
      JJ = JJ-1
      IF (JJ.GT.0) GO TO 10
   20 BB(6,NRP) = FF(59)
      BB(5,NRP) = FF(60)
      BB(7,NRP) = FF(63)
      SI(1) = 0.
      SI(2) = 0.
      SI(3) = 0.
      SI(4) = 1.
C     SET UP CONSTANTS USED FOR INITIAL FUNCTION
      CE(8) = CMP(1) - CE(2)
      CE(9) = CSQRT(CE(8),ONE)
      IF (NK.GE.0.OR.BB(7,NRP).NE.1.) GO TO 30
      CE(9) = CMPLX(REAL(CE(9)),0.)
   30 CONTINUE
C     SET UP U,X1,X2 AND TAO AT ETA = ZERO
      Z = (0.,0.)
      ETA(1) = Z
      U(1,1) = ONE
      U(2,1) = Z
      CALL TOFH (Z,U,TAO)
      B = AIMAG(TAO(1,1))
      TMP = -CD*B-CMP(3)
      TMP = TMP/CABS(TMP)
      X1(2,1) = CMPLX(CABS(CE(9)),0.)
C     CHECK FOR BP=0
      IF (REAL(CMP(4)*CMP(5)).NE.0) X1(2,1) =
     1 X1(2,1)*TMP*CMP(5)/CABS(CMP(5))
      X1(1,1) = -TAO(1,1)*X1(2,1)
      TMP = X1(2,1)*TAO(2,2)
```

```
      U(3,1) = C(1)*(TMP+CONJG(TMP))
      U(4,1) = CMPLX(AIMAG(TMP)/B,0.)
      C(17) = REAL(4.*CMP(2)*x1(2,1)*B*CMP(6))
      C(16) = CD*C(17)
      BB(4,NRP) = (1.-TR)*CD*C(17)*C(1)
C     COMPUTE U,X1, AND TAO UP TO THE INITIAL CHARACTERISTIC
      DO 40 J = 2,N
   40 ETA(J) = ETA(J-1)+H
      CALL INVAL (2,N)
      DO 50 J = 2,N
      TMP = CONJG(TAO(2,J))
      TAO(2,J) = CONJG(TAO(1,J))
   50 TAO(1,J) = TMP
      DO 60 K = 1,4
   60 TEMP(K+4) = U(K,N)
      DO 70 I = 1,N
      ETA(I) = CONJG(ETA(I))
      DO 70 K = 1,4
   70 U(K,I) = CONJG(U(K,I))
      CALL XAB (2,N)
C     STORE THE RESULTS
      NM1 = N-1
      DO 80 J = 1,NM1
      ETA(J) = U(3,J)
      T(J,1) = U(4,J)
      DO 80 I = 1,2
      X3(I,J) = U(I,J)
   80 X1(I,J) = TAO(I,J)
      RETURN
      END


      SUBROUTINE TAIL (NO)
C     MAKE RUNS TO EVALUATE THE AUTOMATED PARAMETERS
      COMPLEX T,H,U,X1,X3,TAO,ETA,Z,TB,TEMP,BP,ONE
      COMMON /A/ C(40)
      COMMON U(4,540),X1(2,360),X3(2,360),TAO(2,360),ETA(360),T(2,360),Z
      COMMON /C/ TEMP(20),BB(8,33)
      COMMON /D/ AA,N,M,MRP,NN,NR,II,JJ,KK,IP,NP,LBM
      COMMON /E/ FF(66),NK,NCR,LC(31)
      COMMON /G/ N1,N2,N6,N7
      DIMENSION B(8,1)
      EQUIVALENCE (B(1,1),U(1,1)), (ONE,C(21)), (BP,C(27)), (TB,C(31))
      DATA J,LT/-1,-0/
      K = IABS(NK)
      LBP = LBM + LBM/2
      IF (NP.EQ.0) GO TO 10
      JMAX = MAX0(0,-NP)
      IF (K.GT.1) GO TO 20
      NO = 1
   10 WRITE (N2,140)
      RETURN
C     SET AUTOMATED PARAMETERS TO ZERO
   20 DO 30 I = 2,K
      KT = LC(I)
      IF(MOD((KT+1)/2,2).EQ.0) GO TO 105
   30 FF(KT) = 0.
   40 ETA(N) = CONJG(ETA(N))
      JJ = N
      IF (J.GT.0) WRITE (N2,110) J
```

```
      CALL AANDB (N,NN,ETA,JJ,1)
      IF (JJ.EQ.N) JJ = NN
      L = JJ
      IF (J.GT.0) JJ = N-JJ
C     J IS NEGATIVE FOR NOSE AUTOMATION
C     J IS POSITIVE FOR LEAST SQUARES AUTOMATION
C     J IS ZERO FOR THE TAIL AUTOMATION
      IF (J.NE.0) GO TO 50
      H = (1.,-1.)*(ONE-ETA(NN)*ETA(NN)-TB*ETA(NN))/(ETA(NN)+BP)
      WRITE (N2,120)
      H = (.5*AA*H)/(CABS(H)*FLOAT(MRP))
      ETA(NN+1) = ETA(NN)
      ETA(NN) = ETA(NN)-H
      A = CABS(ETA(NN)-ETA(NN-1))
C     ADD POINTS TO THE PATH ON EITHER SIDE OF THE TAIL
      NN = NN+2
      ETA(NN) = ETA(NN-1)+H
      D = CABS(ETA(NN)-ETA(NN-3))
      IF (D.GE.A) GO TO 50
      H = ETA(NN)
      ETA(NN) = ETA(NN-2)
      ETA(NN-2) = H
   50 DO 60 I = N,NN
   60 ETA(I) = CONJG(ETA(I))
      CALL STEP (-1)
C     FIND THE SOLUTION ON THE PATH FOR EACH AUTOMATED PARAMETER
      DO 70 I = 2,K
      KT = LC(I-1)
      FF(KT) = 0.
      KT = LC(I)
      FF(KT) = 1.
   70 CALL STEP (-1)
      FF(KT) = 0.
      IF (J.LE.0) GO TO 90
      JJ = 1+4*(NN+JJ-N)
      IF(NN+JJ.GT.LBP) GO TO 100
      DO 80 I = 1,JJ,4
      LT = LT-1
      KT = NN+I
      WRITE (N1,160) ETA(L),(B(LL,KT),LL = 1,K)
   80 L = L + 1
   90 J = J+1
      IF (J.LE.JMAX) GO TO 40
      IF (NP.LT.0) NP = LT
      LT = -LT
      WRITE (N2,130) LT
      RETURN
  100 WRITE (N2,150) NN,JJ
      CALL EXIT
  105 WRITE (N2,170) KT
      CALL EXIT
  110 FORMAT (22H BEGIN AUTOMATION PATH,I4)
  120 FORMAT (25H NOSE AUTOMATION COMPLETE)
  130 FORMAT (10H THERE ARE,I4,30H POINTS USED FOR LEAST SQUARES)
  140 FORMAT (22H NO AUTOMATION IS DONE)
  150 FORMAT (31H DIMENSION STATEMENTS TOO SMALL, 2I5)
C     ****CHANGE (4020) TO (20A4) ON IBM 360****
  160 FORMAT (4020)
  170 FORMAT (10H PARAMETER,I3,28H REFERS TO A NON-LINEAR TERM)
```

```
      END

      SUBROUTINE AANDB (NA,NB,ALP,MPSI,IND)
C     READS IN THE PATHS ON THE COMPLEX CHARACTERISTICS AND SETS UP THE
C     INITIAL GRID
C     PATHS ARE PRESCRIBED IN THE ETA OR ETA PRIME PLANE AND THE
C     GRID IS SET UP IN THE XI PLANE
      COMPLEX ALP(1),H,BP,CSQRT,A,ONE,BS
      COMMON /A/ C(40)
      COMMON /D/ AA,N,M,MRP,NN,NR,II,JJ,KK,IP,NP,LBM,TIME
      COMMON /G/ N1,N2,N6,N7
      EQUIVALENCE (ONE,C(21)), (BS,C(35)), (BP,C(27))
      EXTERNAL CSQRT
      IF (IND.GE.0) GO TO 20
C     AUTOMATION, USE THE SAME PATH AGAIN.  CHANGE FROM XI TO ETA
      NP1 = NA+1
      DO 10 I = NP1,NB
   10 ALP(I) = CONJG(ALP(I))
      RETURN
   20 READ (N6,100) MQ,KK
C     ****CHECK FOR END OF FILE****
      IF (EOF(N6).NE.0) GO TO 80
C     MQ IS POSITIVE FOR PATHS IN THE ETA PRIME PLANE
C     MQ IS NEGATIVE FOR PATHS IN THE ETA PLANE
C     IABS(MQ) IS THE NUMBER OF POINTS ON THE PATH TO BE READ IN
      MA = IABS(MQ)
      K = NA
      DO 60 I = 1,MA
      READ (N6,110) A,LL
      IF (MQ.GE.0) A = A*CSQRT(ONE+BS/(A*A),ONE)-BP
      A = CONJG(A)
      MM = CABS(A-ALP(K))/AA+.999
      KN = K+1
      IF (LL.EQ.0) LL = 1
      MM = MM*MRP*IABS(LL)
      IF (LL.GT.0) GO TO 50
      MPSI = K+MM
      IF (KK.GT.0) CALL ADJ (1,1,A)
   50 H = (A-ALP(K))/FLOAT(MM)
      K = K+MM
      DO 60 J = KN,K
   60 ALP(J) = ALP(J-1)+H
      NB = K
      CALL ADJ (MPSI,NB,ALP)
      IF (KK.GT.0) GO TO 70
      K = 2*NB-NA
   70 IF (LBM.GE.K) RETURN
      WRITE (N2,120) NB,K
      CALL EXIT
   80 WRITE (N2,130)
      CALL SECOND (T1)
      TIME = T1-TIME
      WRITE (N2,90) TIME
      CALL EXIT
   90 FORMAT (17H TOTAL CP TIME IS,F6.1,8H SECONDS)
  100 FORMAT (3I3)
  110 FORMAT (2E20.12,I5)
  120 FORMAT (/35H  THE GRID IS TOO LARGE FOR PROGRAM,I5,3H K=I4)
  130 FORMAT (13H OUT OF PATHS)
```

```
      END

      SUBROUTINE ADJ (K,L,X)
C     MODIFIES THE INITIAL PATH
C     SUBSONIC PATHS ARE TRUNCATED AT .999*EM
C     SUPERSONIC PATHS ARE PASTED TO THE SONIC LOCUS
      COMPLEX CB1,CB2,CB3,S,X(1),CSQRT
      COMMON /A/ C(40)
      COMMON /D/ AA,N,M,MRP,NN,NR,II,JJ,KK,IP,NP,LBM
      EQUIVALENCE (CB1,C(29)), (CM1,C(19)), (CM2,C(20)), (CB2,C(37)), (C
     1B3,C(33))
      EXTERNAL CSQRT
      DO 20 I = K,L
      S = 1.-X(I)*(X(I)+CB3)
      T = CABS(S)
      IF (KK.GT.0) GO TO 10
C     MAKES SURE THE PATH REMAINS SUBSONIC
      IF (T-CM1) 20,30,30
C     FOR SUPERSONIC RUN THE POINT IS PLACED ON THE SONIC LOCUS
   10 S = S*CM1/T
      X(I) = CSQRT(CB2-S,X(I))-CB1
   20 CONTINUE
      RETURN
   30 L = I
      S = CM2*S/T
      X(L) = CSQRT(CB2-S,X(L))-CB1
      RETURN
      END

      SUBROUTINE CUSP (A,D,G,DD,H)
C     SOLVES THE EQUATIONS FOR THE AUTOMATED PARAMETERS
      COMPLEX Z,TEMP,G(1),ET,ETO
      COMMON /A/ C(40)
      COMMON /C/ TEMP(20),BB(8,33)
      COMMON /D/ AA,N,M,MRP,NN,NR,II,JJ,KK,IP,NP,LBM
      COMMON /E/ FF(66),NK,NCR,LC(31)
      COMMON /G/ N1,N2,N6,N7
      DIMENSION A(4,1), D(24), DD(40,41), H(31,5), SI(5)
      EQUIVALENCE (SI(1),BB(5,2))
      DATA Z/(0.,0.)/
      NR = IABS(NK)
      NRP = NR+1
      XR = BB(7,NRP)
      FNOR = FLOAT(MRP*MRP)/(AA*AA)
      BB(1,NRP) = 1.
      BB(2,NRP) = 0.
      BB(3,NRP) = 0.
      BB(8,NRP) = 0.
      NCR = MINO(NCR,NR)
      IF (NK.GT.0) GO TO 10
      NCR = NR-1
      BB(7,NRP) = 0.
   10 REWIND N1
C     READ IN DATA FOR NOSE AUTOMATION
      DO 20 J = 1,NR
      READ (N1,190) I,M,I,((A(K,L),K=1,4),G(L),D(L),L=1,M)
C     XU AT THE NOSE
      BB(6,J) = (A(3,M)-A(3,M-1))/A(1,M-1)
C     YU AT THE NOSE
```

```
      BB(5,J) = (A(4,M)-A(4,M-1))/A(1,M-1)
      BB(1,J) = 1.
C     -PSI AT THE NOSE
      H(J,1) = -D(M)
C     -X AT THE NOSE
      H(J,2) = -A(3,M)
C     -Y AT THE NOSE
   20 H(J,3) = -A(4,M)
      ETO = G(M)
C     ETA AT THE NOSE
C     COMPUTE (DEL V/DEL U) AT THE NOSE
      RAT = A(2,M-1)/A(1,M-1)
      RA = FLOAT(MRP)/AA
      DO 30 J = 1,NR
C     READ IN DATA FOR TAIL AUTOMATION
      READ (N1,190) I,M,I,((A(K,L),K=1,4),G(L),D(L),L=1,M)
C     -X AT THE TAIL
      H(J,4) = -A(3,M-1)
C     -Y AT THE TAIL
      H(J,5) = -A(4,M-1)
C     YUU AT THE TAIL
      BB(7,J) = FNOR*(2.*A(4,M-1)-A(4,M)-A(4,M-2))
      IF (NK.EQ.7) BB(7,J) = FNOR*(D(M)+H(J,1))/RHO(0.)
C     DELTA X AT THE TAIL
      BB(2,J) = RA*(A(3,M)-A(3,M-2))
C     DELTA Y AT THE TAIL
      BB(3,J) = RA*(A(4,M)-A(4,M-2))
C     PSI TAIL - PSI NOSE
      BB(4,J) = H(J,1)+D(M-1)
C     XUU AT THE TAIL
      BB(8,J) = FNOR*(2.*A(3,M-1)-A(3,M)-A(3,M-2))
   30 CONTINUE
      NPT = MAX0(0,-NP)
      IF(NP.EQ.0)  NPT = 1000
      L = NRP+NCR
      DO 40 K = 1,L
      DO 40 J = 1,40
   40 DD(J,K) = 0.
      DO 50 J = 1,NR
      DO 50 K = 1,NCR
      JJ = NR+K
      DD(JJ,J) = BB(K,J)
   50 DD(J,JJ) = BB(K,J)
      G(1) = CMPLX(A(1,M-1),A(2,M-1))
C     U AND V AT THE TAIL
      ET = G(M-1)
C     ETA AT THE TAIL
      SUM = 1.
      IF (NPT.EQ.0) GO TO 90
C     READ IN LEAST SQUARES PATHS
      DO 70 L = 1,NPT
      SUM = 0.
      READ (N1,190) G(L+1),(D(J),J = 1,NR)
C     ****CHECK FOR END OF FILE****
      IF (EOF(N1).NE.0) GO TO 75
      DO 60 J = 1,NR
      D(J) = D(J)+H(J,1)
   60 SUM = SUM+D(J)*D(J)
      SUM = SUM*CABS((G(L+1)-ETO)*(G(L+1)-ET))
```

```
      SUM = FLOAT(NR)/SUM
      DO 70 J = 1,NR
      DO 70 K = J,NR
      DD(J,K) = DD(J,K)+D(J)*D(K)*SUM
   70 DD(K,J) = DD(J,K)
   75 IF(NP.EQ.0)  NPT = L - 1
      IF(NPT.EQ.0)  GO TO 90
      SUM = 0.
      DO 80 J = 1,NR
   80 SUM = SUM+DD(J,J)
      WRITE (N2,160) SUM
      SUM = 100.*BB(7,NRP)*FLOAT(NR)/SUM
      BB(7,NRP) = 0.
   90 DO 100 J = 2,NR
      XX = 1./SUM
      I = LC(J)
C     WEIGHT THE ELLIPSE TERM AND ETA TERM LESS
      IF (I.GE.49.AND.I.LE.54.AND.NK.GT.0) XX = .2*XX
  100 DD(J,J) = XX+DD(J,J)
      L = NRP+NCR
      DO 110 K = 1,NCR
      JJ = NR+K
  110 DD(JJ,L) = BB(K,NRP)
C     SOLVE THE SYSTEM OF LINEAR EQUATIONS FOR THE AUTOMATED
C     PARAMETERS
      CALL LEQ (DD,DD(1,L),L-1,1,40,40,XX)
      NRP = 5*L
      WRITE (N2,180) XX
C     COMPUTE XU AND XV
      FF(59) = DD(1,L)*BB(6,1)
      FF(60) = DD(1,L)*BB(5,1)
      DO 120 J = 2,NR
      FF(59) = FF(59) + DD(J,L)*BB(6,J)
      FF(60) = FF(60) + DD(J,L)*BB(5,J)
      I = LC(J)
  120 FF(I) = DD(J,L)
C     COMPUTE CORRECTED XV
      UU = RAT*FF(59) + FF(60)
C     COMPUTE CORRECTED -XU
      VV = RAT*FF(60) - FF(59)
C     COMPUTE UU,VV SO THAT VV/UU IS THE SLOPE AT THE NOSE
      VV = .1E-10*(VV-SQRT(UU*UU+VV*VV))
      UU = .1E-10*UU
      DO 130 K = 1,5
      SI(K) = DD(1,L)*H(1,K)
      DO 130 J = 2,NR
  130 SI(K) = SI(K)+DD(J,L)*H(J,K)
C     SI(1) IS -PSI AT THE NOSE
C     SI(2) IS -X AT THE NOSE
C     SI(3) IS -Y AT THE NOSE
      SI(4) = SI(2)-SI(4)
      SI(5) = SI(3)-SI(5)
      REWIND N1
      SI(4) = 1./SI(4)
C     SI(4) = 1/CHORD
C     SI(5) IS Y AT THE TAIL
      XX = C(16)*SI(4)
      SUM = C(17)*SI(4)
C     NORMALIZE FOR UNIT CHORD LENGTH
```

```
      SI(1) = SI(1)*SI(4)
      SI(5) = SI(5)*SI(4)
      REWIND N7
C     TRANSMIT INPUT DATA TO TAPE1
      READ (N7,240) (D(J),J = 1,24)
      I = 16
      IF (NK.GT.16) I = 24
      WRITE (N1,240) (D(J),J = 1,I)
      WRITE (N1,200) (FF(J),J = 1,62),XR
      REWIND N6
  140 READ (N6,210) I,J
      L = IABS(I)
      IF (J.EQ.0) WRITE (N1,210) I,J
      DO 150 I = 1,L
      READ (N6,220) ETO,K
      IF (J.GE.0) WRITE (N1,220) ETO,K
  150 CONTINUE
      IF (J.EQ.0) GO TO 140
      IF (NPT.GT.0) WRITE (N1,190)  NPT,(G(L+1),L = 1,NPT)
      C(8) = 1./(C(1)*C(3)*C(8)*C(8))
      C(16) = 1./(C(8)*C(11))
      RA = 1.
      WRITE (N1,190) C(8),C(11),C(16),C(19),SUM,XX,UU,VV,Z,G(1),RA,SI(5)
      C(17) = SQRT((C(10))/(C(3)+1.))
      JJ = N+1
      IF ((NRP+NN).LE.LBM) RETURN
C     CHECK TO SEE IF WE HAVE EXCEEDED GRID SIZE
      WRITE (N2,230)
      CALL EXIT
      RETURN
  160 FORMAT (9H TRACE = ,E12.5)
  180 FORMAT (14H DETERMINANT =,E12.5)
C     ****CHANGE (4020) TO (20A4) ON IBM 360****
  190 FORMAT (4020)
  200 FORMAT (8F10.4)
  210 FORMAT (2I3)
  220 FORMAT (2E20.12,I5)
  230 FORMAT (40H NON ENOUGH STORAGE TO COMPLETE THIS RUN)
C     ****CHANGE (8A10) TO (20A4) ON IBM 360****
  240 FORMAT (8A10)
      END

      SUBROUTINE LEQ (A,B,NEQS,NSOLNS,IA,IB,DET)
C     LINEAR EQUATIONS SOLUTIONS WRITTEN AT AEC COMPUTING CENTER (NYU)
C     SOLVE A SYSTEM OF LINEAR EQUATIONS OF THE FORM AX=B BY A MODIFIED
C     GAUSS ELIMINATION SCHEME
C     NEQS = NUMBER OF EQUATIONS AND UNKNOWNS
C     NSOLNS = NUMBER OF VECTOR SOLUTIONS DESIRED
C     IA = NUMBER OF ROWS OF A AS DEFINED BY DIMENSION STATEMENT ENTRY
C     IB = NUMBER OF ROWS OF B AS DEFINED BY DIMENSION STATEMENT ENTRY
C     ADET = DETERMINANT OF A, AFTER EXIT FROM LEQ
      DIMENSION A(IA,IA), B(IB,IB)
      NSIZ = NEQS
      NBSIZ = NSOLNS
C     NORMALIZE EACH ROW BY ITS LARGERT ELEMENT
C     FORM PARTIAL DETERMINANT
      DET = 1.0
      DO 40 I = 1,NSIZ
      BIG = A(I,1)
```

```
      IF (NSIZ.LE.1) GO TO 130
      DO 10 J = 2,NSIZ
      IF (ABS(BIG).GE.ABS(A(I,J))) GO TO 10
      BIG = A(I,J)
   10 CONTINUE
      BG = 1.0/BIG
      DO 20 J = 1,NSIZ
   20 A(I,J) = A(I,J)*BG
      DO 30 J = 1,NBSIZ
   30 B(I,J) = B(I,J)*BG
      DET = DET*BIG
   40 CONTINUE
C     START SYSTEM REDUCTION
      NUMSYS = NSIZ-1
      DO 120 I = 1,NUMSYS
C     SCAN FIRST COLUMN OF CURRENT SYSTEM FOR LARGEST ELEMENT
C     CALL THE ROW CONTAINING THIS ELEMENT, ROW NBGRW
      NN = I+1
      BIG = A(I,I)
      NBGRW = I
      DO 50 J = NN,NSIZ
      IF (ABS(BIG).GE.ABS(A(J,I))) GO TO 50
      BIG = A(J,I)
      NBGRW = J
   50 CONTINUE
      BG = 1.0/BIG
C     SWAP ROW I WITH ROW NBGRW UNLESS I=NBGRW
      IF (NBGRW.EQ.I) GO TO 80
C     SWAP A-MATRIX ROWS
      DO 60 J = I,NSIZ
      TEMP = A(NBGRW,J)
      A(NBGRW,J) = A(I,J)
   60 A(I,J) = TEMP
      DET = -DET
C     SWAP B-MATRIX ROWS
      DO 70 J = 1,NBSIZ
      TEMP = B(NBGRW,J)
      B(NBGRW,J) = B(I,J)
   70 B(I,J) = TEMP
C     ELIMINATE UNKNOWNS FROM FIRST COLUMN OF CURRENT SYSTEM
   80 DO 110 K = NN,NSIZ
C     COMPUTE PIVOTAL MULTIPLIER
      PMULT = -A(K,I)*BG
      IF (PMULT.EQ.0.) GO TO 110
C     APPLY PMULT TO ALL COLUMNS OF THE CURRENT A-MATRIX ROW
      DO 90 J = NN,NSIZ
   90 A(K,J) = PMULT*A(I,J)+A(K,J)
C     APPLY PMULT TO ALL COLUMNS OF MATRIX B
      DO 100 L = 1,NBSIZ
  100 B(K,L) = PMULT*B(I,L)+B(K,L)
  110 CONTINUE
  120 CONTINUE
C     DO BACK SUBSTITUTION WITH B-MATRIX COLUMN = NCOLB
  130 DO 170 NCOLB = 1,NBSIZ
C     DO FOR ROW = NROW
      DO 160 I = 1,NSIZ
      NROW = NSIZ+1-I
      TEMP = 0.0
C     NUMBER OF PREVIOUSLY COMPUTED UNKNOWNS = NXS
```

```
      NXS = NSIZ-NROW
C     ARE WE DOING THE BOTTOM ROW
      IF (NXS.EQ.0) GO TO 150
      DO 140 K = 1,NXS
      KK = NSIZ+1-K
  140 TEMP = TEMP+B(KK,NCOLB)*A(NROW,KK)
  150 B(NROW,NCOLB) = (B(NROW,NCOLB)-TEMP)/A(NROW,NROW)
C     HAVE WE FINISHED ALL ROWS FOR B-MATRIX COLUMN = NCOLB
  160 CONTINUE
C     HAVE WE JUST FINISHED WITH B-MATRIX COLUMN NCOLB=NSIZ
  170 CONTINUE
C     NOW FINISH COMPUTING THE DETERMINANT
      DO 180 I = 1,NSIZ
  180 DET = DET*A(I,I)
      RETURN
      END


      SUBROUTINE STEP (LL)
C     THIS IS THE MAIN CALLING ROUTINE FOR FINDING THE SOLUTION
C     FORKS ARE CALLED FROM STP2
      COMPLEX U,TAO,ARG,ARG2,ETA,X1,X3,TEMP,SS,S(1),PI,UU,TT,T,Z
      COMMON /A/ C(40),ARG(5),ARG2(5)
      COMMON U(4,540),X1(2,360),X3(2,360),TAO(2,360),ETA(360),T(2,360),Z
      COMMON /C/ TEMP(20),SS(6),SI(5)
      COMMON /D/ AA,N,M,MRP,NN,NR,II,JJ,KK,IP,NP,LBM
      COMMON /F/ XP(4),UU(8),TT(8)
      COMMON /G/ N1,N2,N6,N7
      EQUIVALENCE (PF,C(1)), (S(1),T(1,1)), (PI,C(23))
      NM1 = N-1
C     RETRIEVE SOLUTION FROM THE ORIGIN TO THE INITIAL CHARACTERISTIC
      DO 10 I = 1,NM1
      U(3,I) = ETA(I)
      U(4,I) = T(I,1)
      DO 10 J = 1,2
      U(J,I) = X3(J,I)
   10 TAO(J,I) = X1(J,I)
      ARG(1) = ARG2(5)
      DO 20 I = 1,4
      ARG(I+1) = ARG2(I+1)
   20 U(I,N) = TEMP(I+4)
      ETA(N) = CONJG(ETA(N))
      CALL TOFH (ETA(N),U(1,N),TAO(1,N))
      CALL AANDB (N,NN,ETA,II,LL)
C     READ IN ETA PATH
      IF (LL.EQ.0) CALL CUSP (X1(3,NN),T(3,NN),TAO(3,NN),U(5,NN),X3(3,N)
     1)
      M = 0
      NP1 = N+1
C     COMPUTE X1,Y1,U,V,X2,Y2 ON ETA =0.
      CALL INVAL (NP1,NN)
      DO 30 K = 1,4
   30 TEMP(K+8) = U(K,NN)
      DO 40 I = NP1,NN
      DO 40 K = 1,4
   40 U(K,I) = CONJG(U(K,I))
      ARG2(1) = ARG2(5)
      DO 50 I = N,NN
      ETA(I) = CONJG(ETA(I))
      T(1,I) = TAO(1,I)
```

```
      TAO(1,I) = CONJG(TAO(2,I))
      TAO(2,I) = CONJG(T(1,I))
   50 T(2,I) = PF*(TAO(1,I)+TAO(1,I-1))
      TEMP(19) = Z
      CALL XAC (2,N,NN)
      IF (KK.GT.0) GO TO 60
      NR = NN+1
      IP = NR+NN
      S(IP) = CMPLX(SI(1),0.)
C     SET THE VALUE OF THE STREAM FUNCTION IN THE REAL PLANE AT
C     THE INITIAL CHARACTERISTIC
      TEMP(4) = X1(2,N)
      CALL SAVE (U(3,N),N,N,X1(1,NR),S(IP))
      CALL XAB (NP1,NN)
      CALL TPE (X1(1,NR),S(IP),ETA(N),U(5,NN))
      RETURN
C     THE S ARRAY CONTAINS THE XI CHARACTERISTIC
   60 S(N) = CONJG(ETA(N))
      DO 70 K = 1,4
   70 UU(K) = TEMP(K+4)
      CALL TOFH (S(N),UU,TT(5))
C     READ IN THE XI PATH
      KK1 = MIN0(3,KK)
      CALL AANDB (N,MM,S,JJ,LL)
      KK = 3*MIN0(2,KK-1) + KK1
      NR = NP1
      IP = MM+1
      S(IP) = CMPLX(SI(1),0.)
      DO 90 I = 1,NM1
      J = N-I
      DO 80 K = 1,4
   80 U(K,J+1) = CONJG(U(K,J))
      TAO(1,J+1) = CONJG(TAO(2,J))
   90 TAO(2,J+1) = CONJG(TAO(1,J))
      TEMP(4) = X1(2,N)
      DO 100 K = 1,4
      ARG(K+1) = ARG2(K+1)
  100 SS(K) = U(K,N)
C     SS CONTAINS U,V,X, AND Y AT THE INITIAL CHARACTERISTICS
      SS(5) = 1./ETA(N)
      SS(6) = CLOG(-ETA(N))-PI
      SS(3) = X1(2,N)*SS(5)
      SS(4) = -TT(5)*SS(3)+U(3,N)*SS(6)+X3(1,N)
      SS(3) = SS(3)+U(4,N)*SS(6)+X3(2,N)
      CALL XAC (NP1,JJ,NN)
      CALL TPE (X1(1,NR),S(IP),ETA,U)
      L = MM-JJ
      DO 110 I = 1,L
      JJPI = JJ+I
      M = 0
C     COMPUTE THE SOLUTION IN THE TRIANGLE
      CALL XAC (JJPI,JJPI,NN-I)
  110 CALL TPE (X1(1,NR),S(IP),ETA,U)
      II = N
      IF(KK.GE.9) RETURN
C     STORE THE SUPERSONIC PATHS ON TAPE1
      K = NN-NM1
      WRITE (N1,120) K,(ETA(I),I = N,NN)
      K = IP-N
```

```
      WRITE (N1,120) K,(S(I),I = N,MM)
      RETURN
C     ****CHANGE (4O2O) TO (20A4) ON IBM 360****
  120 FORMAT (4O2O)
      END


      SUBROUTINE STP2
C     THIS ROUTINE ENABLES US TO BRANCH OFF INTO MANY PATHS ON THE
C     INITIAL CHARACTERISTIC
      COMPLEX U,X1,X3,TAO,ETA,T,TEMP,ARG,ARG2,Z,S(1),ARG3
      COMMON /A/ C(40),ARG(5),ARG2(5),ARG3(4)
      COMMON U(4,540),X1(2,360),X3(2,360),TAO(2,360),ETA(360),T(2,360),Z
      COMMON /C/ TEMP(20)
      COMMON /D/ AA,N,M,MRP,NN,MM,II,JJ,KK,IP
      EQUIVALENCE (PF,C(1)), (S(1),T(1,1))
      NP1 = NN+1
      ETA(NN) = CONJG(ETA(NN))
      DO 10 K = 1,4
      ARG(K+1) = ARG3(K)
   10 U(K,NN) = TEMP(K+8)
      CALL TOFH (ETA(NN),U(1,NN),TAO(1,NN))
C     READ IN FORK
      CALL AANDB (NN,NR,ETA,NN,1)
C     COMPUTE X1,Y1,U,V,X2,Y2 ON ETA =0.
      CALL INVAL (NP1,NR)
      DO 20 I = NP1,NR
      DO 20 K = 1,4
   20 U(K,I) = CONJG(U(K,I))
      TEMP(17) = T(2,NN)
      DO 30 I = NN,NR
      ETA(I) = CONJG(ETA(I))
      T(1,I) = TAO(1,I)
      TAO(1,I) = CONJG(TAO(2,I))
      TAO(2,I) = CONJG(T(1,I))
   30 T(2,I) = PF*(TAO(1,I)+TAO(1,I-1))
      T(2,NN) = TEMP(17)
      TEMP(19) = TEMP(13)
      M = 1
      X1(3,NR) = TEMP(14)
      X1(4,NR) = TEMP(15)
      T(3,NR) = TEMP(16)
      MM = NR+1
      IP = NR+MM
C     COMPUTE THE SOLUTION IN THE RECTANGLE
      CALL XAC (2,NN,NR)
      CALL XAB (NP1,NR)
C     STORE REAL SOLUTION ON TAPE
      CALL TPE (X1(1,MM),S(IP),ETA(NN))
      RETURN
      END


      SUBROUTINE INVAL (K,NB)
C     COMPUTES U AND V ALONG THE CHARACTERISTIC ETA = 0.
C     ALSO COMPUTES X1,Y1 AND X2,Y2 ALONG ETA = 0.
      COMPLEX U,X1,X3,TAO,ETA,Z,H,S(8),Y,R,T
      COMMON /A/ PF,FAC
      COMMON U(4,540),X1(2,360),X3(2,360),TAO(2,360),ETA(360),T(2,360),Z
      DO 10 I = K,NB
      H = PF*(ETA(I)-ETA(I-1))
```

```
      S(1) = TAO(1,I)
      S(2) = TAO(2,I)
C     MIDPOINT EVALUATION
      CALL TOFH (ETA(I)-H,U(1,I-1),S(4))
C     ENDPOINT EVALUATION
      CALL TOFH (ETA(I),U(1,I-1),TAO(1,I))
C     SIMPSONS RULE IS USED FOR THIS QUADRATURE
      Y = FAC*H*(S(1)+4.*S(6)+TAO(3,I))
      X1(2,I) = X1(2,I-1)*CEXP(-Y)
      X1(1,I) = PF*S(6)*(X1(2,I)+X1(2,I-1))
      R = TAO(4,I)*X1(2,I)
      U(4,I) = (U(3,I-1)+S(5)*U(4,I-1)-R)/(S(5)-TAO(1,I))
   10 U(3,I) = R-TAO(1,I)*U(4,I)
      RETURN
      END

      SUBROUTINE INVAL2 (I,Y)
C     COMPUTES U,V,X2, AND Y2 ALONG XI=0.
      COMPLEX UU,Y(4),TT,ETA,H,XX(4),R,U,X1,X3,TAO,T,Z,S(1)
      COMMON /A/ PF,FAC
      COMMON U(4,540),X1(2,360),X3(2,360),TAO(2,360),ETA(360),T(2,360),Z
      COMMON /F/ XP(4),UU(8),TT(8)
      EQUIVALENCE (T(1),S(1))
      H = PF*(S(I)-S(I-1))
C     MIDPOINT EVALUATION
      CALL TOFH (S(I)-H,UU,XX)
C     ENDPOINT EVALUATION
      CALL TOFH (S(I),UU,TT(5))
C     QUADRATURE BY SIMPSONS RULE
      H = FAC*H*(TT(3)+4.*XX(3)+TT(7))
      Y(4) = Y(2)*CEXP(-H)
      Y(3) = PF*XX(3)*(Y(4)+Y(2))
      R = TT(8)*Y(4)
      UU(8) = (UU(3)-R+XX(2)*UU(4))/(XX(2)-TT(5))
      UU(7) = R-TT(5)*UU(8)
      RETURN
      END

      SUBROUTINE XAB (K,NB)
C     SOLUTION IS SOLVED FOR IN THE TRIANGLE ETA.GE.CONJ(XI)
C     FOR SUBSONIC RUNS ONLY, SINCE SYMMETRY IS EXPLOITED
      COMPLEX U,X1,X3,TAO,ETA,ARG,T,TEMP,CI,SS
      COMMON /A/ C(40),ARG(5)
      COMMON U(4,540),X1(2,360),X3(2,360),TAO(2,360),ETA(360),T(2,360),Z
      COMMON /C/ TEMP(20),SS(6)
      COMMON /D/ AA,N
      EQUIVALENCE (CI,C(25)), (PF,C(1))
      DO 40 I = K,NB
C     REFLECT U,V,X2,Y2,LAMBDA(+,-) ABOUT XI=CONJ(ETA)
      DO 10 L = 1,4
   10 U(L,I-1) = CONJG(U(L,I))
      TAO(1,I-1) = CONJG(TAO(2,I))
      TAO(2,I-1) = CONJG(TAO(1,I))
      ARG(1) = CI
      IF (I.LE.N) GO TO 20
      X3(1,I-1) = CONJG(X3(1,I))
      X3(2,I-1) = CONJG(X3(2,I))
      SS(1) = CONJG(PF*(ETA(I)+ETA(I-1)))
      TEMP(1) = X1(1,I)
```

```
      TEMP(2) = CONJG(T(2,I))
      TEMP(3) = T(1,I)
      TEMP(4) = X1(2,I)
   20 CALL NEXT (I,I,NB,CONJG(ETA(I)-ETA(I-1)))
      DO 30 L = 1,4
   30 U(L,I-1) = U(L,NB)
C     STORE RESULTS AT THE END OF THE PATH
      TAO(1,I-1) = TAO(1,NB)
      TAO(2,I-1) = TAO(2,NB)
      IF (I.LE.N) GO TO 40
      X3(1,I-1) = X3(1,NB)
      X3(2,I-1) = X3(2,NB)
   40 CONTINUE
      RETURN
      END


      SUBROUTINE XAC (K,NA,NB)
C     SOLVES THE EQUATIONS IN A RECTANGULAR AREA
      COMPLEX X1,X3,TAO,J,ETA,T,H,TEMP,UU,TT,ARG,ARG2,S(1),SS
      COMMON /A/ C(40),ARG(5),ARG2(5)
      COMMON U(4,540),X1(2,360),X3(2,360),TAO(2,360),ETA(360),T(2,360),Z
      COMMON /C/ TEMP(20),SS(6)
      COMMON /D/ AA,N,M,MRP,NN,NR,II,JJ,KK,IP,NP,LBM
      COMMON /F/ XP(4),UU(8),TT(8)
      EQUIVALENCE (PF,C(1)), (S(1),T(1,1))
      NP1 = NA+1
      DO 90 I = K,NA
      IF (K.GT.2) GO TO 20
C     A SUBSONIC RUN
      DO 10 L = 1,4
   10 U(L,NA) = U(L,I-1)
      TAO(1,NA) = TAO(1,I-1)
      TAO(2,NA) = TAC(2,I-1)
      IF (I-N) 60,60,50
C     A SUPERSONIC RUN
C     FIND THE INITIAL DATA ON THE OTHER CHARACTERISTIC
   20 NP1 = 2
      DO 30 L = 1,4
   30 TT(L) = TT(L+4)
      TEMP(2) = TEMP(4)
      CALL INVAL2 (I,TEMP)
      ARG(1) = ARG2(5)
      TEMP(1) = TEMP(3)
      TEMP(3) = TT(5)
      TAO(1,1) = TEMP(3)
      TEMP(2) = PF*(TT(2)+TT(6))
      DO 40 L = 1,4
      U(L,1) = UU(L+4)
   40 UU(L) = U(L,1)
      TAO(2,1) = TT(6)
      H = S(I)-S(I-1)
      GO TO 60
   50 X3(1,NA) = X3(1,I-1)
      X3(2,NA) = X3(2,I-1)
      ARG(1) = -CONJG(ARG(5))
      H = CONJG(ETA(I)-ETA(I-1))
C     STORE VARIABLES NEEDED FOR THE INHOMOGENEOUS TERM
      SS(1) = CONJG(PF*(ETA(I)+ETA(I-1)))
      TEMP(1) = X1(1,I)
```

```
      TEMP(2) = CONJG(T(2,I))
      TEMP(3) = T(1,I)
      TEMP(4) = X1(2,I)
   60 CALL NEXT (I,NP1,NB,H)
      IF (KK.GE.0) GO TO 80
C     SAVE DATA AT THE END OF THE ROW
      DO 70 L = 1,4
   70 J(L,I-1) = U(L,NB)
      TAO(1,I-1) = TAO(1,NB)
      TAO(2,I-1) = TAO(2,NB)
   80 IF (I.NE.N) GO TO 90
      TEMP(3) = T(1,N)
      CALL GETX3 (NA,NB)
   90 CONTINUE
      RETURN
      END

      SUBROUTINE NEXT (NA,J,NB,DS)
C     FINDS THE SOLUTION ALONG THE CHARACTERISTIC XI(NA) FROM ETA(J)
C     TO ETA(NB)
C     DS = XI(NA)-XI(NA-1)
C     KK IS POSITIVE FOR SUPERSONIC PATHS
      COMPLEX U,X1,X3,SS,A,B,ET,ETA,TAO,EF,GE,Z,X(2),DS,TEMP,T2(2),T3(2)
     1,S(1),CF,T1(2,1),TT,T,CB1,Q1,Q2,Q3,Q4,XX,YY
      COMMON /A/ C(40)
      COMMON U(4,540),X1(2,360),X3(2,360),TAO(2,360),ETA(360),T(2,360),Z
      COMMON /C/ TEMP(20),SS(6),SI(5)
      COMMON /D/ AA,N,M,MRP,NN,NR,II,JJ,KK,IP,NP,LBM
      EQUIVALENCE (T1(1,1),TAO(1,1)), (S(1),T(1,1)), (PF,C(1)),
     1 (CB1,C(31)), (X(1),XX), (X(2),YY)
      CF(Q1,Q2,Q3) = Q1+Q2*Q3
      EF(Q1,Q2,Q3,Q4) = Q4*(Q2-Q3)/Q1
      GE(Q1,Q2,Q3,Q4,A,B) = EF(Q1*Q1,Q2,Q3,Q4)-PF*(A+XX+Q2*(B+YY))/Q1
      L = NA-N
      NQ = NB
      IF ((KK.LE.0).OR.(NA.LT.JJ)) NQ = 0
      DO 90 I = J,NB
      IF (I.EQ.NQ) GO TO 30
      A = U(1,I)-U(1,I-1)
      B = U(2,I-1)-U(2,I)
      TT = CF(A,B,T1(2,I-1))/(T1(2,I-1)-T1(1,I))
C     U,V TO FIRST ORDER ACCURACY
      X(1) = CF(U(1,I),T1(1,I),TT)
      X(2) = U(2,I)+TT
      CALL LAMBDA (X,T2)
      DO 10 K = 1,2
      T3(K) = PF*(T1(K,I-1)+T2(K))
   10 T2(K) = PF*(T1(K,I)+T2(K))
      TT = CF(A,B,T3(2))/(T3(2)-T2(1))
C     U,V COMPUTED TO SECOND ORDER ACCURACY
      U(1,I) = CF(U(1,I),T2(1),TT)
      U(2,I) = U(2,I)+TT
      TT = T1(2,I)
      CALL LAMBDA (U(1,I),T1(1,I))
   20 A = CF(U(3,I-1)-U(3,I),U(4,I-1)-U(4,I),T3(1))/(T3(1)-T2(2))
C     X2 AND Y2 ARE COMPUTED AND STORED AS X(2),X(1)
      X(2) = U(4,I)+A
      X(1) = CF(U(3,I),A,-T2(2))
      IF (L.LE.0.OR.I.LT.N) GO TO 80
```

```
      IF (I.EQ.N) GO TO 50
      ET = PF*(ETA(I)+ETA(I-1))
C     COMPUTE THE INHOMOGENEOUS TERMS
      A = EF(ETA(I),T2(2),TEMP(2),TEMP(1))
      B = GE(ET,T3(1),TEMP(3),TEMP(4),U(3,I-1),U(4,I-1))
      IF (KK) 60,60,70
C     POINT IS ON THE SONIC LINE, U AND V FOUND EXPLICITLY
   30 TT = 1.-ETA(I)*(CB1+ETA(I))
      TT = C(17)*TT/CABS(TT)
      X(2) = CMPLX(-AIMAG(TT),0.)
      X(1) = CMPLX(REAL(TT),0.)
      DO 40 K = 1,2
      T3(K) = PF*(X(K)+U(K,I))
      U(K,I) = X(K)
   40 X(K) = PF*(X(K)+U(K,I-1))
      CALL LAMBDA (T3,T2)
      CALL LAMBDA (X,T3)
      GO TO 20
   50 IF(KK.LE.0) GO TO 80
C     INTEGRATE THE STREAM FUNCTION IN COMPLEX SPACE
      TT = PF*(T1(2,I)+TT)
      X3(1,N) = X3(1,N)+DS*EF(ETA(N),TT,TEMP(2),TEMP(1))
      IF (NB.EQ.NN) CALL GETPSI (N,SS(5)*TEMP(4),SS(6),X,S(IP))
      GO TO 80
C     MAKE ADJUSTMENTS TO EXPLOIT THE SYMMETRY
   60 A = PF*(A+GE(SS(1),T2(2),CONJG(T(1,I)),CONJG(X1(2,I)),
     1U(3,I),U(4,I)))
      B = PF*(B+EF(CONJG(ETA(NA)),T3(1),T(2,I),CONJG(X1(1,I))))
   70 X3(1,I) = X3(1,I)+DS*A
      B = (ETA(I)-ETA(I-1))*B
C     SOLVE FOR X3,Y3
      TT = CF(B+X3(1,I-1)-X3(1,I),X3(2,I-1)-X3(2,I),T3(1))/(T3(1)-T2(2))
      X3(2,I) = X3(2,I)+TT
      X3(1,I) = CF(X3(1,I),TT,-T2(2))
      IF (KK.LE.0.AND.I.EQ.NA.OR.KK.GT.0.AND.NA.GE.JJ) CALL SAVE (X,I,NA
     1-JJ,X1(1,NR),S(IP))
   80 U(4,I) = X(2)
   90 U(3,I) = X(1)
      RETURN
      END


      SUBROUTINE GETX3 (NA,NB)
C     COMPUTES X3 ON THE INITIAL CHARACTERISTIC
      COMPLEX U,X1,X3,TAO,ETA,JAK,A,B,C,H,Z,E,D,TEMP,T,GE,Q,ET
      COMMON /A/ PF
      COMMON U(4,540),X1(2,360),X3(2,360),TAO(2,360),ETA(360),T(2,360),Z
      COMMON /C/ TEMP(20)
      COMMON /D/ AA,N,M,MRP,NN,NR,II,JJ,KK,IP,NP,LBM
      EQUIVALENCE (Q,TEMP(19)), (ET,TEMP(17))
      NP1 = NA+1
      D = CONJG(JAK(ETA(N)))
      E = 1./ETA(N)
      X3(2,NA) = JAK(ETA(NA))
      X3(1,NA) = Q
      DO 20 J = NP1,NB
      H = ETA(J)-ETA(J-1)
      A = PF*(ETA(J)+ETA(J-1))
      X3(2,J) = JAK(ETA(J))
      C = X3(2,J)-X3(2,J-1)
```

```
      B = PF*(TAO(1,J)+TAO(1,J-1))
      ET = CONJG(X1(1,J))
      TEMP(4) = T(2,J)
C     COMPUTE THE INHOMOGENEOUS TERM
      GE = PF*(U(3,J-1)+U(3,J)+B*(U(4,J-1)+U(4,J)))
      GE = X1(2,N)*(B-TEMP(3))/(A*A)-GE/A
      IF (KK.GT.0) GO TO 10
C     SUBSONIC PATHS,EXPLOIT SYMMETRY
      X3(1,J) = X3(1,J-1)+PF*(H*(GE+ET*(B-TEMP(4))*E)-B*C)
      X3(2,J-1) = PF*(X3(2,J-1)+D)
      GO TO 20
C     SUPERSONIC PATHS
   10 X3(1,J) = X3(1,J-1)+H*GE-B*C
   20 CONTINUE
      IF (KK.GT.0) RETURN
      X3(2,NB) = PF*(X3(2,NB)+D)
      Q = X3(1,NB)
      RETURN
      END


      SUBROUTINE SAVE (X,I,K,A,D)
C     FORMS AND STORES U,V,X AND Y IN THE REAL DOMAIN
C     A IS U,V,X,Y
C     D IS PSI
      COMPLEX X(2),ETA,X1,X3,U,TAO,Z,B,TEMP,T,SS,PI
      COMMON /A/ C(40)
      COMMON U(4,540),X1(2,360),X3(2,360),TAO(2,360),ETA(360),T(2,360),Z
      COMMON /C/ TEMP(20),SS(6),SI(5)
      COMMON /D/ AA,N,M,MRP,NN,NR,II,JJ,KK,IP,NP,LBM
      EQUIVALENCE (PI,C(23))
      DIMENSION AO(4), A(4,1), D(1)
      IF (KK.LE.0) GO TO 20
C     SUPERSONIC RUN, CHECK IF XI IS ON THE SONIC LOCUS
      IF (K.GT.0) GO TO 10
      IF (I.GT.II) GO TO 20
      B = CLOG(-ETA(I))-PI
C     COMPUTE THE STREAM FUNCTION IN COMPLEX SPACE
      CALL GETPSI (I,TEMP(4)/ETA(I),B,X,D)
C     SUPERSONIC RUN, CHECK IF ETA IS ON THE SONIC LOCUS
   10 IF (I.LT.II) RETURN
   20 M = M+1
      Q = ALOG(CABS(ETA(I)))
      B = TEMP(4)/ETA(I)
      IF (M.NE.1) GO TO 50
C     FORM X,Y FROM X1,Y1,X2,Y2,X3,Y3 AND ETA
      AO(3) = (REAL(B+X(2)*Q+X3(2,I))+SI(2))*SI(4)
      AO(4) = (REAL(-TEMP(3)*B+X(1)*Q+X3(1,I))+SI(3))*SI(4)
      AO(1) = REAL(U(1,I))
      AO(2) = REAL(U(2,I))
      IF (KK.LE.0.OR.K.LE.0) GO TO 30
      D(1) = PSI(A,AO,D)
   30 DO 40 L = 1,4
   40 A(L,1) = AO(L)
      RETURN
   50 A(1,M) = REAL(U(1,I))
      A(2,M) = REAL(U(2,I))
C     FORM X,Y FROM X1,Y1,X2,Y2,X3,Y3 AND ETA
      A(3,M) = (REAL(B+X(2)*Q+X3(2,I))+SI(2))*SI(4)
      A(4,M) = (REAL(-TEMP(3)*B+X(1)*Q+X3(1,I))+SI(3))*SI(4)
```

```
      D(M) = PSI(A(1,M-1),A(1,M),D(M-1))
      RETURN
      END


      SUBROUTINE TPE (A,D,ETA,B)
C     STORES THE SOLUTION ON TAPE1
C     IF KK IS POSITIVE THE RUN IS SUPERSONIC
C     IF KK IS NOT POSITIVE THE RUN IS SUBSONIC
C     M IS THE NUMBER OF POINTS ON THE PATH
C     A IS U,V,X,Y ALONG THE PATH
C     D IS THE STREAM FUNCTION ALONG THE PATH
C     ETA IS THE PATH
      COMMON /D/ AA,N,M,MRP,NN,NR,II,JJ,KK,IP,NP,LBM
      COMMON /G/ N1,N2,N6,N7
      DIMENSION A(4,1), D(1), B(32,1)
      COMPLEX ETA(1),ET
      DATA ET/(0.,0.)/
      IF (KK.LE.0) GO TO 10
      N4 = 4
      WRITE (N1,40) KK,M,N4,((A(K,L),K = 1,N4),D(L),L = 1,M)
      RETURN
   10 N4 = 6
      IF (JJ.LT.0.AND.NP.LT.0) GO TO 20
      WRITE (N1,40) KK,M,N4,((A(K,L),K = 1,4),ETA(L),D(L),L = 1,M)
      RETURN
C     WRITES INFORMATION FOR LEAST SQUARES
   20 L = M+JJ
      IF (CABS(ET-ETA(M)).NE.0.) LL = 1
      N4 = M-L
      DO 30 K = 1,L
      KX = K+N4
   30 B(LL,K) = D(KX)
      LL = LL+1
      ET = ETA(M)
      RETURN
C     ****CHANGE (4020) TO (20A4) ON IBM 360****
   40 FORMAT (4020)
      END


      SUBROUTINE TOFH (A,U,TT)
C     GIVEN THE VALUE OF ETA, THIS ROUTINE COMPUTES LAMBDA+ AND LAMBDA-
C     AS WELL AS FUNCTIONS WHICH ARE USED IN THE QUADRATURE FORMULAS
C     ALONG THE CHARACTERISTIC THROUGH W = 1.
C     A IS THE VALUE OF ETA
C     U IS U,V AT THE PREVIOUS POINT
C     TT WILL CONTAIN LAMBDA (+,-) AND THE FUNCTIONS USED IN THE
C     QUADRATURE FORMULAS
      COMPLEX A,T,D,D3,U(6),P,P2,QS,CS,TT(4),TQ,TTH,HP,ARG,CB1,CB2
      COMMON /A/ C(40),ARG(5)
      COMMON /F/ HP,QS
      COMPLEX CSQRT,P3,D2,D4,R,D6
      EQUIVALENCE (CB2,C(31)), (CB1,C(33)), (R,ARG(5)), (CM1,C(9)), (CG1
     1,C(4)), (CG2,C(7)), (CM2,C(14))
      EXTERNAL CSQRT
      T = 1.-A*(A+CB1)
      CALL VELOC (T,U)
      CS = CM1-CG1*QS
      D6 = CS*(QS-CS)
      R = CSQRT(D6,R)
```

```
      P = U(6)*U(6)
      P2 = U(5)*U(6)
      D4 = -U(5)*U(5)
      P3 = 1./(CS+D4)
      D = P2+P2
      D2 = -CG1+D4/QS
      D3 = QS-(P+P)
      TT(1) = (R+P2)*P3
      P = CG2*QS+CM2
      TT(2) = (P2-R)*P3
      D4 = P2/QS+P/R
      TQ = (D4-TT(1)*D2)*P3/HP
      TTH = (0.,.5)*(D3-TT(1)*D)*P3
      P2 = 1./(TT(1)-TT(2))
      CS = A+A+CB1
      TT(3) = CS*(TTH/T-TQ)*P2
      TT(4) = -CB2*(TQ*T+TTH)
      RETURN
      END


      SUBROUTINE VELOC (T,U)
C     TRANSFORMS CHARACTERISTIC VARIABLES TO HODOGRAPH VARIABLES
C     GIVEN T AND THE VELOCITY AT THE PRECEDING POINT, THE VELOCITY IS
C     COMPUTED ALONG THE INITIAL CHARACTERISITC S = 1, AT T = T
      COMPLEX T,U(6),QS,HSH,HP,H1,W,WS,QO,ARG,CSQRT
      COMMON /A/ C(40),ARG(5)
      COMMON /F/ HP,QS
      COMMON /G/ N1,N2,N6,N7
      DIMENSION R(2)
      EQUIVALENCE (W,ARG(3)), (R(1),H1), (PF,C(1))
      EXTERNAL CSQRT
C     ***CHANGE ER TO 1E-10 FOR SINGLE PRECISION IBM 360***
      DATA ER/.1E-21/
      QO = U(1)*U(1)+U(2)*U(2)
C     DO AT MOST 50 NEWTON ITERATIONS
      DO 10 I = 1,50
      H1 = HSH(QO)-T
      QS = QO-H1/HP
      IF (R(1)*R(1)+R(2)*R(2).LE.ER) GO TO 20
   10 QO = QS
      WRITE (N2,30)
      CALL EXIT
   20 W = CSQRT(QS/T,W)
      WS = W*T
      U(5) = PF*(W+WS)
      U(6) = (0.,.5)*(W-WS)
      RETURN
   30 FORMAT (17H STOPPED AT VELOC)
      END


      COMPLEX FUNCTION HSH(Q)
C     COMPUTES THE FUNCTION H**2 AND ITS DERIVATIVE HP
C     Q = U*U + V*V
      COMPLEX Q,HP,TH1,TH2,S1,S2,T,ARG,T1,T2,CSQRT
      COMMON /A/ C(40),ARG(5)
      COMMON /F/ HP
      EQUIVALENCE (S1,ARG(4)), (S2,ARG(2)), (CG1,C(3)), (CG2,C(6)), (CM1
     1,C(13)), (CM2,C(10)), (CM3,C(18)), (CM4,C(15))
      EXTERNAL CSQRT
```

```
      TH1 = CG1-CM1*Q
      TH2 = CM2-CG1*Q
      T1 = TH1*TH1-1.
      S1 = CSQRT(T1,S1)
      T2 = TH2*TH2-Q*Q
      S2 = CSQRT(T2,S2)
      T = CEXP(CG2*CLOG(TH1-S1))
      T = CM3*T/(TH2+S2)
      HSH = Q*T
      HP = CM4*HSH/S1+CM2*T/S2
      RETURN
      END


      SUBROUTINE LAMBDA (X,Y)
C     COMPUTES LAMBDA+ AND LAMBDA- GIVEN U AND V
C     X IS U,V
C     Y IS LAMBDA+,LAMBDA-
      COMPLEX X(2),Y(2),Q,CS,ARG,R,CSQRT,XX,YY
      COMMON /A/ C(40),ARG(5)
      EQUIVALENCE (CM,C(9)), (CG,C(4)), (Q,ARG(1))
      EXTERNAL CSQRT
      XX = X(1)
      YY = X(2)
      R = XX*XX+YY*YY
      CS = CM-CG*R
      Q = CSQRT(CS*(R-CS),Q)
      R = CS-YY*YY
      Y(1) = R/(XX*YY-Q)
      Y(2) = R/(XX*YY+Q)
      RETURN
      END


      COMPLEX FUNCTION JAK(T)
C     COMPUTES THE INITIAL CHARACTERISTIC DATA
C     THIS ROUTINE CAN BE REPLACED BY ANY OTHER ANALYTIC FUNCTION
C     T IS THE VALUE OF ETA
C     Z IS THE VALUE OF THE INITIAL FUNCTION, G(ETA)
      COMPLEX T,Z,CC,CSQRT,ZP,Y,ONE,CE(1),FF
      COMMON /A/ C(40)
      COMMON /E/ FF(33)
      EQUIVALENCE (FF(25),CE(1)), (C(21),ONE), (C(25),CC)
      EXTERNAL CSQRT
C     ELLIPTIC CYLINDER FUNCTION
      Y = T - CE(4)
      ZP = CSQRT(CE(2)*Y*Y+CE(8),ONE)
      Z = CE(1)*CE(2)*(Y/(ZP+CE(9))+Y/ZP)
C     ETA, ETA**2, AND ETA**3 TERMS
      Z = Z+CE(3)*T+CE(5)*T*T+CE(7)*T*T*T
C     NOSE LOGS
      DO 10 J = 1,7,2
      Y = FF(J+1)-T
   10 Z = Z+FF(J)*CLOG(Y)
C     TAIL LOGS
      DO 20 J = 9,15,2
      Y = T-FF(J+1)
   20 Z = Z+FF(J)*CLOG(Y)
C     SIDE LOGS
      DO 30 J = 17,23,2
      Y = CC*(FF(J+1)-T)
```

```
   30 Z = Z+FF(J)*CLOG(Y)
      JAK = Z
      RETURN
      END

      FUNCTION PSI (X,Y,R)
C     COMPUTES THE STREAM FUNCTION PSI IN THE REAL HODOGRAPH PLANE
C     R IS THE PREVIOUS VALUE OF THE STREAM FUNCTION
C     X IS THE PREVIOUS VALUE OF U,V,X,Y
C     Y IS THE CURRENT VALUE OF U,V,X,Y
      DIMENSION X(4), Y(4)
      COMMON /A/ PF
      U = PF*(X(1)+Y(1))
      V = PF*(X(2)+Y(2))
      DY = Y(4)-X(4)
      DX = Y(3)-X(3)
      Q = U*U+V*V
      PSI = R+RHO(Q)*(U*DY-V*DX)
      RETURN
      END

      FUNCTION RHO (Q)
C     COMPUTES THE DENSITY RHO
C     Q = U*U + V*V
C     RHO = 1. AT Q=1.
      COMMON /A/ C(40)
      EQUIVALENCE (CG,C(5)), (CM1,C(12)), (CM2,C(11))
      RHO = (CM1-CM2*Q)**CG
      RETURN
      END

      SUBROUTINE GETPSI (I,E,Q,Y,R)
C     FORMS THE SOLUTION X,Y AT A COMPLEX POINT AND CALLS CPSI
C     E IS X1/ETA
C     Q IS LOG(ETA)
C     TEMP(3) IS LAMBDA+
C     U(1,I) IS U,V AT THE CURRENT POINT
C     Y IS X2,Y2
C     X3(1,I) IS X3,Y3
C     SS IS THE PREVIOUS VALUE OF U,V,X,Y
C     R IS THE PREVIOUS VALUE OF THE STREAM FUNCTION
C     TT IS THE CURRENT COMPLEX VALUE OF U,V,X,Y
      COMPLEX U,X1,X3,TAO,ETA,T,Z,Y(2),SS,TT(4),TEMP,Q,E
      COMMON U(4,540),X1(2,360),X3(2,360),TAO(2,360),ETA(360),T(2,360),Z
      COMMON /C/ TEMP(20),SS(6),SI(5)
      TT(3) = E+Y(2)*Q+X3(2,I)
      TT(4) = -TEMP(3)*E+Y(1)*Q+X3(1,I)
      TT(1) = U(1,I)
      TT(2) = U(2,I)
      R = CPSI(TT,R)
      DO 10 K = 1,4
   10 SS(K) = TT(K)
      RETURN
      END

      FUNCTION CPSI (Y,R)
C     COMPUTES THE COMPLEX STREAM FUNCTION PSI
C     R IS THE PREVIOUS VALUE OF THE STREAM FUNCTION
C     SS IS THE PREVIOUS VALUE OF U,V,X,Y
```

```
C       Y IS THE CURRENT VALUE OF U,V,X,Y
C       SI(4) SCALES THE CHORD LENGTH TO 1.
        COMPLEX TEMP,SS,Y(4),Q,CRHO,U,V,DY,DX
        COMMON /A/ C(40)
        COMMON /C/ TEMP(20),SS(6),SI(5)
        EQUIVALENCE (CG,C(5)), (CM1,C(12)), (CM2,C(11)), (PF,C(1))
        U = PF*(SS(1)+Y(1))
        V = PF*(SS(2)+Y(2))
        DY = Y(4)-SS(4)
        DX = Y(3)-SS(3)
        Q = U*U+V*V
        CRHO = CEXP(CG*CLOG(CM1-CM2*Q))
        CPSI = REAL(CRHO*(U*DY-V*DX))
        CPSI = R+SI(4)*CPSI
        RETURN
        END

        COMPLEX FUNCTION CSQRT(X,Y)
C       COMPUTES THE COMPLEX SQUARE ROOT OF X AND CHOOSES THE BRANCH
C       THE BRANCH LINE OF THE SQUARE ROOT IS A STRAIGHT LINE FROM THE
C       ORIGIN PASSING THROUGH -Y
        DIMENSION X(2), Y(2)
        DATA PF/.5/
        XX = X(1)
        YY = X(2)
        R = XX*XX+YY*YY
        IF (R.EQ.0.) GO TO 40
        Q = SQRT(PF*(SQRT(R)+ABS(XX)))
        IF (XX.GE.0.) GO TO 10
        R = Q
        Q = PF*YY/R
        GO TO 20
   10   R = PF*YY/Q
   20   IF (Q*Y(1)+R*Y(2)) 30,40,40
   30   CSQRT = CMPLX(-Q,-R)
        RETURN
   40   CSQRT = CMPLX(Q,R)
        RETURN
        END




C       PROGRAM C-PRINTS ABBREVIATED TELETYPE GRAPHS

        PROGRAM C(OUTPUT,TAPE1,TAPE2=OUTPUT)
C       GENERATES SMALL P-N DIAGRAMS FOR TELETYPE
        COMPLEX BP,GG
        INTEGER HN,HP
C       ****CHANGE DIMENSION OF PG TO 255 ON IBM 360****
        COMMON /F/ PG(102),XMIN,YMIN,XFAC,YFAC,NCH,LSZ,NLIN,IWD,JLN,KCH
        DIMENSION CC(6),IG(64),A(6,250),PSI(250)
        DATA K,LM/0,250/
        DATA HN,HP/1HN,1HP/
        N1 = 1
        N2 = 2
        REWIND N1
```

```
      READ (N1,140) NP,NRN,MRP,EM,BP,NK
C     ****CHANGE TO LL=80 ON IBM 360****
      LL = 32
C     ****CHANGE TO LL=90 ON IBM 360****
      IF (NK.GT.15) LL = 36
C     SKIP PAST THE REST OF TAPE7 DATA
      READ (N1,200) (GG,I = 1,LL)
      IF (NP.EQ.0) GO TO 20
      JJ = MAX0(2,2-NP)
C     READ IN AUTOMATION PATHS
      DO 10 LL = 1,JJ
      READ (N1,160) II,L
      II = IABS(II)
      DO 10 J = 1,II
   10 READ (N1,170) GG,L
      IF (NP.GT.0) GO TO 30
C     SKIP PAST LEAST SQUARES AUTOMATION POINTS
   20 READ (N1,150) L,(GG,J = 1,L)
   30 CONTINUE
      READ (N1,150) (CC(I),I=1,6),GG,GG,GG,GG
      WRITE (N2,120)
C     SET UP AXES FOR THE P-N DIAGRAM
      CALL PNAXIS ((0.,0.))
      INN = MRP
C     READ DATA FOR A PATH OR FORK
   40 READ (N1,150) KK,L,IM,((A(I,J),I = 1,IM),PSI(J),J = 1,L)
C     ****CHECK FOR END OF FILE****
      IF (EOF(N1).NE.0) GO TO 100
C     CHECK TO SEE IF DIMENSION STATEMENTS ARE BIG ENOUGH
      IF (L.GT.LM) GO TO 110
C     CHECK FOR SUPERSONIC PATH
      IF (KK.GT.0) GO TO 70
C     WE ARE ON A SUBSONIC PATH OR FORK
C     PUT SYMBOL P AT POINTS ON PATH OR FORK WHERE PSI IS POSITIVE
C     PUT SYMBOL N AT POINTS ON PATH OR FORK WHERE PSI IS NEGATIVE
      LN = L
      DO 60 I = 1,LN
      L = HP
      IF (PSI(I).LT.0.) L = HN
   60 CALL PN (A(5,I),L)
      GO TO 40
C     CONSTRUCT P-N TRIANGLE FOR SUPERSONIC PATH
   70 IF (INN*(K/INN).NE.K) GO TO 90
      J = 0
      DO 80  M = 1,L,INN
      J = J+1
      LN = HP
      IF (PSI(M).LT.0.) LN = HN
   80 IG(J) = LN
      WRITE (N2,180) (IG(M),M = 1,J)
   90 K = K + 1
      IF(L.GT.1) GO TO 40
      WRITE (N2,120)
      K = 0
      IF (KK.GT.9) GO TO 40
C     SKIP PAST SUPERSONIC PATHS
      READ (N1,150) L,(GG,I = 1,L)
      READ (N1,150) L,(GG,I = 1,L)
      GO TO 40
```

```
  100 WRITE (N2,130) PG
      CALL EXIT
  110 WRITE (N2,190)
      GO TO 40
  120 FORMAT(///)
C     ****CHANGE TO (1X15A4) ON IBM 360****
  130 FORMAT (1X6A10)
  140 FORMAT (3I5,20X,3F5.3)
C     ****CHANGE (4020) TO (20A4) ON IBM 360****
  150 FORMAT (4020)
  160 FORMAT (2I3)
  170 FORMAT (2E20.12,I5)
  180 FORMAT (62(1X,A1))
  190 FORMAT (21H TOO MANY MESH POINTS)
C     ****CHANGE TO (20A4) ON IBM 360****
  200 FORMAT (8A10)
      END

      SUBROUTINE PN (X,L)
C     PUT CHARACTER L INTO ROW AND COLUMN DETERMINED BY POSITION X
      DIMENSION X(2), IJ(10)
      COMMON /F/ PG(102),XMIN,YMIN,XFAC,YFAC,NCH,LSZ,NLIN,IWD,JLN,KCH
C     XMIN,YMIN IS THE LOWER LEFT HAND CORNER OF THE GRAPH
C     XFAC,YFAC ARE THE SCALING INCREMENTS FOR X AND Y
C     NCH IS THE NUMBER OF CHARACTERS IN A MACHINE WORD.10 FOR CDC 6600
C     LSZ IS THE NUMBER OF CHARACTERS WHICH WILL COMPRISE A PRINT LINE
C     NLIN IS THE NUMBER OF LINES THE GRAPH WILL HAVE
C     THE CHARACTER L WILL APPEAR IN THE  IWD  WORD ON LINE JLN
C     KCH IS THE NUMBER OF THE CHARACTER WITHIN THE WORD WHICH WILL BE
C     REPLACED BY THE THE CHARACTER CONTAINED IN L
C     THE DIMENSION OF PG MUST BE NLIN*LSZ/NCH
C     SEE BLOCK DATA FOR THE DEFINITION OF ELEMENTS IN THIS BLOCK
C     COMPUTE THE CHARACTER NUMBER
      IWD = (X(1)-XMIN)*XFAC+1.5
C     COMPUTE THE LINE NUMBER - ONE
      JLN = FLOAT((NLIN-IFIX((X(2)-YMIN)*YFAC)))-.5
C     CHECK TO SEE IF WE ARE WITHIN PRESCRIBED LIMITS
      IF ((IWD.LE.0).OR.(JLN.LT.0).OR.(IWD.GT.LSZ).OR.(JLN.GT.NLIN)) RET
     1URN
C     COMPUTE THE WORD NUMBER
      I = 1+(IWD+JLN*LSZ)/NCH
C     COMPUTE THE CHARACTER NUMBER
      KCH = 1+MOD(IWD,NCH)
C     REPLACE THE CHARACTER BY L
C     ****NON-ANSI - SEE WRITEUP AT END****
      DECODE (NCH,10,PG(I)) (IJ(K),K = 1,NCH)
      IJ(KCH) = L
C     ****NON-ANSI - SEE WRITEUP AT END****
      ENCODE (NCH,10,PG(I)) (IJ(K),K = 1,NCH)
      RETURN
   10 FORMAT (10A1)
      END

      SUBROUTINE PNAXIS (X)
C     DRAW AXES THROUGH THE POINT X
C     THE X-AXIS WILL CONSIST OF ---+-- WHERE THE + APPEARS EVERY 10
C     CHARACTERS ON THE LINE
C     THE Y-AXIS CONSISTS OF + EVERY FIVE LINES FROM THE POINT X
      INTEGER PG,HB,HP,HM
```

```
      DIMENSION X(2), XX(2)
      COMMON /F/ PG(102),XMIN,YMIN,XFAC,YFAC,NCH,LSZ,NLIN,IWD,JLN,KCH
      DATA HP,HM,HB/1H+,1H-,1H /
C     SEE SUBROUTINE PN FOR THE MEANING OF THE ELEMENTS IN THIS BLOCK
C     SET THE GRAPH TO ALL BLANKS
      II = NLIN*LSZ/NCH
      DO 10 I = 1,II
   10 PG(I) = HB
      H1 = 1./XFAC
      CALL PN (X,HP)
      II = IWD
      XX(2) = X(2)
C     DO X-AXIS
      LS = LSZ-1
      DO 20 I = 1,LS
      XX(1) = XMIN+FLOAT(I-1)*H1
      L = HM
      IF (MOD(I-II,10).EQ.0) L = HP
   20 CALL PN (XX,L)
C     DO Y-AXIS
      H1 = 1./YFAC
      II = 1+NLIN-JLN
      XX(1) = X(1)
      DO 30 I = 1,NLIN
      IF (MOD(I-II,5).NE.0) GO TO 30
      XX(2) = YMIN+FLOAT(NLIN-I)*H1
      CALL PN (XX,HP)
   30 CONTINUE
      RETURN
      END

      BLOCK DATA
      COMMON /F/ PG(102),XMIN,YMIN,XFAC,YFAC,NCH,LSZ,NLIN,IWD,JLN,KCH
C     ****CHANGE NCH TO 4 FOR IBM360****
      DATA XMIN,YMIN,XFAC,YFAC,NCH,LSZ,NLIN/-1.2,-.6,25.,12.5,10,60,17/
      END




C     PROGRAM D-PRINTS X,Y COORDINATES AND CALCOMP GRAPH

      PROGRAM D(OUTPUT,TAPE1,TAPE2 = OUTPUT,TAPE3 = 1002,TAPE4,FILMPL =
     1TAPE4)
C     THIS PART FINDS THE AIRFOIL AND DOES THE PLOTTING
      COMPLEX BP,BB,GG,CSQRT
      COMMON /A/ BP,CC(6),FF(64),EM,NRN,NP,NK,MRP
      COMMON /C/ SF,SIZE,ANG,XMAX,YMAX,XOR,YOR,PGSIZ
C     ****CHANGE DIMENSION OF PG TO 930 FOR IBM 360****
      COMMON /F/ PG(403),XMIN,YMIN,XFAC,YFAC,NCH,LSZ,NLIN,IWD,JLN,KCH
      COMMON /G/ N1,N2,N3,N4
      COMMON C(5,500),A(6,250),BB(250),PSI(250),AR(2,41,40)
      EXTERNAL CSQRT
      DATA NNX,NN/0,1/
C     DRAWS AND LABELS AXES AND SETS PLOT PARAMETERS
C     READS THE DATA TO BE PLOTTED
      N1 = 1
```

```
      N2 = 4
      N3 = 3
      N4 = 4
      REWIND N1
      READ (N1,40) NP,NRN,MRP,EM,BP,NK
C     ****CHANGE TO LL=80 ON IBM 360****
      LL = 32
C     ****CHANGE TO LL=90 ON IBM 360****
      IF (NK.GT.15) LL = 36
C     SKIP PAST THE REST OF TAPE7 DATA
      READ (N1,110) (GG,I = 1,LL)
      IF (NP.EQ.0) GO TO 20
      JJ = MAXO(2,2-NP)
C     READ IN AUTOMATION PATHS
      DO 10 LL = 1,JJ
      READ (N1,60) II,L
      II = IABS(II)
      DO 10 J = 1,II
   10 READ (N1,70) GG,L
      IF (NP.GT.0) GO TO 30
C     SKIP PAST LEAST SQUARES AUTOMATION POINTS
   20 READ (N1,50) L,(GG,J = 1,L)
   30 REWIND N3
      READ (N1,50) (CC(I),I = 1,6),(C(I,2),I = 1,4),(C(I,1),I = 1,4)
      GG = -CSQRT(1.+BP*BP,(1.,0.))-BP
      C(5,2) = ATAN2(AIMAG(GG),REAL(GG))
      WRITE (N2,100)
C     SET UP AXES FOR THE P-N DIAGRAM
      CALL PNAXIS ((0.,0.))
      CALL GOPLOT
      CALL CPLOT ((3.,2.5),-3)
      SF = 6.
      CALL GRF (NN,NNX)
      WRITE (N2,80)
      WRITE (N2,90) PG
      WRITE (N2,100)
      SF = 1.
      CALL CPLOT ((14.9,-13.),-3)
      XMAX = 22.
      CALL CPLOT ((11.2,5.5),-3)
      CALL LOCUS (NNX,NN)
      ANG = 0.
      CALL XYAXES ((0.,0.),7.0,7.0,.2)
      ANG = 90.
      CALL XYAXES ((0.,0.),3.,3.,.2)
      CALL CPLOT ((0.,0.),999)
      CALL EXIT
   40 FORMAT (3I5,20X,3F5.3)
C     ****CHANGE (4020) TO (20A4) ON IBM 360****
   50 FORMAT (4020)
   60 FORMAT (2I3)
   70 FORMAT (2E20.12,I5)
   80 FORMAT (1H1////////)
C     ****CHANGE TO (1X30A4) ON IBM 360****
   90 FORMAT (1X13A10)
  100 FORMAT (1H1)
C     ****CHANGE TO (20A4) ON IBM 360****
  110 FORMAT (8A10)
      END
```

```
      SUBROUTINE GRF (NN,NNX)
C     READS DATA AND CONSTRUCTS P-N DIAGRAMS
      COMPLEX ETA(200),SEE(200),BP,BB
      INTEGER HP,HN
      DIMENSION AA(6), IG(62)
      COMMON /A/ BP,CC(6),FF(64),EM,NRN,NP,NK,MRP
      COMMON C(5,500),A(6,250),BB(250),PSI(250),AR(2,41,40)
      COMMON /G/ N1,N2,N3,N4
      EQUIVALENCE (AR(1,1,1),IA), (AR(2,1,1),IB), (AR(1,2,1),ETA(1)), (A
     1R(1,1,21),SEE(1)), (IG(1),FF(1))
      DATA ZO,XT,MX,LM,MXMAX,NNXMAX,K/0.,1.,3,250,500,250,0/
      DATA HP,HN/1HP,1HN/
      IN = MRP
      INN = (IN+1)/2
C     READ DATA FOR A PATH OR FORK
   10 READ (N1,210) KK,L,IM,((A(I,J),I = 1,IM),PSI(J),J = 1,L)
C     ****CHECK FOR END OF FILE****
      IF (EOF(N1).NE.0) GO TO 160
C     CHECK TO SEE IF DIMENSION STATEMENTS ARE BIG ENOUGH
      IF (L.GT.LM) GO TO 170
      LN = L-1
C     CHECK FOR SUPERSONIC PATH
      IF (KK.GT.0) GO TO 40
C     WE ARE ON A SUBSONIC PATH OR FORK
C     PUT SYMBOL P AT POINTS ON PATH OR FORK WHERE PSI IS POSITIVE
C     PUT SYMBOL N AT POINTS ON PATH OR FORK WHERE PSI IS NEGATIVE
      LN = L
      DO 30 I = 1,LN
      L = HP
      IF (PSI(I).LT.0.) L = HN
   30 CALL PN (A(5,I),L)
      IF (KK.LT.0) GO TO 10
C     WE ARE ON A FORK, LOOK FOR BODY POINTS
   40 IF (LN.LT.3) GO TO 100
      DO 90 J = 3,LN
      CALL INTERP (PSI(J-2),ZO,A(1,J-2),AA,M,IM)
C     M IS POSITIVE IF A BODY POINT HAS BEEN FOUND IN THE INTERVAL
      IF (M.EQ.0) GO TO 90
C     STORE U,V,X AND Y IN C ARRAY
      DO 50 N = 1,4
   50 C(N,MX) = AA(N)
      N = MX
C     INCREMENT MX IF WE HAVE NOT EXCEEDED MAXIMUM SIZE
      IF (MX.LE.MXMAX) MX = MX+1
C     CHECK FOR SUPERSONIC FLOW
      IF (KK.GT.0) GO TO 110
C     INCREMENT NNX IF WE HAVE NOT EXCEEDED DIMENSION SIZE
      IF (NNX.LE.NNXMAX) NNX = NNX+1
C     STORE ETA AT PSI=ZO FOR PLOTTING IN THE HODOGRAPH PLANE
      BB(NNX) = CMPLX(AA(5),AA(6))
C     ELIMINATE ERRONEOUS POINTS
      IF (C(1,N).LT.-.1) GO TO 80
C     LOOK FOR POINTS ON THE CENTRAL STREAMLINE
      IF (C(3,N).LT.0.) GO TO 70
      IF (C(3,N).GT.XT) GO TO 80
C     COMPUTE ANGLE IN ETA PLANE FOR LATER SORTING
   60 C(5,N) = ATAN2(AA(6),AA(5))
      GO TO 90
   70 IF (ABS(C(1,N)).LE.ABS(C(2,N))) GO TO 60
```

```
C     ELIMINATE THIS POINT
   80 MX = N
   90 CONTINUE
  100 IF (KK.LE.0) GO TO 10
C     SUPERSONIC PATH WITH NO SIGN CHANGE
      L = LN+1
      GO TO 130
  110 C(5,N) = SIGN(1.57,PSI(1))-.001*C(2,N)
      L = LN+1
      IF (MOD(K,IN).NE.0) GO TO 130
C     PLOT EVERY  IN  CHARACTERISTIC FROM THE BODY TO THE SONIC LINE
      CALL CPLOT (AA(3),3)
      DO 120 I = J,L
  120 CALL CPLOT (A(3,I),2)
C     CONSTRUCT P-N TRIANGLE FOR SUPERSONIC PATH
  130 IF (INN*(K/INN).NE.K) GO TO 150
      J = 0
      DO 140 M = 1,L,INN
      J = J+1
      LN = HP
      IF (PSI(M).LT.0.) LN = HN
  140 IG(J) = LN
      WRITE (N2,180) (IG(M),M = 1,J)
C     PLOT OTHER FAMILY OF CHARACTERISTICS
  150 CALL BE (K,L,IN)
      IF (L.NE.1) GO TO 10
      WRITE (N2,200)
C     CHECK TO SEE IF SUPERSONIC PATHS ARE TO BE READ IN
      IF(KK.GE.9) GO TO 10
C     READ IN SUPERSONIC PATHS
      READ (N1,210) IA,(ETA(I),I = 1,IA)
      READ (N1,210) IB,(SEE(I),I = 1,IB)
      NN = -KK
      GO TO 10
  160 CALL SORT (MX-1)
      RETURN
  170 WRITE (N2,190)
      GO TO 10
  180 FORMAT (62(1X,A1))
  190 FORMAT (21H TOO MANY MESH POINTS)
  200 FORMAT (1H1)
C     ****CHANGE (4020) TO (20A4) ON IBM 360****
  210 FORMAT (4020)
      END


      SUBROUTINE BE (J,N,IN)
C     PLOTS CHARACTERISTICS IN THE SUPERSONIC REGION
      COMPLEX BB
      COMMON C(5,500),A(6,250),BB(250),PSI(250),AR(2,41,40)
      COMMON /G/ N1,N2,N3,N4
      DIMENSION M(41), DD(41)
      DATA NAR,MA/41,40/
   10 L = 0
C     CHECK FOR FIRST LINE
      IF (J.GT.0) GO TO 30
      FAC = -PSI(1)/ABS(PSI(1))
      DO 20 I = 1,N,IN
      L = L+1
      AR(1,L,1) = A(3,I)
```

```
      AR(2,L,1) = A(4,I)
      DD(L) = PSI(I)
   20 M(L) = 1
      J = 1
      LL = L-1
C     CHECK TO SEE IF WE HAVE EXCEEDED THE DIMENSION OF AR
      IF (L.LE.NAR) RETURN
      WRITE (N2,100)
      IN = IN+IN
      GO TO 10
   30 J = J+1
      DO 70 I = 1,N,IN
      L = L+1
      IF (FAC*PSI(I).LE.0.) GO TO 60
C     POINT IS OUTSIDE THE BODY
      M(L) = M(L)+1
      IF (M(L).EQ.2) GO TO 50
C     CHECK FOR DIMENSION OF AR
      IF (M(L).LE.MA) GO TO 60
      M(L) = 2
      CALL CPLOT (AR(1,L,1),3)
      DO 40 K = 2,MA
   40 CALL CPLOT (AR(1,L,K),2)
      AR(1,L,1) = AR(1,L,MA)
      AR(2,L,1) = AR(2,L,MA)
      GO TO 60
C     FIND THE BODY BY LINEAR INTERPOLATION
   50 R2 = PSI(I)-DD(L)
      R1 = PSI(I)/R2
      R2 = -DD(L)/R2
      AR(1,L,1) = R1*AR(1,L,1)+R2*A(3,I)
      AR(2,L,1) = R1*AR(2,L,1)+R2*A(4,I)
C     STORE THE POINT FOR PLOTTING
   60 K = M(L)
      AR(1,L,K) = A(3,I)
      AR(2,L,K) = A(4,I)
   70 DD(L) = PSI(I)
      IF (N.GT.1) RETURN
C     WE HAVE FINISHED THIS SUPERSONIC PATH
C     FINISH PLOTTING CHARACTERISTICS
      DO 90 I = 1,LL
      L = M(I)
      IF (L.LE.1) GO TO 90
      CALL CPLOT (AR(1,I,1),3)
      DO 80 K = 1,L
   80 CALL CPLOT (AR(1,I,K),2)
   90 CONTINUE
      J = 0
      RETURN
  100 FORMAT (27H TOO MANY SUPERSONIC POINTS)
      END

      SUBROUTINE INTERP (Y,T,U,W,J,N)
C     COMPUTES POINTS ON THE BODY BY QUADRATIC INTERPOLATION
C     THE BODY IS THE STREAMLINE PSI=T
C     Y(1),Y(2),Y(3) ARE PSI AT THREE ADJACENT POINTS
C     U IS A SIX-COMPONENT VECTOR,U,V,X,Y,ETA
      DIMENSION Y(1), U(1), V(6), W(1)
      DATA N2/12/
```

```
      H(A,B,C,D,E) = (A*C-B*D)/E
      J = 0
      XB = Y(2)-T
      XC = Y(3)-T
C     CHECK FOR A SIGN CHANGE BETWEEN SECOND AND THIRD INTERVAL
      IF (XB*XC) 20,10,50
C     CHECK TO SEE IF BOTH XB AND XC ARE ZERO
   10 IF (XB+XC) 20,50,20
   20 J = 1
C     COMPUTE DELTA PSI
      EA = Y(3)-Y(2)
      EB = Y(3)-Y(1)
      EC = Y(2)-Y(1)
      XA = Y(1)-T
      DO 30 I = 1,N
C     DO LINEAR INTERPOLATION BETWEEN POINTS 2 AND 3
      K = N2+I
      V(I) = H(U(I+6),U(K),XC,XB,EA)
      W(I) = H(U(I),U(K),XC,XA,EB)
C     DO QUADRATIC INTERPOLATION
   30 W(I) = H(W(I),V(I),XB,XA,EC)
      IF (EA*EC.GT.0) RETURN
C     IF PSI IS NOT MONOTONIC USE LINEAR INTERPOLATION
      DO 40 I = 1,N
   40 W(I) = V(I)
      J = -1
   50 RETURN
      END


      SUBROUTINE TITLE (TC)
C     PRINTS THE TITLE PAGE OF THE OUTPUT
      COMPLEX T,CSQRT,ONE,BP,BB
      COMMON /A/ BP,CC(6),FF(64),EM,NRN,NP,NK,MRP
      COMMON C(5,500),A(6,250),BB(250),PSI(250),AR(2,41,40)
      COMMON /G/ N1,N2,N3,N4
      EXTERNAL CSQRT
      DATA ONE/(1.,0.)/
      CALL DATE (IDATE)
C     DATE IS A CDC ROUTINE WHICH GIVES THE MONTH, DAY AND YEAR
      WRITE (N2,120) IDATE,NRN,EM,CC(5),CC(6),TC
      REWIND N1
      READ (N1,40) (PSI(I),I = 1,12)
      READ (N1,50) (PSI(I),I = 13,28)
      IF (NK.GT.15) READ (N1,50) (PSI(I),I = 29,44)
      READ (N1,60) (FF(I),I = 1,64)
      I = MAX0(2,2-NP)
      DO 20 LL = 1,I
      READ (N1,70) II,JJ
      WRITE (N2,130) II,JJ
      II = IABS(II)
      DO 10 J = 1,II
      READ (N1,80) T,JJ
   10 WRITE (N2,140) T,JJ
      IF (LL.NE.2) GO TO 20
C     CONVERT TAIL FROM ETA PRIME TO ETA PLANE
      T = T*CSQRT(1.+BP*BP/(T*T),ONE)-BP
      CC(5) = REAL(T)
      CC(6) = AIMAG(T)
      C(5,1) = ATAN2(CC(6),CC(5))
```

```
      JJ = 13+IABS(NK)
      WRITE (N2,90) (PSI(J),J = 1,JJ)
      WRITE (N2,100) (FF(J),J = 1,63)
      IF (NP,GE,0) GO TO 30
      WRITE (N2,110)
   20 CONTINUE
   30 WRITE (N2,150)
      RETURN
   40 FORMAT (3(1X,A4),9F5.3)
   50 FORMAT (16(1X,A4))
   60 FORMAT (8F10.4)
   70 FORMAT (2I3)
   80 FORMAT (2E20.12,I5)
   90 FORMAT (///38X,6HTAPE 7///4X,3A4,2F7.3,F6.3,F6.2,F6.3,2F7.3,
     1 2F6.3/4X,16A4/4X,16A4)
  100 FORMAT (//4(4X,4F7.3,5X,4F7.3/4X,4F7.3,5X,4F7.3//))
  110 FORMAT (1H1,35X,16HAUTOMATION PATHS)
  120 FORMAT (1H //60X,A10//////37X,4HRUN=,I5//20X,12HCIRCULATORY ,
     1 30HFLOW ABOUT A TRANSONIC AIRFOIL///20X,2HM=,F5.3,3X,3HCL=,
     2 F5.3,3X,3HCD=,F5.3,3X,4HT/C=,F5.3/////35X,14HTAPE 6, PATH 0/)
  130 FORMAT (/31X,2I3)
  140 FORMAT (31X,2F8.3,I4)
  150 FORMAT (1H1//10X,1HU,14X,1HV,14X,1HX,14X,1HY,13X,2HCP////)
      END

      SUBROUTINE SORT (N)
      COMPLEX BP,BB
      DIMENSION RR(6)
      COMMON /A/ BP,CC(6),FF(64),EM,NRN,NP,NK,MRP
      COMMON C(5,500),A(6,250),BB(250),PSI(250),AR(2,41,40)
      COMMON /C/ SF,SIZE,ANG,XMAX,YMAX,XOR,YOR,PGSIZ
      COMMON /G/ N1,N2,N3,N4
      EQUIVALENCE (CC(1),C1), (CC(2),C2), (CC(3),C3)
      Q(I) = 1.-C(1,I)*C(1,I)-C(2,I)*C(2,I)
C     COMPUTES THE COEFFICIENT OF PRESSURE
      PE(I) = C1*(AMAX1(0.,1.+C2*Q(I))**C3-1.)
C     FIND THE THICKNESS TO CHORD RATIO TC
      CPMAX = 1.5
      YMN = C(4,1)
      YMX = YMN
      DO 10 J = 2,N
      YMN = AMIN1(YMN,C(4,J))
   10 YMX = AMAX1(YMX,C(4,J))
      TC = YMX-YMN
      CC(6) = AMAX1(.1E-30,CC(6))
C     ****NON-ANSI - SEE WRITEUP AT END****
      ENCODE (60,80,RR) EM,CC(5),CC(6),TC
      CALL TITLE (TC)
      WRITE (3,90) RR,NRN,N
C     DRAW CP AXIS AND LABEL THE GRAPH
      ANG = 90.
      CALL XYAXES ((-.5,5.5),3.,2.,-.5)
      ANG = 0.
      SF = 1.
C     COMPUTE AND PLOT CRITICAL SPEED
      C(1,N+1) = SQRT((C2+1.)-(C2+1.)/(C3+C3-1.))/EM
      C(2,N+1) = 0.
      YMX = 5.5-2.*PE(N+1)
      SIZE = .28
```

-162-

```
      CALL CSYMBL   (CMPLX(-.5,YMX),15,-1)
      SIZE = .14
      CALL CSYMBL ((-.3,7.1),1HC,1)
      CALL CSYMBL ((-.15,6.98),1HP,1)
      CALL CSYMBL   ((0.,-1.5),RR,60)
      SF = 6.
      SIZE = .07
C     ORDER THE POINTS AROUND THE BODY FROM TAIL TO TAIL
      DO 20 K = 2,N
      IF (C(5,K).LT.C(5,1)) C(5,K) = C(5,K)+6.283
   20 CONTINUE
      DO 50 K = 2,N
      YMN = C(5,K-1)
      L = K-1
      DO 30 J = K,N
      IF (C(5,J).GE.YMN) GO TO 30
      YMN = C(5,J)
      L = J
   30 CONTINUE
      IF (L.EQ.(K-1)) GO TO 50
      DO 40 J = 1,5
      C(J,N+1) = C(J,L)
      C(J,L) = C(J,K-1)
   40 C(J,K-1) = C(J,N+1)
   50 CONTINUE
      ANG = 90.
      DO 60 J = 2,N
      C(5,J) = PE(J)
      WRITE (N2,100) (C(I,J),I = 1,5)
      WRITE (N3,110) (C(I,J),I = 1,5)
      ANG = 180.*ATAN2(C(2,J),C(1,J))/3.14159
      CALL CSYMBL   (C(3,J),15,-1)
      C(5,1) = PE(1)
   60 CONTINUE
      WRITE (N2,100) (C(I,1),I = 1,5)
      WRITE (N3,110) (C(I,1),I = 1,5)
      ANG = 0.
      YOR = YOR+5.5
      SS = 2./SF
      DO 70 K = 1,N
      IF (ABS(C(5,K)).GT.CPMAX) GO TO 70
      C(4,K) = -SS*C(5,K)
      CALL CSYMBL   (C(3,K),3,-1)
   70 CONTINUE
      RETURN
   80 FORMAT (3H M=,F4.3,5X,3HCL=,F5.3,5X,3HCD=,F5.4,5X,4HT/C=,F4.3)
C     ****CHANGE TO (15A4,I5) ON IBM 360****
   90 FORMAT (6A10,2I5)
  100 FORMAT (F13.5,4F15.5)
C     ****CHANGE (4020) TO (20A4) ON IBM 360****
  110 FORMAT (4020)
      END

      SUBROUTINE LOCUS (M,NN)
C     DOES THE PLOTTING IN THE HODOGRAPH PLANE
      COMPLEX S,DD,X,BB,CSQRT,T,ETA(1),SEE(1),TH,ONE,BP,BAD,ES
      COMMON C(5,500),A(6,250),BB(250),PSI(250),AR(2,41,40)
      COMMON /A/ BP,CC(6),FF(64),EM,NRN,NP,NK,MRP
      COMMON /C/ SF,SIZE,ANG,XMAX,YMAX,XOR,YOR,PGSIZ
```

```
      COMMON /G/ N1,N2,N3,N4
      EQUIVALENCE (CA,CC(4)), (T,CC(5))
      EQUIVALENCE (AR(1,1,1),IA), (AR(2,1,1),IB), (AR(1,2,1),ETA(1)), (A
     1R(1,1,21),SEE(1))
      EXTERNAL CSQRT
      ES(S) = CA/(ONE-S*(S+T))
      BAD(S) = CSQRT(DD-ES(S),X)
      DATA ONE,TH,N,SX/(1.,0.),(0.,.05),252,5./
      SF = SX
C     PLOT THE STAGNATION POINT
      DD = 1.+BP*BP
      X = -CSQRT(DD,ONE)-BP
      CALL CSYMBL  (X,11,-1)
C     PLOT THE BRANCH POINT
      ANG = 45.
      CALL CSYMBL  (-BP,3,-1)
      ANG = 0.
C     PLOT THE LOCATION OF THE CUSP AT THE TAIL
      CALL CSYMBL  (T,11,-1)
C     PLOT THE POINTS WHERE PSI = 0.
      DO 10 I = 1,M
   10 CALL CSYMBL  (BB(I),3,-1)
C     PLOT THE SONIC LOCUS
      X = CSQRT(DD-CA,-TH)-BP
      CALL CPLOT (X,3)
      DO 20 I = 1,N
      S = CA*CEXP(FLOAT(I)*TH)
      X = CSQRT(DD-S,X)-BP
   20 CALL CPLOT (X,2)
      IF ((NN.GE.0).OR.(NN.LE.-9)) GO TO 50
      CA = CA*CA
      T = BP+BP
      BP = - BP
      IF (MOD(-NN,3).NE.1) GO TO 32
C     PLOT THE SUPERSONIC PATHS
      CALL CPLOT (ETA,3)
      DO 30 I = 2,IA
   30 CALL CPLOT (ETA(I),2)
   32 IF (MOD(-NN,3).NE.2) GO TO 36
C     PLOT BAD POINTS OF ETA
      X = BAD(ETA(1))
      CALL CPLOT (BP-CONJG(X),3)
      DO 34 I = 2,IA
      X = BAD(ETA(I))
   34 CALL CPLOT (BP-CONJG(X),2)
   36 IF (NN.LT.-6) GO TO 50
      IF (NN.LT.-3) GO TO 42
      CALL CPLOT (CONJG(SEE(1)),3)
      DO 40 I = 2,IB
   40 CALL CPLOT (CONJG(SEE(I)),2)
      GO TO 50
C     PLOT BAD POINTS OF XI
   42 X = BAD(CONJG(SEE(1)))
      CALL CPLOT(BP-CONJG(X),3)
      DO 44 I = 2,IB
      X = BAD(CONJG(SEE(I)))
   44 CALL CPLOT(BP-CONJG(X),2)
   50 SIZE = .28
      SX = SIZE/(SX+SX)
```

```
C     PUT ARROWS AT THE LOCATION OF THE LOGS IN THE DIRECTION OF THE CUT
      DO 90 I = 1,45,4
      IF (FF(I).EQ.0..AND.FF(I+1).EQ.0.) GO TO 90
      CONVX = 0.
      CONVY = 0.
      IF (I.GE.17) GO TO 60
      ANG = 0.
      CONVX = SX
      GO TO 80
   60 IF (I.GE.33) GO TO 70
      ANG = 180.
      CONVX = -SX
      GO TO 80
   70 ANG = -90.
      CONVY = -SX
   80 CALL CSYMBL   (CMPLX(CONVX+FF(I+2),CONVY+FF(I+3)),20,-1)
   90 CONTINUE
      SIZE = .07
      IF ((NP.GT.0).OR.(NRN.LE.0)) RETURN
C     READ AND PLOT LEAST SQUARES POINTS
      READ (N1,110) IA,(ETA(I),I = 1,IA)
      DO 100 I = 1,IA
  100 CALL CSYMBL   (ETA(I),26,-1)
      RETURN
C     ****CHANGE TO (20A4) ON IBM 360****
  110 FORMAT (4020)
      END

      SUBROUTINE XYAXES (X,BOT,TOP,SCF)
C     X IS THE LOCATION OF THE ORIGIN ON THE AXIS
C     BOT IS THE LENGTH OF THE AXIS TO THE LEFT OF THE ORIGIN
C     TOP IS THE LENGTH TO THE RIGHT OF THE ORIGIN
      COMPLEX ZB,ZT,H,COR
      COMMON /C/ SF,SIZE,ANG,XMAX,YMAX,XOR,YOR,PGSIZ
      DIMENSION X(2), Y(2)
      ANGO = ANG
      SFO = SF
      SIZO = SIZE
      Y(1) = XOR
      Y(2) = YOR
      ANG = 0.
      SF = 1.
      SIZE = .14
      XOR = X(1)+XOR
      YOR = X(2)+YOR
      ZB = CMPLX(-BOT,0.)
      ZT = CMPLX(TOP,0.)
      COR = (-.25,-.3)
      NC = 16
      IF (ABS(ANGO).NE.90.) GO TO 10
C     VERTICAL Y-AXIS
      ZB = (0.,1.)*ZB
      ZT = (0.,1.)*ZT
      COR = (-.6,0.)
      NC = 15
C     DRAW LINE FOR THE AXIS
   10 CALL CPLOT (ZT,3)
      CALL CPLOT (ZB,2)
      K = BOT
```

```
      L = TOP
      N = 1+K+L
      S = -FLOAT(K)*SCF
      H = ZT/TOP
      ZB = -FLOAT(K)*H
      ZT = ZB+COR
      DO 20 I = 1,N
C     DRAW HATCH MARK
      CALL CSYMBL (ZB,NC,-1)
      B = S+FLOAT(I-1)*SCF
C     ****NON-ANSI - SEE WRITEUP AT END****
      ENCODE (10,30,A) B
C     LABEL AXIS
      CALL CSYMBL (ZT,A,4)
      ZB = ZB+H
   20 ZT = ZT+H
      SF = SFO
      SIZE = SIZO
      ANG = ANGO
      XOR = Y(1)
      YOR = Y(2)
      RETURN
   30 FORMAT (F4.1)
      END


      SUBROUTINE CSYMBL (X,N,L)
      COMMON /C/ SF,SIZE,ANG,XMAX,YMAX,XOR,YOR,PGSIZ
      DIMENSION X(2)
C     CHANGE RELATIVE MOVEMENTS TO ABSOLUTE INCHES
      XX = XOR+SF*X(1)
      YY = YOR+SF*X(2)
C     CHECK TO SEE IF WE ARE WITHIN THE PAGE
      IF ((XX.LT.0.).OR.(YY.LT.0.).OR.(XX.GT.XMAX).OR.(YY.GT.YMAX))
     1RETURN
      CALL SYMBOL (XX,YY,SIZE,N,ANG,L)
      RETURN
      END


      SUBROUTINE CPLOT (X,N)
      COMMON /C/ SF,SIZE,ANG,XMAX,YMAX,XOR,YOR,PGSIZ
      DIMENSION X(2)
C     CHANGE RELATIVE MOVEMENTS TO ABSOLUTE INCHES
      XX = XOR+SF*X(1)
      YY = YOR+SF*X(2)
C     CHECK TO SEE IF WE ARE WITHIN THE PAGE
      IF ((XX.LT.0.).OR.(YY.LT.0.).OR.(XX.GT.XMAX).OR.(YY.GT.YMAX))
     1 GO TO 20
   10 CALL PLOT (XX,YY,IABS(N))
      IF (N.GT.0) RETURN
      XOR = XX
      YOR = YY
      RETURN
   20 IF (N.LT.0) GO TO 30
      XX = AMAX1(0.,AMIN1(XX,XMAX))
      YY = AMAX1(0.,AMIN1(YY,YMAX))
      GO TO 10
C     GO TO NEXT PAGE
   30 XOR = 0.
      YOR = 0.
```

```
      CALL PLOT (PGSIZ,0.,N)
      RETURN
      END


      SUBROUTINE PN (X,L)
C     PUT CHARACTER L INTO ROW AND COLUMN DETERMINED BY POSITION X
      DIMENSION X(2), IJ(10)
      COMMON /F/ PG(403),XMIN,YMIN,XFAC,YFAC,NCH,LSZ,NLIN,IWD,JLN,KCH
C     XMIN,YMIN IS THE LOWER LEFT HAND CORNER OF THE GRAPH
C     XFAC,YFAC ARE THE SCALING INCREMENTS FOR X AND Y
C     NCH IS THE NUMBER OF CHARACTERS IN A MACHINE WORD,10 FOR CDC 6600
C     LSZ IS THE NUMBER OF CHARACTERS WHICH WILL COMPRISE A PRINT LINE
C     NLIN IS THE NUMBER OF LINES THE GRAPH WILL HAVE
C     THE CHARACTER L WILL APPEAR IN THE  IWD  WORD ON LINE JLN
C     KCH IS THE NUMBER OF THE CHARACTER WITHIN THE WORD WHICH WILL BE
C     REPLACED BY THE THE CHARACTER CONTAINED IN L
C     THE DIMENSION OF PG MUST BE NLIN*LSZ/NCH
C     SEE BLOCK DATA FOR THE DEFINITION OF ELEMENTS IN THIS BLOCK
C     COMPUTE THE CHARACTER NUMBER
      IWD = (X(1)-XMIN)*XFAC+1.5
C     COMPUTE THE LINE NUMBER - ONE
      JLN = FLOAT((NLIN-IFIX((X(2)-YMIN)*YFAC)))-.5
C     CHECK TO SEE IF WE ARE WITHIN PRESCRIBED LIMITS
      IF ((IWD.LE.0).OR.(JLN.LT.0).OR.(IWD.GT.LSZ).OR.(JLN.GT.NLIN)) RET
     1URN
C     COMPUTE THE WORD NUMBER
      I = 1+(IWD+JLN*LSZ)/NCH
C     COMPUTE THE CHARACTER NUMBER
      KCH = 1+MOD(IWD,NCH)
C     REPLACE THE CHARACTER BY L
C     ****NON-ANSI - SEE WRITEUP AT END****
      DECODE (NCH,10,PG(I)) (IJ(K),K = 1,NCH)
      IJ(KCH) = L
C     ****NON-ANSI - SEE WRITEUP AT END****
      ENCODE (NCH,10,PG(I)) (IJ(K),K = 1,NCH)
      RETURN
   10 FORMAT (10A1)
      END


      SUBROUTINE PNAXIS (X)
C     DRAW AXES THROUGH THE POINT X
C     THE X-AXIS WILL CONSIST OF ---+-- WHERE THE + APPEARS EVERY 10
C     CHARACTERS ON THE LINE
C     THE Y-AXIS CONSISTS OF + EVERY FIVE LINES FROM THE POINT X
      INTEGER HP,HM
      DIMENSION X(2), XX(2)
      COMMON /F/ PG(403),XMIN,YMIN,XFAC,YFAC,NCH,LSZ,NLIN,IWD,JLN,KCH
C     SEE SUBROUTINE PN FOR THE MEANING OF THE ELEMENTS IN THIS BLOCK
C     SET THE GRAPH TO ALL BLANKS
      DATA HB,HP,HM/1H ,1H+,1H-/
      II = NLIN*LSZ/NCH
      DO 10 I = 1,II
   10 PG(I) = HB
      H1 = 1./XFAC
      CALL PN (X,HP)
      II = IWD
      XX(2) = X(2)
C     DO X-AXIS
      LS = LSZ-1
```

```fortran
      DO 20 I = 1,LS
      XX(1) = XMIN+FLOAT(I-1)*H1
      L = HM
      IF (MOD(I-II,10).EQ.0) L = HP
   20 CALL PN (XX,L)
C     DO Y-AXIS
      H1 = 1./YFAC
      II = 1+NLIN-JLN
      XX(1) = X(1)
      DO 30 I = 1,NLIN
      IF (MOD(I-II,5).NE.0) GO TO 30
      XX(2) = YMIN+FLOAT(NLIN-I)*H1
      CALL PN (XX,HP)
   30 CONTINUE
      RETURN
      END


      COMPLEX FUNCTION CSQRT(X,Y)
C     COMPUTES THE COMPLEX SQUARE ROOT OF X AND CHOOSES THE BRANCH
C     THE BRANCH LINE OF THE SQUARE ROOT IS A STRAIGHT LINE FROM THE
C     ORIGIN PASSING THROUGH -Y
      DIMENSION X(2), Y(2)
      DATA PF/.5/
      XX = X(1)
      YY = X(2)
      R = XX*XX+YY*YY
      IF (R.EQ.0.) GO TO 40
      Q = SQRT(PF*(SQRT(R)+ABS(XX)))
      IF (XX.GE.0.) GO TO 10
      R = Q
      Q = PF*YY/R
      GO TO 20
   10 R = PF*YY/Q
   20 IF (Q*Y(1)+R*Y(2)) 30,40,40
   30 CSQRT = CMPLX(-Q,-R)
      RETURN
   40 CSQRT = CMPLX(Q,R)
      RETURN
      END


      SUBROUTINE GOPLOT
C     INITIATE PLOT
C     ****************************************************************
C     THIS SUBROUTINE SHOULD BE REPLACED BY ANY ROUTINE WHICH INSTRUCTS
C     THE SYSTEM TO INITIATE A PLOT
C     ****************************************************************
      COMMON /A/ BP,CC(6),FF(64),EM,NRN,NP,NK,MRP
      COMPLEX BP
      DIMENSION ID(6), LTAB(8), NAME(16)
      DATA MS,NU/777777770000000B,16/
      DATA NAME/10HGARABEDIAN,7H 110204,10HDAVID KORN,7H 109201,10H F. B
     1AUER ,7H 110205,10HN. KASHDAN,7H 110208,10HGARABEDIAN,7H 146202,10
     2HDAVID KORN,7H 141201,9HF. BAUER ,7H 143207,10HN. KASHDAN,7H 14620
     31/
      DATA LTAB/34343337B,34334434B,34343340B,34343343B,34374135B,343734
     134B,34373642B,34374134B/
      ISHIFT(XXX,YYY) = SHIFT(XXX,YYY)
      CALL READCP (ID,21B,1)
      ID(1) = ISHIFT(ID(2).AND.MS,-18)
```

```
      N = IABS(NRN)
      DO 10 L = 1,NU,2
      J = L/2+1
      IF (LTAB(J)-ID(1)) 10,20,10
   10 CONTINUE
      L = NU+1
   20 ENCODE (60,30,ID) NAME(L),NAME(L+1),N
      CALL PLOTS (60,ID,30,1,11.,11.)
      RETURN
   30 FORMAT (A10,5H --- ,A7,11X,I3)
      END


      BLOCK DATA
      COMMON /C/ SF,SIZE,ANG,XMAX,YMAX,XOR,YOR,PGSIZ
      COMMON /F/ PG(403),XMIN,YMIN,XFAC,YFAC,NCH,LSZ,NLIN,IWD,JLN,KCH
C     ****CHANGE NCH TO 4 FOR IBM360****
C     ****CHANGE LSZ TO 120 ON IBM 360****
      DATA XMIN,YMIN,XFAC,YFAC,NCH,LSZ,NLIN/-1.2,-.6,50.,25.,10,130,31/
      DATA SF,SIZE,ANG,XMAX,YMAX,XOR,YOR,PGSIZ/1.0,.14,0.,11.,11.,0.,0.,
     111.30/
      END




C     PROGRAM E-CHANGES PATHS, TAPE 6

      PROGRAM E(TAPE6,INPUT,OUTPUT,TAPE2 = OUTPUT,TAPE5 = INPUT)
C     THIS PROGRAM IS DESIGNED TO MAKE CHANGES TO DATA ON TAPE6 BY
C     GIVING EDITING INSTRUCTIONS LIKE ADD, REPLACE, AND DELETE
      INTEGER DE,RE,AD,EN
      DIMENSION A(1)
      COMMON MO,M(40),N(2000),M2(40),K,J,IM
      COMMON /B/ KK
      COMMON /G/ N2,N5,N6
      EQUIVALENCE (N(1),A(1))
      DATA AD,DE,RE,EN,I,ISW,IMAX/2HAD,2HDE,2HRE,2HEN,1,0,2000/
C     M IS POINTER LIST WHICH POINTS TO THE FIRST ELEMENT OF EACH PATH
      KK = 2
      K = -1
      N2 = 2
      N5 = 5
      N6 = 6
C     READS IN THE OLD SET OF PATHS
      REWIND N6
   10 READ (N6,250) N(I),N(I+1)
C     ****CHECK FOR END OF FILE****
      IF (EOF(N6).NE.0) GO TO 60
C     CHECK  FOR FIRST NON-AUTOMATED PATH
      IF (ISW.NE.0.AND.N(I+1).EQ.0) GO TO 30
      ISW = IABS(N(I+1))
      K = K+1
C     ADD ONE TO THE NUMBER OF PATHS
      M(K) = I
   30 II = I+2
      JJ = 3*IABS(N(I))+I+1
      DO 40 J = II,JJ,3
```

```
   40 READ (N6,260) A(J),A(J+1),N(J+2)
      I = JJ+1
C     CHECK TO SEE IF WE HAVE EXCEEDED DIMENSION SIZE
      IF (I.LE.IMAX) GO TO 10
   50 WRITE (N2,270)
      CALL EXIT
C     DATA HAS BEEN READ IN
   60 IM = I
      IF (K.GE.0) GO TO 65
      WRITE (N2,330)
      K = 1
      M(K-1) = 1
      M(K) = 9
      IM = 17
      N(1) = 2
      N(2) = 0
      A(3) = -.8
      A(4) = 0.
      N(5) = 2
      A(6) = -.9999999
      A(7) = 0.
      N(8) = 1
      N(9) = 2
      N(10) = 0
      A(11) = .3
      A(12) = .05
      N(13) = 1
      A(14) = .52
      A(15) = -.39
      N(16) = 1
C     KM IS THE NUMBER OF PATHS
   65 KM = K
      WRITE (N2,280) KM,IM
      K = K+1
      M(K) = IM
   70 CALL READR (X,INST,1HA,16HINSTRUCTION       )
C     CHECK FOR END INSTRUCTION
      IF (EN.EQ.INST) GO TO 220
      CALL READR (X,II,1HI,16HPATH NUMBER       )
      IF (II.LE.KM) GO TO 80
      IF ((II.EQ.K).AND.(AD.EQ.INST)) GO TO 80
      WRITE (N2,290)
      KK = 30
      GO TO 70
   80 CALL READR (X,JJ,1HI,16HFORK NUMBER       )
      J = M(II)
   90 IF (JJ.LE.0) GO TO 100
C     LOCATE LOCATION OF FIRST ELEMENT OF THIS FORK
      J = J+2+3*IABS(N(J))
      JJ = JJ-1
      GO TO 90
C     J WILL POINT TO FIRST ELEMENT OF PATH II,FORK JJ
  100 IF (AD.NE.INST) GO TO 110
C     ADD PATH OR FORK OR CARD
      CALL ADD (II,1)
      KM = K-1
C     CHECK TO SEE IF ADDING PATH HAS CAUSED US TO EXCEED DIMENSION
      IF (IM-IMAX) 70,70,50
  110 IF (RE.NE.INST) GO TO 120
```

```
C     REPLACE PATH,FORK, OR CARD
      CALL ADD (II,0)
      GO TO 70
C     CHECK FOR DELETE INSTRUCTION
 120  IF (DE.NE.INST) GO TO 170
      CALL READR (X,NC,1HI,16HCARD NUMBER        )
      IF (NC.LE.0) GO TO 130
C     DELETE ONLY ONE CARD
      L = IABS(N(J))-1
      IF (L.EQ.0) GO TO 130
      IF (N(J).LT.0) L = -L
      N(J) = L
      J = J+3*NC-1
      CALL MOVE (-3,II+1)
      GO TO 70
 130  IF (J.NE.M(II)) GO TO 160
C     DELETE PATH AND ALL THE FORKS
      L = M(II+1)-M(II)
      K = K-1
      KM = KM-1
      IM = IM-L
      DO 140 JJ = J,IM
      NC = JJ+L
 140  N(JJ) = N(NC)
      DO 150 JJ = II,K
 150  M(JJ) = M(JJ+1)-L
      GO TO 70
C     DELETE PATH II,FORK,JJ
 160  CALL MOVE (-2-3*IABS(N(J)),II+1)
      L = M(II)+1
      N(L) = N(L)+1
      GO TO 70
 170  IF (JJ.GE.0.AND.J.LE.IM) GO TO 200
C     WRITE OUT A MAP SHOWING WHERE FIRST ELEMENT OF EACH PATH IS STORED
      WRITE (N2,280) KM,IM
      WRITE (N2,300) (M(L-1),L = 1,K)
      DO 180 L = 1,K
      II = M(L-1)
 180  M2(L) = N(II)
      WRITE (N2,300) (M2(L),L = 1,K)
      DO 190 L = 1,K
      II = M(L-1)+1
 190  M2(L) = N(II)
      WRITE (N2,300) (M2(L),L = 1,K)
      WRITE (N2,310) J
      GO TO 70
C     WRITE OUT PATH II,FORK JJ
 200  WRITE (N2,250) N(J),N(J+1)
      II = J+2
      JJ = 3*IABS(N(J))+J+1
      DO 210 L = II,JJ,3
 210  WRITE (N2,320) A(L),A(L+1),N(L+2)
      GO TO 70
C     WRITE OUT NEW TAPE6
 220  REWIND N6
      I = 1
 230  WRITE (N6,250) N(I),N(I+1)
      II = I+2
      JJ = 3*IABS(N(I))+I+1
```

```
      DO 240 J = II,JJ,3
  240 WRITE (N6,260) A(J),A(J+1),N(J+2)
      I = JJ+1
      IF (I.LT.IM) GO TO 230
      CALL EXIT
  250 FORMAT (2I3)
  260 FORMAT (2F20.12,I5)
  270 FORMAT (20H TOO MANY DATA CARDS)
  280 FORMAT (1X,I3,6H PATHS,3X,I4,14H DATA ELEMENTS/)
  290 FORMAT (25H PATH NUMBER OUT OF RANGE)
  300 FORMAT (1X,17I4/)
  310 FORMAT (I4)
  320 FORMAT (2F8.3,I4)
  330 FORMAT (19H DEFAULT TAPE6 USED /)
      END


      SUBROUTINE ADD (I,LL)
C     ADD OR REMOVE PATH,FORK, OR CARD
C     I IS THE PATH NUMBER
C     LL = 1 FOR ADD AND LL=0 FOR REPLACE
C     J HAS THE VALUE OF THE LOCATION OF THE FIRST CARD OF THE FORK
      COMMON MO,M(40),N(2000),M2(40),K,J,IM
      DIMENSION A(1)
      EQUIVALENCE (A(1),N(1))
      IP = I+1
      CALL READR (X,NC,1HI,16HCARD NUMBER       )
      IF (NC.GT.0) GO TO 60
      CALL READR (X,II,1HI,16HNUMBER OF POINTS)
      IQ = IABS(II)
      CALL READR (X,JJ,1HI,16HTYPE OF PATH      )
C     CHECK FOR REPLACEMENT OF THE FIRST CARD OF THE PATH OR FORK
      IF ((LL.EQ.0).AND.(NC.EQ.0)) GO TO 70
C     ADD OR REPLACE A PATH OR FORK
      L = J+LL
      IF ((M(I)+1).NE.L) GO TO 20
C     PATH IS TO BE ADDED
      K = K+1
      KL = K+IP
      DO 10 NN = IP,K
      KK = KL-NN
   10 M(KK) = M(KK-1)
      GO TO 30
   20 KL = M(I)+LL
      N(KL) = N(KL)-LL
   30 CALL MOVE (2+3*IQ+(LL-1)*(2+3*IABS(N(L))),IP)
      N(J) = II
      N(J+1) = JJ
      JJ = J+1+3*IQ
      II = J+2
   40 DO 50 L = II,JJ,3
      CALL READR (A(L),NX,1HF,16HREAL ETA         )
      CALL READR (A(L+1),NX,1HF,16HIMAGINARY ETA   )
   50 CALL READR (X,N(L+2),1HI,16HREFINEMENT       )
      RETURN
C     ADD OR REPLACE ONLY ONE CARD
   60 II = J+3*NC-1
      JJ = II
      IF (LL.EQ.0) GO TO 40
      L = IABS(N(J))+1
```

```
       IF (N(J).LT.0) L = -L
       N(J) = L
       J = J+3*NC-1
       CALL MOVE (3,IP)
       GO TO 40
C      REPLACE FIRST CARD ONLY
   70  N(J) = II
       N(J+1) = JJ
       RETURN
       END

       SUBROUTINE MOVE (I,NN)
C      IF I IS POSITIVE STORAGE IS MOVED DOWN TO MAKE ROOM FOR NEW DATA
C      IF I IS NEGATIVE STORAGE IS MOVED UP I ELEMENTS
C      NN IS THE PATH NUMBER + 1
       COMMON MO,M(40),N(2000),M2(40),K,J,IM
C      CHANGE POINTER LIST
       DO 10 L = NN,K
   10  M(L) = M(L)+I
       IF (I.GT.0) GO TO 40
       DO 20 L = J,IM
       KK = L-I
   20  N(L) = N(KK)
   30  IM = IM+I
       RETURN
   40  L = IM+1
   50  L = L-1
       KK = L+I
       N(KK) = N(L)
       IF (L-J) 50,30,50
       END

       SUBROUTINE READR (X,I,T,II)
C      READS IN DATA CARDS
C      T IS THE TYPE, A FOR HOLLERITH,I FOR INTEGER,F FOR FLOATING POINT
C      II IS THE MESSAGE WHICH WILL PRINT IF ANOTHER LINE HAS TO BE READ
C      I WILL CONTAIN THE VARIABLE TO BE READ IN IF T=A OR T=I
C      X WILL CONTAIN THE VARIABLE FOR READING FLOATING POINT
       INTEGER BL
C      ****CHANGE DIMENSION OF L TO 90 ON IBM 360****
       COMMON /A/ N(72),L(30)
C      ****CHANGE DIMENSION OF II TO 4 ON IBM360****
       DIMENSION II(2), ITM(5)
       COMMON /B/ KK
       COMMON /G/ N2,N5,N6
       DATA K,HO,BL/1,1HA,2H  /
C      ****USE KWD=3 ON IBM 360****
       DATA KWD/1/
C      CHECK TO SEE IF LIST HAS BEEN EXHAUSTED
       IF (KK.LE.K) GO TO 10
       KK = 1
       WRITE (N2,60) II
C      CREATE A NEW LIST IN L
       READ (N5,70) N
       CALL PRCSS (K)
   10  IF (T.EQ.HO) GO TO 20
C      CONVERT RIGHT JUSTIFIED HOLLERITH TO FLOATING POINT
C      ****NON-ANSI - SEE WRITEUP AT END****
       DECODE (10,80,L(KK)) X
```

```
      I = X
      KK = KK+KWD
      RETURN
C     HOLLERITH, FIND FIRST TWO NON-BLANK CHARACTERS
C     ****NON-ANSI - SEE WRITEUP AT END****
   20 DECODE (10,90,L(KK) )ITM
      DO 30 J = 1,4
      IF (ITM(J).NE.BL) GO TO 40
   30 CONTINUE
      I = ITM(5)
      GO TO 50
   40 I = J
      JJ = ITM(I)
C     ****NON-ANSI - SEE WRITEUP AT END****
      DECODE (10,100,L(KK) )ITM
      IF (ITM(I).EQ.BL) JJ = ITM(I+1)
      I = JJ
   50 KK = KK + KWD
      RETURN
   60 FORMAT (1X2A10/)
   70 FORMAT (72A1)
   80 FORMAT (F10.0)
   90 FORMAT (5A2)
  100 FORMAT (A1,4A2)
      END


      SUBROUTINE PRCSS (K)
C     BREAK UP LINE READ IN INTO 10 CHARACTER RIGHT JUSTIFIED WORDS
C     ELIMINATE BLANKS
C     / ACTS AS A DELIMITER
C     K WILL BE THE TOTAL NUMBER OF WORDS ON THE LINE
      INTEGER BL,SL
      COMMON /A/ N(72),L(30)
      DIMENSION LL(10)
C     ****USE KWD=3 ON IBM 360****
      DATA BL,SL,KWD/1H ,1H/,1/
      K = 1
      KK = 1
      LL(1) = BL
      DO 40 I = 1,72
      M = N(I)
      IF (M.EQ.BL) GO TO 40
      IF (M.NE.SL) GO TO 30
      KK = MAX0(1,KK-1)
      JJ = 10-KK
      IF (JJ.EQ.0) GO TO 10
C     ****NON-ANSI - SEE WRITEUP AT END****
      ENCODE (10,60,L(K) )(BL,J = 1,JJ),(LL(J),J = 1,KK)
      GO TO 20
C     ****NON-ANSI - SEE WRITEUP AT END****
   10 ENCODE (10,60,L(K) )LL
   20 LL(1) = BL
      KK = 1
      K = K+KWD
      GO TO 40
   30 LL(KK) = M
      KK = KK+1
   40 CONTINUE
C     PROCESS THE LAST WORD
```

```
      IF (KK.EQ.1) RETURN
      KK = KK-1
      JJ = 10-KK
      IF (JJ.EQ.0) GO TO 50
C     ****NON-ANSI - SEE WRITEUP AT END****
      ENCODE (10,60,L(K) )(BL,J = 1,JJ),(LL(J),J = 1,KK)
      RETURN
C     ****NON-ANSI - SEE WRITEUP AT END****
   50 ENCODE (10,60,L(K) )LL
      RETURN
   60 FORMAT (10A1)
      END




C     PROGRAM F-COMPUTES TURBULENT BOUNDARY LAYER CORRECTION

      PROGRAM F(TAPE3,OUTPUT,TAPE4,TAPE2=OUTPUT)
C     CALCULATES THE DISPLACEMENT THICKNESS OF THE BOUNDARY LAYER AND
C     DETERMINES WHETHER SEPARATION OCCURS
      COMMON /G/ N2,N3,N4
      DIMENSION C(5,250), U(250), V(250), X(250), Y(250), CP(250), S(250
     1), UE(250), EM(250), T(250), DS(250), DUDS(250), DELS(250), SEP(25
     20), CO(250), YS(250), THET2(250), H2(250), X1(250), ALF(250), DX(2
     350), DY(250), CUR(250)
C     **ALTER THIS CARD TO CHANGE PHYSICAL PARAMETERS IN THE PROGRAM**
      DATA RN,TR,GAM,RTH,TE1,TE2,PCH,SP,ANG/20.0E06,.3424,1.4,320.0,5.0E
     1-03,5.0E-05,-.500,.004,-.17453/
      N2 = 2
      N3 = 3
      N4 = 4
      REWIND N3
      REWIND N4
      READ (N3,620) EMF,CL,CD,TTC,NRN,NP
      CM = 1.+.2*EMF**2
      DO 10 J = 1,NP
      READ (N3,870) (C(I,J),I = 1,5)
   10 CONTINUE
C     NP IS TOTAL NUMBER OF POINTS FROM PROGRAM D
      WRITE (N4,630) NRN
      WRITE (N4,640) EMF,CL,CD,TTC
      WRITE (N4,650) NP
      WRITE (N4,660) RN
      WRITE (N4,670) RN,TR,GAM,RTH,TE1,TE2,PCH,SP,ANG
      CRL = 1.
      XMIN = 1.
      KM = 1
      DO 20 J = 1,NP
      IF (C(3,J).GE.XMIN) GO TO 20
      KM = J
      XMIN = C(3,J)
   20 CONTINUE
      DO 30 J = 1,KM
      NPS = NP-J+1
      KMJ = KM-J+1
      U(NPS) = C(1,KMJ)
```

```
      V(NPS) = C(2,KMJ)
      X(NPS) = C(3,KMJ)
      Y(NPS) = C(4,KMJ)
   30 CP(NPS) = C(5,KMJ)
      KM1 = KM+1
      DO 40 J = KM1,NP
      LK = J-KM1+1
      U(LK) = C(1,J)
      V(LK) = C(2,J)
      X(LK) = C(3,J)
      Y(LK) = C(4,J)
   40 CP(LK) = C(5,J)
C     OPTIONAL TEST TO ELIMINATE DUPLICATE OR EXTRANEOUS POINTS
      IF (ANG.LE.0.) GO TO 100
      NPT = NP
      DO 90 J = 1,NPT
      IF (X(J).GE..9999) GO TO 100
      D1 = X(J+1)-X(J)
      D2 = Y(J+1)-Y(J)
      TEMP = ATAN2(DY,DX)
      ALF1 = ATAN2(V(J),U(J))
      IF (ABS(TEMP-ALF1).LT.ANG) GO TO 90
      D1 = X(J+2)-X(J)
      D2 = Y(J+2)-Y(J)
      TEMP = ATAN2(DY,DX)
      IF (ABS(TEMP-ALF1).GE.ANG) GO TO 60
      JR = J+1
      NP1 = NP-1
      DO 50 JK = JR,NP1
      CP(JK) = CP(JK+1)
      X(JK) = X(JK+1)
      U(JK) = U(JK+1)
      V(JK) = V(JK+1)
   50 Y(JK) = Y(JK+1)
      NP = NP-1
      GO TO 90
   60 D1 = X(J+2)-X(J+1)
      D2 = Y(J+2)-Y(J+1)
      TEMP = ATAN2(DY,DX)
      ALF1 = ATAN2(V(J+1),U(J+1))
      IF (ABS(TEMP-ALF1).GE.ANG) GO TO 80
      NP1 = NP-1
      DO 70 JK = J,NP1
      CP(JK) = CP(JK+1)
      X(JK) = X(JK+1)
      U(JK) = U(JK+1)
      V(JK) = V(JK+1)
   70 Y(JK) = Y(JK+1)
      NP = NP-1
      GO TO 90
   80 WRITE (N2,680)
   90 CONTINUE
  100 CONTINUE
      DO 110 J = 1,NP
      IF (CP(J).LT.0.) GO TO 120
  110 JP = J
  120 JP = JP+1
      DO 130 J = JP,NP
      IF (X(J).LT..99999) GO TO 130
```

```
      JT = J
      GO TO 140
  130 CONTINUE
C     TEST TO DETERMINE START OF BOUNDARY LAYER CORRECTION. IF PCH IS
C     NEGATIVE TRANSITION BEGINS AT MAXIMUM CP IN THE SUPERSONIC REGION
  140 IF (PCH.LT.0.) GO TO 180
      DO 170 JJ = 1,JT
      IF (X(JJ)-PCH) 170,150,160
  150 KST = JJ
      GO TO 200
  160 T1 = X(JJ)-PCH
      T2 = ABS(X(JJ-1)-PCH)
      IF (T1.LE.T2) GO TO 150
      KST = JJ-1
      GO TO 200
  170 CONTINUE
C     FIND X CORRESPONDING TO PEAK CP
  180 PK = ABS(CP(JP))
      DO 190 J = JP,JT
      IF (ABS(CP(J)).LE.PK) GO TO 190
      PK = ABS(CP(J))
      KST = J
  190 CONTINUE
  200 CONTINUE
C     FIND CORRESPONDING X FOR TRANSITION ON BOTTOM SURFACE
      NP1 = NP+1
      NBT = NP-JT
      DO 210 J = 1,NBT
      KBST = NP1-J
      IF (X(KBST).GE.X(KST)) GO TO 220
  210 CONTINUE
  220 T1 = ABS(X(KBST)-X(KST))
      T2 = ABS(X(KBST+1)-X(KST))
      IF (T1.GT.T2) KBST = KBST+1
C     COMPUTES V/U,M,DS,UE,AND CURVATURE
      NP1 = NP
      DO 250 J = 1,NP1
      IF (U(J).NE.0.) GO TO 230
      ALF(J) = 0.
      GO TO 240
  230 ALF(J) = V(J)/U(J)
  240 CONTINUE
      TEST = (5.*(CM/(1.+.7*CP(J)*EMF**2)**(.2857143)-1.))
      EM(J) = 0.
      IF (TEST.GT.0.) EM(J) = SQRT(TEST)
  250 CONTINUE
      DO 260 J = 2,NP1
      DX(J) = X(J)-X(J-1)
  260 DY(J) = Y(J)-Y(J-1)
      KBSTP1 = KBST+1
      DO 270 J = KST,KBSTP1
      S(J) = SQRT(X(J)**2+Y(J)**2)
      D = 1.+.2*EM(J)**2
      T(J) = CM/D
  270 UE(J) = EM(J)/EMF*SQRT(T(J))
      KS = KST+1
      DO 280 J = 2,NP1
  280 DS(J) = SQRT(DX(J)**2+DY(J)**2)
      DO 290 J = 2,NP1
```

```
      IF ((U(J).EQ.0.).OR.(U(J-1).EQ.0.)) GO TO 290
      CUR(J) = (V(J)*U(J-1)-U(J)*V(J-1))/((U(J)*U(J-1)+V(J)*V(J-1))*DS(J
     1))
  290 CONTINUE
      DX(1) = X(1)-X(NP1)
      DY(1) = Y(1)-Y(NP1)
      DS(1) = SQRT(DX(1)**2+DY(1)**2)
      IF ((U(1).EQ.0.).OR.(U(NP1).EQ.0.)) GO TO 300
      CUR(1) = (V(1)*U(NP1)-U(1)*V(NP1))/((U(1)*U(NP1)+V(1)*V(NP1))*DS(1
     1))
      GO TO 310
  300 CUR(1) = 0.
  310 CONTINUE
      CURT = CUR(1)
      DO 320 K = 2,JT
  320 CUR(K-1) = CUR(K)
      JTP = JT+1
      DO 330 K = JTP,NP1
  330 CUR(K-1) = CUR(K)
      CUR(NP1) = CURT
      WRITE (N4,690)
      WRITE (N4,700) X(KBST),Y(KBST),ALF(KBST),CUR(KBST),EM(KBST)
      KB1 = KBST+1
      DO 360 J = KB1,NP1
      IF (X(J).NE.0.) GO TO 350
      WRITE (N4,710) X(J),Y(J),ALF(J),CUR(J),EM(J)
      GO TO 360
  350 WRITE (N4,730) X(J),Y(J),ALF(J),CUR(J),EM(J)
  360 CONTINUE
      KT1 = KST-1
      WRITE (N4,730) (X(J),Y(J),ALF(J),CUR(J),EM(J),J = 1,KT1)
      WRITE (N4,740) X(KST),Y(KST),ALF(KST),CUR(KST),EM(KST)
      DO 370 J = KS,JT
  370 DUDS(J) = (UE(J)-UE(J-1))/DS(J)
C     CALL INTEGRATION ROUTINE FOR THE TOP SURFACE WHERE THETA IS
C     COMPUTED BY SOLVING THE NASH MACDONALD DIFFERENTIAL EQUATION BY A
C     MODIFIED EULER SCHEME
      CALL INTEG (KST,EM,UE,DUDS,DS,JT,CM,TE1,TE2,TR,RN,CRL,GAM,RTH,THET
     12,H2)
C     COMPUTATION OF DELX,SEPARATION AND CORRECTED Y-COORDINATE
      DO 380 J = KS,JT
      DELS(J) = H2(J)*THET2(J)
  380 SEP(J) = -THET2(J)*DUDS(J)/UE(J)
      CALL COSD (KST,JT,X,Y,CO)
      DO 390 J = KS,JT
  390 YS(J) = Y(J)-DELS(J)*CO(J)
      WRITE (N4,750)
      JTM = JT-1
      WRITE (N4,760)
      WRITE (N4,770)(X(J),YS(J),ALF(J),CUR(J),EM(J),THET2(J),DELS(J),SEP
     1(J),H2(J),J = KS,JTM)
      WRITE (N4,780)X(JT),YS(JT),ALF(JT),EM(JT),THET2(JT),DELS(JT),SEP(J
     1T),H2(JT)
      NN = 1
      SM = 0.
      JM = KST
      DO 410 J = KS,JT
      IF (SM.GE.SEP(J)) GO TO 410
      SM = SEP(J)
```

```
      JM = J
      GO TO (400,410), NN
  400 IF (SM.LT.SP) GO TO 410
      JM1 = J
      NN = 2
  410 CONTINUE
      GO TO (430,420), NN
  420 WRITE (N2,790)
      WRITE (N2,800) X(JM1)
      WRITE (N2,810) SM,X(JM)
      GO TO 440
  430 WRITE (N2,820)
      WRITE (N2,810) SM,X(JM)
C     WRITE COORDINATES OUT ON TAPE3 WITH Y REPLACED BY YS.  TAPE3 IS
C     INPUT TO PROGRAM G. YS ON BOTTOM NOT COMPUTED YET.  YS FOR BOTTOM
C     IS WRITTEN ON TAPE3 AT END
  440 CONTINUE
      DO 450 J = 1,KST
      C(1,J) = U(J)
      C(2,J) = V(J)
      C(3,J) = X(J)
      C(4,J) = Y(J)
  450 C(5,J) = CP(J)
      DO 460 J = KS,JT
      C(1,J) = U(J)
      C(2,J) = V(J)
      C(3,J) = X(J)
      C(4,J) = YS(J)
  460 C(5,J) = CP(J)
      DO 470 J = KBST,NP1
      C(1,J) = U(J)
      C(2,J) = V(J)
      C(3,J) = X(J)
      C(4,J) = Y(J)
  470 C(5,J) = CP(J)
      HDT = H2(JT)
      THETDT = THET2(JT)
      EMDT = EM(JT)
      NP = NP-1
      NR = NP-JT+1
      KSB = NP1+1-KBST
C     REORDER DATA ON BOTTOM FOR INTEGRATION SUBROUTINE
      CALL RESHUF (X,X1,NP,NR)
      CALL RESHUF (Y,X1,NP,NR)
      CALL RESHUF (U,X1,NP,NR)
      CALL RESHUF (V,X1,NP,NR)
      CALL RESHUF (CP,X1,NP,NR)
      CALL RESHUF (T,X1,NP,NR)
      CALL RESHUF (UE,X1,NP,NR)
      CALL RESHUF (EM,X1,NP,NR)
      NR = NR+1
      NR1 = NR+1
      DO 480 J = 2,NR1
      DX(J) = X(J)-X(J-1)
  480 DY(J) = Y(J)-Y(J-1)
      DO 490 J = 3,NR
  490 DS(J) = SQRT(DX(J)**2+DY(J)**2)
      DO 500 J = 3,NR
  500 DUDS(J) = (UE(J)-UE(J-1))/DS(J)
```

```
C     CORRECT THE BOTTOM SURFACE
      CALL INTEG (KSB,EM,UE,DUDS,DS,NR,CM,TE1,TE2,TR,RN,CRL,GAM,RTH,THET
     12,H2)
      NR = NR-1
      KS1 = KSB+1
      DO 510 J = KS1,NR
      DELS(J) = H2(J)*THET2(J)
  510 SEP(J) = -THET2(J)*DUDS(J)/UE(J)
      CALL COSD (KSB,NR,X,Y,CO)
      RAT = EMDT*SQRT(CM/(1.+.2*EMDT**2))/EMF
      DRAGT = THETDT*RAT**(.5*HDT+2.5)/CRL
      DRAGB = THET2(NR)*RAT**(.5*H2(NR)+2.5)/CRL
C     FRICTION DRAG
      DRAG = DRAGT+DRAGB
      DO 520 J = KS1,NR
      ALF(J) = 0.
      IF (U(J).NE.0.) ALF(J) = V(J)/U(J)
  520 CONTINUE
      DO 530 J = KS1,NR
  530 YS(J) = Y(J)+DELS(J)*CO(J)
      WRITE (N4,830)
      WRITE (N4,760)
      J1 = NR-KSB
      DO 540 J = 1,J1
      J2 = NR-J+1
      JK = JT+J
      WRITE (N4,770)X(J2),YS(J2),ALF(J2),CUR(JK),EM(J2),THET2(J2),DELS(J
     12),SEP(J2),H2(J2)
  540 CONTINUE
      WRITE (N4,840) DRAG
      NN = 1
      SM = 0.
      JM = KSB
      DO 560 J = KS1,NR
      IF (SM.GE.SEP(J)) GO TO 560
      SM = SEP(J)
      JM = J
      GO TO (550,560), NN
  550 IF (SM.LT.SP) GO TO 560
      JM1 = J
      NN = 2
  560 CONTINUE
      GO TO (580,570), NN
  570 WRITE (N2,850)
      WRITE (N2,800) X(JM1)
      WRITE (N2,810) SM,X(JM)
      GO TO 585
  580 WRITE (N2,860)
      WRITE (N2,810) SM,X(JM)
  585 DO 590 J = 1,J1
      J2 = NR-J+1
      J3 = JT+J
      C(1,J3) = U(J2)
      C(2,J3) = V(J2)
      C(3,J3) = X(J2)
      C(4,J3) = YS(J2)
  590 C(5,J3) = CP(J2)
      DO 600 J = 1,KM
      KJM = NP1+J-KM
```

```
       U(J) = C(1,KJM)
       V(J) = C(2,KJM)
       X(J) = C(3,KJM)
       Y(J) = C(4,KJM)
  600  CP(J) = C(5,KJM)
       NPK = NP1-KM
       DO 610 J = 1,NPK
       LK = KM+J
       U(LK) = C(1,J)
       V(LK) = C(2,J)
       X(LK) = C(3,J)
       Y(LK) = C(4,J)
  610  CP(LK) = C(5,J)
       REWIND N3
       CD = .1E-30
       NRN = -NRN
       WRITE (N3,620) EMF,CL,CD,TTC,NRN,NP1
       DO 615 J = 1,NP1
  615  WRITE (N3,870) U(J),V(J),X(J),Y(J),CP(J)
       CALL EXIT
  620  FORMAT (3X,F4.3,8X,F5.3,8X,F5.3,9X,F4.3,14X,2I5)
  630  FORMAT (27H1 INVISCID CASE RUN NUMBER=I4)
  640  FORMAT (1H0,3H M=F5.3,4H CL=F5.3,14H FORM DRAG CD=F5.3,5H T/C=F5.3
      1)
  650  FORMAT (19H0 NUMBER OF POINTS=I4/)
  660  FORMAT (1H0,50HRESULT OF TURBULENT BOUNDARY LAYER CORRECTION,  R=1
      1PE9.2)
  670  FORMAT (39H0DATA RN,TR,GAM,RTH,TE1,TE2,PCH,SP,ANG//6X1PE8.1,1H,0
      1PF5.4,1H,F3.1,1H,F5.1,1H,E7.1,1H,E7.1,1H,F5.3,1H,F4.3,1H,F7.5/)
  680  FORMAT (39H TEST FOR ERRONEOUS POINT DOES NOT WORK)
  690  FORMAT (5X1HX7X1HY8X3HV/U8X1HK5X1HM)
  700  FORMAT (1H ,2F8.5,F9.4,F9.2,F7.4,22H  TRANSITION AT BOTTOM)
  710  FORMAT (1H ,2F8.5,F9.4,F9.2,F7.4,19H  STAGNATION POINT )
  730  FORMAT (1H ,2F8.5,F9.4,F9.2,F7.4)
  740  FORMAT (1H ,2F8.5,F9.4,F9.2,F7.4,19H  TRANSITION AT TOP)
  750  FORMAT (1H0,23X24HCORRECTED OUTPUT FOR TOP/)
  760  FORMAT (5X1HX7X2HYS6X3HV/U6X1HK5X1HM4X5HTHETA3X4HDELS4X3HSEP4X1HH)
  770  FORMAT (1H ,2F8.5,F8.4,F7.2,F7.4,2F7.5,F8.5,F6.2)
  780  FORMAT (1H ,2F8.5,F8.4,7XF7.4,2F7.5,F8.5,F6.2,5H TAIL)
  790  FORMAT (25H SEPARATION OCCURS ON TOP)
  800  FORMAT (30H SEPARATION FIRST OCCURS AT X=F8.5)
  810  FORMAT (28H MAXIMUM NASH MACDONALD SEP=F8.5,6H AT X=F8.5)
  820  FORMAT (21H NO SEPARATION ON TOP)
  830  FORMAT (1H023X27HCORRECTED OUTPUT FOR BOTTOM/)
  840  FORMAT (1H0,18H FRICTION DRAG CD=F6.5)
  850  FORMAT (28H SEPARATION OCCURS ON BOTTOM)
  860  FORMAT (24H NO SEPARATION ON BOTTOM)
C      ****CHANGE (4020) TO (20A4) ON IBM 360****
  870  FORMAT (4020)
       END

       SUBROUTINE INTEG (NST,EM,UES,DUDS,DS,JT,CM,TE1,TE2,TR,RN,CRL,GAM,R
      1TH,THET2,H2)
C      ROUTINE FOR INTEGRATING THETA USING MIDPOINT VALUES AND CENTERED
C      DIFFERENCES
       COMMON /G/ N2,N3,N4
       DIMENSION EM(1), UES(1), DUDS(1), DS(1), THET2(1), H2(1)
       DIMENSION H(250)
       JM0 = CRL/RN
```

```
      JT1 = JT-1
      DO 140 J = NST,JT1
      EMT = (EM(J+1)+EM(J))/2.
      UESA = (UES(J+1)+UES(J))/2.
      VM = 1.+.2*EMT**2
      T = CM/VM
      RFT = UESA*(T+TR)*T/(UM0*(1.+TR))
      IF (J-NST) 10,20,30
   10 WRITE (N4,150)
      CALL EXIT
   20 THET1 = 320./RFT
      THET2(J) = THET1
      GE = 6.5
   30 FC = 1.+0.066*EMT**2-.008*EMT**3
      FR = 1.-0.134*EMT**2+.027*EMT**3
      IND = 0
   40 IND = IND+1
      TAU = 1./(FC*(2.4711*ALOG(FR*RFT*THET1)+4.75)+1.5*GE+1724./(GE**2+
     1200.)-16.87)**2
      HB = 1./(1.-GE*SQRT(TAU))
      H(J) = (HB+1.)*(1.+.178*EMT**2)-1.
      PI = -H(J)*THET1*DUDS(J+1)/(UESA*TAU)
      IF (PI.LT.-1.5) GO TO 60
      IF (PI.GT.1.E4) GO TO 70
   50 CONTINUE
      G = 6.1*SQRT(PI+1.81)-1.7
      GO TO 90
   60 PI = -1.5
      GO TO 80
   70 PI = 1.E4
   80 CONTINUE
      GO TO 50
   90 CONTINUE
      T2 = ABS(G-GE)/GE
      GE = G
      DT2 = DT
      DT = -(H(J)+2.-EMT**2)*THET1*DUDS(J+1)/UESA+TAU
      IF (IND.GT.1) GO TO 100
      THT = THET2(J)
      THET1 = DT*DS(J+1)+THT
      THET1 = .5*(THET1+THT)
      GO TO 40
  100 DT = (DT2+DT)/2.
      TI = ABS((DT-DT2)/DT)
      IF (TI.LT.TE2) GO TO 120
  110 THET1 = DT*DS(J+1)+THT
      THET1 = .5*(THET1+THT)
      IF (IND.LE.1000) GO TO 40
      IF (PI.EQ.-1.5) GO TO 130
      WRITE (N4,160) TI,J,EM(J),EMT,DUDS(J+1),UESA
      GO TO 130
  120 IF (T2.GE.TE1) GO TO 110
  130 THET2(J+1) = DT*DS(J+1)+THT
      THET1 = .5*(THET2(J+1)+THT)
      H2(J+1) = H(J)
  140 CONTINUE
      RETURN
  150 FORMAT (33H  ERROR IN J . J IS LESS THAN NST)
  160 FORMAT (5H0 TI=E12.5,3H J=I4,4H EM=E12.5,5H EMT=E12.5,6H DUDS=E12.
```

```
    15,6H UESA=E12.5)
    END

    SUBROUTINE COSD (NST,NFSH,X,Y,CO)
    DIMENSION X(1), Y(1), CO(1)
    NS = NST+1
    DO 10 J = NS,NFSH
    DX = X(J)-X(J-1)
    DY = Y(J)-Y(J-1)
 10 CO(J) = 1./SQRT(1.+(DY/DX)**2)
    RETURN
    END

    SUBROUTINE RESHUF (XB,XT,KBST,NR)
    DIMENSION XB(1), XT(1)
    XT(1) = XB(KBST+1)
    DO 10 J = 1,NR
    NR1 = KBST-J
 10 XT(J+1) = XB(NR1+1)
    NR1 = NR+1
    DO 20 J = 1,NR1
 20 XB(J) = XT(J)
    RETURN
    END




C    PROGRAM G-DOES ANALYSIS OF FLOW WITH SHOCKS

     PROGRAM G(INPUT = 66,OUTPUT = 500,TAPE3 = 500,TAPE4 = 400,TAPE2 =
    1OUTPUT,TAPE5 = INPUT)
     COMMON PHI(162,31),FP(162,31)
     COMMON /B/ AA(100),BB(100)
     COMMON /C/ M,MM,MP,N,NN,LL,LP,I,IM,IMM,IM3,II,JJ,IK,JK,IZ,ITYP,MXP
    1,NS,NCY,TE,PI,RAD,TP,TPI,DT,DR,DELTH,DELR,RA,RAS,RA2,RA3,RA4,RA5,E
    2M,QCRIT,C1,C2,C4,C5,C6,C7,BET,EPSIL,TC,CL,CHD,ALP,ALPO,DPHI,XPHI,C
    3N,SN,EP,C3,RA7,RA8,RA9,EL,XM,XS,FSYM,ST,X,Y,YM,XA,YA,AQ,BQ,KP,YR,E
    4MO,EE,IDIM,NFC,NMP,IS,N2,N3,N4,N5,M4,NRN
     DIMENSION COMC(85)
     EQUIVALENCE (COMC(1),M)
C    ***NON-ANSI***
     NAMELIST /P/ EM,ALP,M,N,NS,ITYP,NCY,XS,XM,XPHI,YA,KP,II,JJ,IZ,EP,
    1 ST,FSYM,NFC,NMP,IS,TE,NRN
     DATA GAM,IMO/1.4,0/
     N2 = 2
     N3 = 3
     N4 = 4
     N5 = 5
     M4 = N4
     REWIND N4
 10 WRITE (N2,180)
C    ****NON-ANSI****
     READ (N5,P)
     NTPE = N4
C    SELECT OUTPUT TAPE
     N4 = M4
```

```
      IF (IZ.GE.80) N4 = N2
      ALP = ALP/RAD
      IF (NS.NE.0) GO TO 40
C     CHECK FOR TERMINATE,RETRIEVE, OR STORE INSTRUCTIONS
      IF (ITYP.EQ.0) GO TO 170
      REWIND N3
      IF (ITYP.LT.0) GO TO 30
C     ****CHANGE BINARY READ TO (20A4) ON IBM 360****
      READ (N3) COMC
      CALL RETRIV
      GO TO 140
   30 ITYP = -ITYP
C     ****CHANGE BINARY WRITE TO (20A4) ON IBM 360****
      WRITE (N3) COMC
      CALL STORE
      GO TO 140
C     COMPUTE CONSTANTS NEEDED IN CALCULATION
   40 RA7 = 1.+EP
      RA8 = 1.+3.*EP
      RA9 = 1.+RA8
      C3 = 2.+EP
      EL = 2.*RA7
      IF (EM.EQ.EMO) GO TO 50
C     NEW MACH NUMBER, ADJUST CONSTANTS WHICH DEPEND ON MACH NUMBER
      EMO = AMAX1(EM,.1E-40)
      EM = EMO
      C2 = .5*(GAM-1.)
      C1 = C2+1./(EM*EM)
      C5 = 1./(.5*GAM*EM*EM)
      C6 = C2*EM*EM
      C4 = C6+1.
      C7 = 1./(C5*C6)
      BET = SQRT(1.-EM*EM)
      IMO = 1
   50 QCRIT = 5.*C1/6.
      IF (NS.GT.0) GO TO 70
      IF (ITYP.EQ.0) GO TO 60
      NS = 0
C     GO TO CRUDE GRID IF ITYP.GT.0
      IF (ITYP.GT.0) CALL CRUDER
      GO TO 140
   60 REWIND N3
      CALL RETRIV
      NS = -NS
      CALL RESTRT
      GO TO 140
   70 IF (ITYP) 80,90,100
C     GO BACK TO FINER GRID
   80 CALL REFINE
      GO TO 140
C     SET UP CONSTANTS AND DO CONFORMAL MAPPING
   90 CALL AIRFOL
      CALL RESTRT
      GO TO 140
  100 IF (IMO.LE.0) GO TO 110
      IMO = 0
      CALL PHIRR
  110 CONTINUE
C     CHECK TO SEE IF ANGLE OF ATTACK HAS CHANGED
```

```
      IF (ABS(ALP-ALPO).GT.1.E-8) CALL SICO
      Y = (XS-XM)/(1.-QCRIT)
      YM = XS-Y
      IF (XPHI.EQ.0.) YA = YA/(2.*CHD)
C     DO AT MOST NS CYCLES
      WRITE (N4,210)
      IF (N4.NE.N2) WRITE (N2,210)
      DO 120 K = 1,NS
C     WRITE ON TAPE2 EVERY KP CYCLES
      IF (MOD(K-1,KP).EQ.0) NTPE = N2
C     ALL OTHER CYCLES GO ON N4
      WRITE (NTPE,190) MXP,YR,YA,CL,PHI(II,JJ),IK,JK
      NTPE = N4
      CL = 2.*DPHI*CHD
      CALL SWEEP
C     CHECK TO SEE IF WE HAVE SATISFIED CONVERGENCE CRITERIA
      IF (AMAX1(YR,ABS(YA)).LT.ST) GO TO 130
      IF (XPHI.EQ.0.) YA = 0.
      YA = YA/XPHI
  120 CONTINUE
  130 WRITE (N4,190) MXP,YR,YA,CL,PHI(II,JJ),IK,JK
C     KEEP TRACK OF THE TOTAL NUMBER OF CYCLES
      NCY = NCY-1+K
  140 ALP = RAD*ALP
      ITYP = IABS(ITYP)
      CALL SECOND(TIME)
  150 WRITE (NTPE,200) EM,ALP,EP,M,N,NCY,NS,XS,XM,XPHI,ST,TIME
      IF (NTPE.EQ.N2) GO TO 160
      NTPE = N2
      GO TO 150
  160 IF (ITYP.GE.2) CALL GETCP
      GO TO 10
  170 ITYP = 4
      ALP = ALP*RAD
      CALL GETCP
C     TERMINATE PLOT
      CALL CPLOT ((0.,0.),999)
      CALL EXIT
  180 FORMAT (7H READ P/)
  190 FORMAT (I3,2E12.3,2F11.5,I4,I3)
  200 FORMAT (4H EM=F4.3,3X4HALP=F5.2,3X3HEP=F4.2,3X4HM*N=I3,1H*,I2,
     1 3X4HNCY=,I4,3X3HNS=,I4/4H XS=,F4.2,3X,3HXM=,F4.2,3X5HXPHI=,F4.2
     2 ,3X,3HST=,E7.1,3X5HTIME=,F7.2//)
  210 FORMAT (4H MXP,6X,3HRES,9X,2HYA,10X,2HCL,9X,3HPHI,3X2HIK,2X2HJK)
      END

      SUBROUTINE RESTRT
      COMMON PHI(162,31),FP(162,31)
      COMMON /B/ AA(100),BB(100)
      COMMON /C/ M,MM,MP,N,NN,LL,LP,I,IM,IMM,IM3,II,JJ,IK,JK,IZ,ITYP,MXP
     1,NS,NCY,TE,PI,RAD,TP,TPI,DT,DR,DELTH,DELR,RA,RAS,RA2,RA3,RA4,RA5,E
     2M,QCRIT,C1,C2,C4,C5,C6,C7,BET,EPSIL,TC,CL,CHD,ALP,ALPO,DPHI,XPHI,C
     3N,SN,EP,C3,RA7,RA8,RA9,EL,XM,XS,FSYM,ST,X,Y,YM,XA,YA,AQ,BQ,KP,YR,E
     4MO,EE,IDIM,NFC,NMP,IS,N2,N3,N4,N5,M4,NRN
      COMPLEX Z
      COMMON /A/ A(40),B(40),C(40),D(40),E(40),RHO(40),RP(40),R(41),RS(4
     11),RI(41),SI(162),CO(162),Z(162),FM(162),PHIR(162)
C     SET UP CONSTANTS
      TP = PI+PI
```

```
      TPI = 1./TP
      RAD = 180./PI
      ITYP = 1
      IF ((N+1).NE.NN.OR.(M+1).NE.MM) NCY = 0
      MM = M+1
      MP = MM+1
      LL = MP/2
      LP = LL+2
      NN = N+1
      DR = -1./FLOAT(N)
      DT = TP/FLOAT(M)
      DELR = .5/DR
      DELTH = .5/DT
      RA = DT/DR
      RAS = RA*RA
      RA2 = -.5*RA
      RA3 = -.125/DELTH
      RA4 = .25/(DELTH*DELTH)
      RA5 = -RA*(RA3+RA3)
      DO 10 K = 1,N
      R(K) = 1.+DR*FLOAT(K-1)
      RS(K) = R(K)*R(K)
      RI(K) = 1./R(K)
   10 CONTINUE
      R(NN) = 0.
      RS(NN) = 0.
      DO 20 L = 1,MP
      TH = FLOAT(L-1)*DT
      CO(L) = COS(TH)
   20 SI(L) = SIN(TH)
      IF (NCY.LE.0) GO TO 24
      CALL MAP2
      GO TO 26
   24 CALL MAP
   26 BQ = -4.
      DPHI = PI*SN/(CHD*BET)
      CL = TP*SN/BET
      DO 60 L = 1,M
      X = CO(L)
      CO(L) = X*CN-SI(L)*SN
      SI(L) = SI(L)*CN+X*SN
      PHIR(L) = ATAN2(-SI(L)*BET,-CO(L))
   30 IF (PHIR(L).GE.BQ) GO TO 40
      PHIR(L) = PHIR(L)+TP
      GO TO 30
   40 BQ = PHIR(L)
      DO 50 J = 1,NN
   50 PHI(L,J) = R(J)*CO(L)+DPHI*PHIR(L)*TPI
   60 CONTINUE
      PHIR(MM) = PHIR(1)+TP
      PHIR(MP) = PHIR(2)+TP
      DO 70 J = 1,NN
      PHI(MM,J) = PHI(1,J)+DPHI
   70 PHI(MP,J) = PHI(2,J)+DPHI
      CALL INIT
      RETURN
      END

      SUBROUTINE INIT
```

```
      COMMON PHI(162,31),FP(162,31)
      COMMON /B/ AA(100),BB(100)
      COMMON /C/ M,MM,MP,N,NN,LL,LP,I,IM,IMM,IM3,II,JJ,IK,JK,IZ,ITYP,MXP
     1,NS,NCY,TE,PI,RAD,TP,TPI,DT,DR,DELTH,DELR,RA,RAS,RA2,RA3,RA4,RA5,E
     2M,QCRIT,C1,C2,C4,C5,C6,C7,BET,EPSIL,TC,CL,CHD,ALP,ALPO,DPHI,XPHI,C
     3N,SN,EP,C3,RA7,RA8,RA9,EL,XM,XS,FSYM,ST,X,Y,YM,XA,YA,AQ,BQ,KP,YR,E
     4MO,EE,IDIM,NFC,NMP,IS,N2,N3,N4,N5,M4,NRN
      COMPLEX Z
      COMMON /A/ A(40),B(40),C(40),D(40),E(40),RHO(40),RP(40),R(41),RS(4
     11),RI(41),SI(162),CO(162),Z(162),FM(162),PHIR(162)
      CO(MP) = CO(2)
      CO(MM) = CO(1)
      SI(MM) = SI(1)
      SI(MP) = SI(2)
      ALPO = ALP
      CN = COS(ALP+BB(1))
      SN = SIN(ALP+BB(1))
      CALL PHIRR
      RETURN
      END

      SUBROUTINE PHIRR
      COMMON PHI(162,31),FP(162,31)
      COMMON /B/ AA(100),BB(100)
      COMMON /C/ M,MM,MP,N,NN,LL,LP,I,IM,IMM,IM3,II,JJ,IK,JK,IZ,ITYP,MXP
     1,NS,NCY,TE,PI,RAD,TP,TPI,DT,DR,DELTH,DELR,RA,RAS,RA2,RA3,RA4,RA5,E
     2M,QCRIT,C1,C2,C4,C5,C6,C7,BET,EPSIL,TC,CL,CHD,ALP,ALPO,DPHI,XPHI,C
     3N,SN,EP,C3,RA7,RA8,RA9,EL,XM,XS,FSYM,ST,X,Y,YM,XA,YA,AQ,BQ,KP,YR,E
     4MO,EE,IDIM,NFC,NMP,IS,N2,N3,N4,N5,M4,NRN
      COMPLEX Z
      COMMON /A/ A(40),B(40),C(40),D(40),E(40),RHO(40),RP(40),R(41),RS(4
     11),RI(41),SI(162),CO(162),Z(162),FM(162),PHIR(162)
C     ADJUST CONDITION AT INFINITY FOR MACH NUMBER AND ANGLE OF ATTACK
      BQ = -4.
      DO 20 L = 1,MP
      PHIR(L) = ATAN2(-BET*SI(L),-CO(L))
   10 IF (PHIR(L).GE.BQ) GO TO 20
      PHIR(L) = PHIR(L)+TP
      GO TO 10
   20 BQ = PHIR(L)
      RETURN
      END

      SUBROUTINE SICO
      COMMON PHI(162,31),FP(162,31)
      COMMON /B/ AA(100),BB(100)
      COMMON /C/ M,MM,MP,N,NN,LL,LP,I,IM,IMM,IM3,II,JJ,IK,JK,IZ,ITYP,MXP
     1,NS,NCY,TE,PI,RAD,TP,TPI,DT,DR,DELTH,DELR,RA,RAS,RA2,RA3,RA4,RA5,E
     2M,QCRIT,C1,C2,C4,C5,C6,C7,BET,EPSIL,TC,CL,CHD,ALP,ALPO,DPHI,XPHI,C
     3N,SN,EP,C3,RA7,RA8,RA9,EL,XM,XS,FSYM,ST,X,Y,YM,XA,YA,AQ,BQ,KP,YR,E
     4MO,EE,IDIM,NFC,NMP,IS,N2,N3,N4,N5,M4,NRN
      COMPLEX Z
      COMMON /A/ A(40),B(40),C(40),D(40),E(40),RHO(40),RP(40),R(41),RS(4
     11),RI(41),SI(162),CO(162),Z(162),FM(162),PHIR(162)
      NCY = 0
C     COMPUTE COS(THETA+ALPO),SIN(THETA+ALPO)
      CN = COS(ALP-ALPO)
      SN = SIN(ALP-ALPO)
      CALL COSI
```

```
      RETURN
      END

      SUBROUTINE COSI
      COMMON PHI(162,31),FP(162,31)
      COMMON /B/ AA(100),BB(100)
      COMMON /C/ M,MM,MP,N,NN,LL,LP,I,IM,IMM,IM3,II,JJ,IK,JK,IZ,ITYP,MXP
     1,NS,NCY,TE,PI,RAD,TP,TPI,DT,DR,DELTH,DELR,RA,RAS,RA2,RA3,RA4,RA5,E
     2M,QCRIT,C1,C2,C4,C5,C6,C7,BET,EPSIL,TC,CL,CHD,ALP,ALPO,DPHI,XPHI,C
     3N,SN,EP,C3,RA7,RA8,RA9,EL,XM,XS,FSYM,ST,X,Y,YM,XA,YA,AQ,BQ,KP,YR,E
     4MO,EE,IDIM,NFC,NMP,IS,N2,N3,N4,N5,M4,NRN
      COMPLEX Z
      COMMON /A/ A(40),B(40),C(40),D(40),E(40),RHO(40),RP(40),R(41),RS(4
     11),RI(41),SI(162),CO(162),Z(162),FM(162),PHIR(162)
      DO 10 L = 1,M
      X = CO(L)
      CO(L) = X*CN-SI(L)*SN
   10 SI(L) = SI(L)*CN+X*SN
      CALL INIT
      RETURN
      END

      SUBROUTINE SWEEP
C     SWEEP THROUGH THE GRID ONE TIME
      COMMON PHI(162,31),FP(162,31)
      COMMON /B/ AA(100),BB(100)
      COMMON /C/ M,MM,MP,N,NN,LL,LP,I,IM,IMM,IM3,II,JJ,IK,JK,IZ,ITYP,MXP
     1,NS,NCY,TE,PI,RAD,TP,TPI,DT,DR,DELTH,DELR,RA,RAS,RA2,RA3,RA4,RA5,E
     2M,QCRIT,C1,C2,C4,C5,C6,C7,BET,EPSIL,TC,CL,CHD,ALP,ALPO,DPHI,XPHI,C
     3N,SN,EP,C3,RA7,RA8,RA9,EL,XM,XS,FSYM,ST,X,Y,YM,XA,YA,AQ,BQ,KP,YR,E
     4MO,EE,IDIM,NFC,NMP,IS,N2,N3,N4,N5,M4,NRN
      COMPLEX Z
      COMMON /A/ A(40),B(40),C(40),D(40),E(40),RHO(40),RP(40),R(41),RS(4
     11),RI(41),SI(162),CO(162),Z(162),FM(162),PHIR(162)
      YR = 0.
      IK = LL
      JK = 1
      DO 10 J = 1,N
   10 RP(J) = PHI(LL-1,J)
      MXP = 0
C     SWEEP THROUGH THE GRID FROM NOSE TO TAIL ON UPPER SURFACE
      DO 30 I = LL,M
      IM = I-1
      IMM = I-2
      IM3 = I-3
      DO 20 J = 1,N
   20 RP(J) = PHI(I+1,J)-RP(J)
   30 CALL MURMAN
      AQ = 0.
      BQ = 0.
      I = MM
      DO 40 J = 1,N
   40 RP(J) = PHI(MP,J)-RP(J)
      CALL MURMAN
C     UPDATE PHI AT THE TAIL FROM UPPER SURFACE
      DO 50 J = 1,N
   50 PHI(1,J) = PHI(MM,J)-DPHI
C     SWEEP THROUGH THE GRID FROM NOSE TO TAIL ON LOWER SURFACE
      DO 60 J = 1,N
```

```
   60 RP(J) = PHI(LL,J)
      DO 80 J = 3,LL
      I = LP-J
      IM = I+1
      IMM = I+2
      IM3 = I+3
      DO 70 L = 1,N
   70 RP(L) = RP(L)-PHI(I-1,L)
   80 CALL MURMAN
C     ADJUST CIRCULATION TO SATISFY THE KUTTA CONDITION
      IF (XPHI.EQ.0.) GO TO 90
      YA = XPHI*((PHI(M,1)-PHI(MP,1))*DELTH+SI(1))
   90 DPHI = DPHI+YA
      YA = YA*TPI
      DO 100 L = 1,MP
      PHI(L,NN) = DPHI*TPI*PHIR(L)
      DO 100 J = 1,N
  100 PHI(L,J) = PHI(L,J)+YA*PHIR(L)
      DO 110 J = 1,N
  110 PHI(MP,J) = PHI(2,J)+DPHI
      RETURN
      END

      SUBROUTINE MURMAN
C     SET UP COEFFICIENT ARRAYS FOR THE TRIDIAGONAL SYSTEM USED FOR LINE
C     RELAXATION AND COMPUTE THE UPDATED PHI ON THIS LINE
      COMMON PHI(162,31),FP(162,31)
      COMMON /B/ AA(100),BB(100)
      COMMON /C/ M,MM,MP,N,NN,LL,LP,I,IM,IMM,IM3,II,JJ,IK,JK,IZ,ITYP,MXP
     1,NS,NCY,TE,PI,RAD,TP,TPI,DT,DR,DELTH,DELR,RA,RAS,RA2,RA3,RA4,RA5,E
     2M,QCRIT,C1,C2,C4,C5,C6,C7,BET,EPSIL,TC,CL,CHD,ALP,ALPO,DPHI,XPHI,C
     3N,SN,EP,C3,RA7,RA8,RA9,EL,XM,XS,FSYM,ST,X,Y,YM,XA,YA,AQ,BQ,KP,YR,E
     4MO,EE,IDIM,NFC,NMP,IS,N2,N3,N4,N5,M4,NRN
      COMPLEX Z
      COMMON /A/ A(40),B(40),C(40),D(40),E(40),RHO(40),RP(40),R(41),RS(4
     11),RI(41),SI(162),CO(162),Z(162),FM(162),PHIR(162)
C     DO THE BOUNDARY
      FAC = FLOAT(IM-IMM)
      KK = 0
      U = RP(1)*DELTH-SI(I)
C     CHECK FOR THE TAIL POINT
      IF (I.EQ.MM) GO TO 10
      BQ = U/FP(I,1)
      AQ = U*BQ
      BQ = AQ*BQ*(FP(I-1,1)-FP(I+1,1))
   10 CS = C1-C2*AQ
      RP(1) = AQ
      C(1) = -CS*RAS
      C(1) = C(1)+C(1)
      A(1) = CS-AQ
      X = CO(I)*(C(1)*DR+RA4*(CS+AQ))
      IF (AQ.LE.QCRIT) GO TO 30
C     FLOW IS SUPERSONIC, BACKWARD DIFFERENCES
      D(1) = A(1)*(RA8*PHI(IMM,1)-RA9*PHI(IM,1)-EP*PHI(IM3,1))+RA3*BQ+X
      A(1) = -(C(1)+A(1)*RA7)
      KK = 1
      GO TO 40
C     FLOW SUBCRITICAL, CENTRAL DIFFERENCES
   30 D(1) = A(1)*(PHI(I+1,1)+PHI(I-1,1))+RA3*BQ+X
```

```
      A(1) = A(1)+A(1)-C(1)
C     DO NON-BOUNDARY POINTS
   40 DO 60 J = 2,N
      DU = RP(J)
      U = DU*R(J)*DELTH-SI(I)
      DV = PHI(I,J+1)-PHI(I,J-1)
      V = DV*RS(J)*DELR-CO(I)
      US = U*U
      VS = V*V
      BQ = 1./FP(I,J)
      US = BQ*US
      VS = BQ*VS
      QS = US+VS
      RP(J) = QS
      CS = C1-C2*QS
      UVS = BQ*QS
      C(J) = RS(J)*(VS-CS)*RAS
      B(J-1) = C(J)
      A(J) = CS-US
      UV = BQ*U*V
      X = RA2*UV*R(J)
C     COMPUTE CONTRIBUTION OF RIGHT-HAND SIDE FROM LOW ORDER TERMS
      D(J) = RA5*(CS+US-VS-VS)*R(J)*DV-DT*UV*DU+RA3*UVS*(RI(J)*U*(FP(I-1
     1,J)-FP(I+1,J))+RA*V*(FP(I,J-1)-FP(I,J+1)))
      IF (QS.LE.QCRIT) GO TO 50
C     SUPERSONIC FLOW, USE BACKWARD DIFFERENCING
      KK = KK+1
      X = X*FAC
      D(J) = D(J)+A(J)*(RA8*PHI(IMM,J)-RA9*PHI(IM,J)-EP*PHI(IM3,J))+X*(E
     1P*(PHI(IMM,J+1)-PHI(IMM,J-1))+EL*(PHI(IM,J-1)-PHI(IM,J+1)))
      A(J) = -(RA7*A(J)+2.*C(J))
      QS = C3*X
      B(J-1) = B(J-1)+QS
      C(J) = C(J)-QS
      GO TO 60
   50 CONTINUE
C     SUBSONIC FLOW, USE CENTRAL DIFFERENCES
      D(J) = D(J)+A(J)*(PHI(I+1,J)+PHI(I-1,J))+X*(PHI(I+1,J+1)+PHI(I-1,J
     1-1)-PHI(I+1,J-1)-PHI(I-1,J+1))
      A(J) = 2.*(A(J)-C(J))
   60 CONTINUE
C     ADJUST FOR BOUNDARY CONDITION AT INFINITY
      D(N) = D(N)-C(N)*PHI(I,NN)
      MXP = MAX0(MXP,KK)
C     SOLVE THE TRIDIAGONAL SYSTEM
      CALL TRID
      DO 80 J = 1,N
C     FIND THE LOCATION OF THE MAXIMUM RESIDUAL
      IF (ABS(E(J)-PHI(I,J)).LE.YR) GO TO 70
      YR = ABS(E(J)-PHI(I,J))
      IK = I
      JK = J
C     COMPUTE RELAXATION FACTOR
   70 X = AMIN1(XS,AMAX1(XM,YM+Y*RP(J)))
C     SAVE OLD VALUE OF PHI
      RP(J) = PHI(I,J)
C     COMPUTE NEW PHI AT EACH POINT ON THE LINE
   80 PHI(I,J) = X*E(J)+(1.-X)*PHI(I,J)
      RETURN
```

```
      END

      SUBROUTINE TRID
C     SOLVE N DIMENSIONAL TRIDIAGONAL SYSTEM OF EQUATIONS
      COMMON PHI(162,31),FP(162,31)
      COMMON /B/ AA(100),BB(100)
      COMMON /C/ M,MM,MP,N,NN,LL,LP,I,IM,IMM,IM3,II,JJ,IK,JK,IZ,ITYP,MXP
     1,NS,NCY,TE,PI,RAD,TP,TPI,DT,DR,DELTH,DELR,RA,RAS,RA2,RA3,RA4,RA5,E
     2M,QCRIT,C1,C2,C4,C5,C6,C7,BET,EPSIL,TC,CL,CHD,ALP,ALPO,DPHI,XPHI,C
     3N,SN,EP,C3,RA7,RA8,RA9,EL,XM,XS,FSYM,ST,X,Y,YM,XA,YA,AQ,BQ,KP,YR,E
     4MO,EE,IDIM,NFC,NMP,IS,N2,N3,N4,N5,M4,NRN
      COMPLEX Z
      COMMON /A/ A(40),B(40),C(40),D(40),E(40),RHO(40),RP(40),R(41),RS(4
     11),RI(41),SI(162),CO(162),Z(162),FM(162),PHIR(162)
      XX = 1./A(1)
      E(1) = XX*D(1)
C     DO ELIMINATION
      DO 10 J = 2,N
      C(J-1) = C(J-1)*XX
      XX = 1./(A(J)-B(J-1)*C(J-1))
   10 E(J) = (D(J)-B(J-1)*E(J-1))*XX
C     DO BACK SUBSTITUTION
      DO 20 J = 2,N
      L = NN-J
   20 E(L) = E(L)-C(L)*E(L+1)
      RETURN
      END


      SUBROUTINE STORE
C     STORES ON TAPE3 ALL DATA NECESSARY TO RESUME RUN
C     ****CHANGE BINARY READS AND WRITES TO (20A4) ON IBM 360****
      COMMON PHI(162,31),FP(162,31)
      COMMON /B/ AA(100),BB(100)
      COMMON /C/ M,MM,MP,N,NN,LL,LP,I,IM,IMM,IM3,II,JJ,IK,JK,IZ,ITYP,MXP
     1,NS,NCY,TE,PI,RAD,TP,TPI,DT,DR,DELTH,DELR,RA,RAS,RA2,RA3,RA4,RA5,E
     2M,QCRIT,C1,C2,C4,C5,C6,C7,BET,EPSIL,TC,CL,CHD,ALP,ALPO,DPHI,XPHI,C
     3N,SN,EP,C3,RA7,RA8,RA9,EL,XM,XS,FSYM,ST,X,Y,YM,XA,YA,AQ,BQ,KP,YR,E
     4MO,EE,IDIM,NFC,NMP,IS,N2,N3,N4,N5,M4,NRN
      COMPLEX Z
      COMMON /A/ A(40),B(40),C(40),D(40),E(40),RHO(40),RP(40),R(41),RS(4
     11),RI(41),SI(162),CO(162),Z(162),FM(162),PHIR(162)
      WRITE (N3) PHI,FP,A,B,C,D,E,RP,RHO,R,RS,RI,SI,CO,Z,FM,PHIR,AA,BB
      RETURN
      END


      SUBROUTINE RETRIV
      COMMON PHI(162,31),FP(162,31)
      COMMON /B/ AA(100),BB(100)
      COMMON /C/ M,MM,MP,N,NN,LL,LP,I,IM,IMM,IM3,II,JJ,IK,JK,IZ,ITYP,MXP
     1,NS,NCY,TE,PI,RAD,TP,TPI,DT,DR,DELTH,DELR,RA,RAS,RA2,RA3,RA4,RA5,E
     2M,QCRIT,C1,C2,C4,C5,C6,C7,BET,EPSIL,TC,CL,CHD,ALP,ALPO,DPHI,XPHI,C
     3N,SN,EP,C3,RA7,RA8,RA9,EL,XM,XS,FSYM,ST,X,Y,YM,XA,YA,AQ,BQ,KP,YR,E
     4MO,EE,IDIM,NFC,NMP,IS,N2,N3,N4,N5,M4,NRN
      COMPLEX Z
      COMMON /A/ A(40),B(40),C(40),D(40),E(40),RHO(40),RP(40),R(41),RS(4
     11),RI(41),SI(162),CO(162),Z(162),FM(162),PHIR(162)
C     READS IN ALL THE DATA NECESSARY TO RESUME RUN
      READ (N3) PHI,FP,A,B,C,D,E,RP,RHO,R,RS,RI,SI,CO,Z,FM,PHIR,AA,BB
      RETURN
```

```
                END

                SUBROUTINE REFINE
C               HALVES THE MESH SIZE.   VALUES OF PHI AT MIDPOINTS ARE FOUND BY
C               LINEAR INTERPOLATION .   THIS SUBROUTINE MAY BE PERFORMED ONLY
C               AFTER SUBROUTINE CRUDER HAS BEEN EXECUTED
                COMMON PHI(162,31),FP(162,31)
                COMMON /B/ AA(100),BB(100)
                COMMON /C/ M,MM,MP,N,NN,LL,LP,I,IM,IMM,IM3,II,JJ,IK,JK,IZ,ITYP,MXP
               1,NS,NCY,TE,PI,RAD,TP,TPI,DT,DR,DELTH,DELR,RA,RAS,RA2,RA3,RA4,RA5,E
               2M,QCRIT,C1,C2,C4,C5,C6,C7,BET,EPSIL,TC,CL,CHD,ALP,ALPO,DPHI,XPHI,C
               3N,SN,EP,C3,RA7,RA8,RA9,EL,XM,XS,FSYM,ST,X,Y,YM,XA,YA,AQ,BQ,KP,YR,E
               4MO,EE,IDIM,NFC,NMP,IS,N2,N3,N4,N5,M4,NRN
                COMPLEX Z
                COMMON /A/ A(40),B(40),C(40),D(40),E(40),RHO(40),RP(40),R(41),RS(4
               11),RI(41),SI(162),CO(162),Z(162),FM(162),PHIR(162)
                X = 2.
                M = M+M
                MM = M+1
                N = N+N
                NN = N+1
                II = II+II-1
                JJ = JJ+JJ-1
                CALL BOTH
                RETURN
                END


                SUBROUTINE CRUDER
C               DOUBLES THE MESH SIZE
                COMMON PHI(162,31),FP(162,31)
                COMMON /B/ AA(100),BB(100)
                COMMON /C/ M,MM,MP,N,NN,LL,LP,I,IM,IMM,IM3,II,JJ,IK,JK,IZ,ITYP,MXP
               1,NS,NCY,TE,PI,RAD,TP,TPI,DT,DR,DELTH,DELR,RA,RAS,RA2,RA3,RA4,RA5,E
               2M,QCRIT,C1,C2,C4,C5,C6,C7,BET,EPSIL,TC,CL,CHD,ALP,ALPO,DPHI,XPHI,C
               3N,SN,EP,C3,RA7,RA8,RA9,EL,XM,XS,FSYM,ST,X,Y,YM,XA,YA,AQ,BQ,KP,YR,E
               4MO,EE,IDIM,NFC,NMP,IS,N2,N3,N4,N5,M4,NRN
                COMPLEX Z
                COMMON /A/ A(40),B(40),C(40),D(40),E(40),RHO(40),RP(40),R(41),RS(4
               11),RI(41),SI(162),CO(162),Z(162),FM(162),PHIR(162)
                X = .5
                M = M/2
                N = N/2
                II = II/2+1
                JJ = JJ/2+1
                CALL BOTH
                RETURN
                END


                SUBROUTINE BOTH
                COMMON PHI(162,31),FP(162,31)
                COMMON /B/ AA(100),BB(100)
                COMMON /C/ M,MM,MP,N,NN,LL,LP,I,IM,IMM,IM3,II,JJ,IK,JK,IZ,ITYP,MXP
               1,NS,NCY,TE,PI,RAD,TP,TPI,DT,DR,DELTH,DELR,RA,RAS,RA2,RA3,RA4,RA5,E
               2M,QCRIT,C1,C2,C4,C5,C6,C7,BET,EPSIL,TC,CL,CHD,ALP,ALPO,DPHI,XPHI,C
               3N,SN,EP,C3,RA7,RA8,RA9,EL,XM,XS,FSYM,ST,X,Y,YM,XA,YA,AQ,BQ,KP,YR,E
               4MO,EE,IDIM,NFC,NMP,IS,N2,N3,N4,N5,M4,NRN
                COMPLEX Z
                COMMON /A/ A(40),B(40),C(40),D(40),E(40),RHO(40),RP(40),R(41),RS(4
               11),RI(41),SI(162),CO(162),Z(162),FM(162),PHIR(162)
```

```
      DIMENSION XY(2)
      EQUIVALENCE (XY(1),Z(1))
      PF = 1./X
      DELR = X*DELR
      DELTH = X*DELTH
      DR = PF*DR
      DT = PF*DT
      RA3 = PF*RA3
      RA4 = PF*PF*RA4
      RA5 = PF*RA5
      NCY = 0
      MP = MM+1
      CALL PERMUT (R,NN,1)
      CALL PERMUT (RS,NN,1)
      CALL PERMUT (RI,NN,1)
      CALL PERMUT (CO,MP,1)
      CALL PERMUT (SI,MP,1)
      CALL PERMUT (PHIR,MP,1)
      CALL PERMUT (Z,MP,2)
      CALL PERMUT (XY(2),MP,2)
      CALL PERMUT (FM,MP,1)
      DO 20 L = 1,NN
      CALL PERMUT (FP(1,L),MP,1)
   20 CALL PERMUT (PHI(1,L),MP,1)
      DO 30 L = 1,MP
      CALL PERMUT (FP(L,1),NN,IDIM)
   30 CALL PERMUT (PHI(L,1),NN,IDIM)
      MM = M+1
      MP = MM+1
      LL = MP/2
      LP = LL+2
      IF (X.EQ..5) GO TO 80
      DO 40 L = 1,M,2
      DO 40 J = 1,NN,2
   40 PHI(L+1,J) = .5*(PHI(L,J)+PHI(L+2,J))
      DO 50 J = 1,N,2
      DO 50 L = 1,MM
   50 PHI(L,J+1) = .5*(PHI(L,J)+PHI(L,J+2))
      DO 60 K = 1,NN
      FP(2,K) = FP(MP,K)
   60 PHI(MP,K) = PHI(2,K)+DPHI
      DO 70 L = 1,MP
      BQ = FLOAT(L-1)*DT
      CO(L) = COS(BQ)
   70 SI(L) = SIN(BQ)
      CALL COSI
      RETURN
   80 NN = N+1
      DO 90 K = 1,NN
      FP(MP,K) = FP(2,K)
   90 PHI(MP,K) = PHI(2,K)+DPHI
      CO(MP) = CO(2)
      SI(MP) = SI(2)
      PHIR(MP) = PHIR(2)+TP
      RETURN
      END

      SUBROUTINE PERMUT (AX,NX,JX)
C     REORDERS POINTS WITHIN AN ARRAY
```

```
      COMMON PHI(162,31),FP(162,31)
      COMMON /B/ AA(100),BB(100)
      COMMON /C/ M,MM,MP,N,NN,LL,LP,I,IM,IMM,IM3,II,JJ,IK,JK,IZ,ITYP,MXP
     1,NS,NCY,TE,PI,RAD,TP,TPI,DT,DR,DELTH,DELR,RA,RAS,RA2,RA3,RA4,RA5,E
     2M,QCRIT,C1,C2,C4,C5,C6,C7,BET,EPSIL,TC,CL,CHD,ALP,ALPO,DPHI,XPHI,C
     3N,SN,EP,C3,RA7,RA8,RA9,EL,XM,XS,FSYM,ST,X,Y,YM,XA,YA,AQ,BQ,KP,YR,E
     4MO,EE,IDIM,NFC,NMP,IS,N2,N3,N4,N5,M4,NRN
      COMPLEX Z
      COMMON /A/ A(40),B(40),C(40),D(40),E(40),RHO(40),RP(40),R(41),RS(4
     11),RI(41),SI(162),CO(162),Z(162),FM(162),PHIR(162)
      DIMENSION AX(1)
      L = 1
      JY = JX+JX
      NY = 2*((NX-1)/2)+1
      NZ = 2*(NX/2)
      IF (X.EQ.2.) GO TO 30
      NY = JX*(NY-1)+1
      NZ = JX*(NZ-1)
      DO 10 J = 1,NY,JY
      A(L) = AX(J)
   10 L = L+1
      DO 20 J = JX,NZ,JY
      A(L) = AX(J+1)
   20 L = L+1
      GO TO 60
   30 DO 40 J = 1,NY,2
      A(J) = AX(L)
   40 L = L+JX
      DO 50 J = 2,NZ,2
      A(J) = AX(L)
   50 L = L+JX
   60 L = 1
      DO 70 J = 1,NX
      AX(L) = A(J)
   70 L = L+JX
      RETURN
      END


      SUBROUTINE GETCP
C     COMPUTE CP,CD, AND CM BY INTEGRATION AND OUTPUT THE SOLUTION ALONG
C     THE BODY
      COMMON PHI(162,31),FP(162,31)
      COMMON /B/ AA(100),BB(100)
      COMMON /C/ M,MM,MP,N,NN,LL,LP,I,IM,IMM,IM3,II,JJ,IK,JK,IZ,ITYP,MXP
     1,NS,NCY,TE,PI,RAD,TP,TPI,DT,DR,DELTH,DELR,RA,RAS,RA2,RA3,RA4,RA5,E
     2M,QCRIT,C1,C2,C4,C5,C6,C7,BET,EPSIL,TC,CL,CHD,ALP,ALPO,DPHI,XPHI,C
     3N,SN,EP,C3,RA7,RA8,RA9,EL,XM,XS,FSYM,ST,X,Y,YM,XA,YA,AQ,BQ,KP,YR,E
     4MO,EE,IDIM,NFC,NMP,IS,N2,N3,N4,N5,M4,NRN
      COMPLEX Z
      COMMON /A/ A(40),B(40),C(40),D(40),E(40),RHO(40),RP(40),R(41),RS(4
     11),RI(41),SI(162),CO(162),Z(162),FM(162),PHIR(162)
      INTEGER A
      REAL MACH
      COMPLEX CLCD,TMP,CI,ZER,CEXP
      DIMENSION QS(1), IMACH(21)
      EQUIVALENCE (QS(1),PHIR(1))
      DATA CI,ZER/(0.,1.),(0.,0.)/
      DATA IMACH/1HQ,1HR,1HS,1HT,1HU,1HV,1HW,1HX,1HY,1HZ,1H0,1H1,1H2,1H3
     1,1H4,1H5,1H6,1H7,1H8,1H9,1H+/
```

```
      MACH(Q) = SQRT(Q/(C1-C2*Q))
      CPR(Q) = C5*(AMAX1(0.,C4-C6*Q)**C7-1.)
      IMC(Q) = MINO(21,IFIX(10.*Q)+1)
C     USE OUTPUT TAPE FOR OUTPUT IF ITYP=2,OTHERWISE USE N4
      IF (ITYP.EQ.2) N4 = N2
      IF (ITYP.GE.3) WRITE (N4,70)
      IF ((IZ.GT.80).AND.(IZ.NE.130)) REWIND M4
C     COMPUTE Q**2 AT EACH POINT ON THE AIRFOIL
      DO 10 L = 2,M
      U = (PHI(L+1,1)-PHI(L-1,1))*DELTH-SI(L)
   10 QS(L) = (U*U)/FP(L,1)
C     INTERPOLATE TO GET CP AT THE TAIL
      QS(1) = .5*(QS(2)+QS(M))
      QS(MM) = QS(1)
      CLCD = ZER
      CM = 0.
      DO 20 L = 1,MM
C     COMPUTE CIRCLE ANGLE IN DEGREES
      TH = RAD*FLOAT(L-1)*DT
C     COMPUTE THE COEFFICIENT OF PRESSURE AT POINT L
      CP = CPR(QS(L))
C     COMPUTE THE MACH NUMBER AS A FUNCTION OF Q**2
      EML = MACH(QS(L))
C     COMPUTE CP*DZ
      TMP = CP*SQRT(FP(L,1))*CEXP(CI*FM(L))
C     SUM UP CL,CD, AND CM
      CLCD = CLCD+TMP
      CM = CM+REAL((CONJG(Z(L))-.25)*TMP)
C     WRITE PUNCH OUTPUT ONTO TAPE4 IF IZ.GT.120
      IF (IZ.GT.120) WRITE (M4,80) Z(L),CP
C     WRITE SOLUTION AT EACH BODY POINT IF ITYP.GT.2
      IF (ITYP.GT.2) WRITE (N4,80) TH,Z(L),CP,EML,PHI(L,1),FP(L,1)
   20 CONTINUE
C     CORRECT CD FOR NON-CLOSED TAIL BY USING AVERAGE CP AT TAIL
      CLCD = -DT*CHD*CI*(CLCD+.5*(CP+CPR(QS(1)))*(Z(MM)-Z(1)))
C     CORRECT CL,CD FOR ANGLE OF ATTACK
      CLCD = CLCD*CEXP(CI*(-ALP/RAD))
      CM = DT*CHD*CM
C     WRITE CD,CL,CM ONTO N4
      WRITE (N4,90) CLCD,CM
C     CONSTRUCT MACH NUMBER DIAGRAM
      I = IMC(EMO)
      I = IMACH(I)
      MA = 130
C     USE PRINT WIDTH OF 130 UNLESS ITYP=2 IN WHICH CASE USE IZ
      IF( ITYP.EQ.2) MA = IZ
      MB = MINO(MM,II+MA/2)
      MA = 1 + MAXO(0,MB-MA)
      DO 30 L = MA,MB
   30 A(L) = I
C     WRITE OUT MACH NUMBERS AT INFINITY
      WRITE (N4,100) (A(L),L = MA,MB)
C     DO MACH NUMBERS ONE LINE AT A TIME DOWN TO THE BODY
      J = N
   40 DO 50 L = 2,MM
      U = (PHI(L+1,J)-PHI(L-1,J))*R(J)*DELTH-SI(L)
      V = (PHI(L,J+1)-PHI(L,J-1))*DELR*RS(J)-CO(L)
      Q = (U*U+V*V)/FP(L,J)
      I = IMC(MACH(Q))
```

```
        A(L) = IMACH(I)
   50 CONTINUE
        A(1) = A(MM)
        WRITE (N4,100) (A(L),L = MA,MB)
        J = J-1
        IF (J.GT.1) GO TO 40
C       DO THE LINE WHICH IS THE BODY
        DO 60 L = MB,MM
        I = IMC(MACH(QS(L)))
   60 A(L) = IMACH(I)
        A(1) = A(MM)
        WRITE (N4,100) (A(L),L = MA,MB)
C       STORE CD IN X
        X = REAL(CLCD)
        IF (ITYP.GE.4) CALL GRAFIC
C       RESTORE PHIR TO VALUE IT HAD ON ENTERING THE ROUTINE
        CALL PHIRR
        ITYP = 1
        IF (IZ.LE.120) RETURN
C       WRITE OUT PARAMETERS ON PUNCH FILE TAPE4
        WRITE (4,110) EM,ALP,TC,CL,X,CM,EP,N,N,NCY
        RETURN
   70 FORMAT (1H14X1HT10X,1HX9X,1HY,8X,2HCP8X,2HEM8X,3HPHI9X,3HMAP/)
   80 FORMAT  (F9.3,5F10.5,2F12.5)
   90 FORMAT (1H1,3X,3HCD=,F8.5,8X,3HCL=,F8.5,8X,3HCM=,F8.5///)
  100 FORMAT (3X,130A1)
  110 FORMAT (7F10.5,I3,I2,I5)
        END


        SUBROUTINE GRAFIC
        COMMON PHI(162,31),FP(162,31)
        COMMON /B/ AA(100),BB(100)
        COMMON /C/ M,MM,MP,N,NN,LL,LP,I,IM,IMM,IM3,II,JJ,IK,JK,IZ,ITYP,MXP
       1,NS,NCY,TE,PI,RAD,TP,TPI,DT,DR,DELTH,DELR,RA,RAS,RA2,RA3,RA4,RA5,E
       2M,QCRIT,C1,C2,C4,C5,C6,C7,BET,EPSIL,TC,CL,CHD,ALP,ALPO,DPHI,XPHI,C
       3N,SN,EP,C3,RA7,RA8,RA9,EL,XM,XS,FSYM,ST,X,Y,YM,XA,YA,AQ,BQ,KP,YR,E
       4MO,EE,IDIM,NFC,NMP,IS,N2,N3,N4,N5,M4,NRN
        COMPLEX Z
        COMMON /A/ A(40),B(40),C(40),D(40),E(40),RHO(40),RP(40),R(41),RS(4
       11),RI(41),SI(162),CO(162),Z(162),FM(162),PHIR(162)
        COMMON /D/ SF,SIZE,ANG,XMAX,YMAX,XOR,YOR,PGSIZ
        DATA NPLOT,PF,EPF,SCF/0,-.5,7.0,6./
        PE(Q) = C5*(AMAX1(0.,C4-C6*Q)**C7-1.)
C       INITIATE PLOT OR GO TO NEXT PAGE
        IF (NPLOT.EQ.0) CALL GOPLOT(NRN)
        IF (NPLOT.GT.0) CALL CPLOT ((13.,-12.),-3)
        NPLOT = 1
C       MOVE THE ORIGIN TO THE LOCATION X=0.,CP=0.
        CALL CPLOT (CMPLX(2.,EPF),-3)
C       PLOT CP CURVE AS A FUNCTION OF X
        CPF = 1./PF
        CCP = CPF*PE(PHIR(1))
        CALL CPLOT (CMPLX(SCF*REAL(Z(1)),CCP),3)
        DO 10 L = 2,MM
        CCP = CPF*PE(PHIR(L))
   10 CALL CPLOT (CMPLX(SCF*REAL(Z(L)),CCP),2)
C       DRAW AND LABEL CP-AXIS
        ANG = 90.
        CALL XYAXES ((-.5,0.),3.,3.,PF)
```

```
      ANG = 0.
C     COMPUTE AND PLOT CRITICAL SPEED
      YMX = CPF*PE(QCRIT)
      SIZE = .28
      CALL CSYMBL (CMPLX(-.5,YMX),15,-1)
      SIZE = .14
      CALL CSYMBL ((-.4,2.5),1HC,1)
      CALL CSYMBL ((-.25,2.38),1HP,1)
C     PLOT BODY
      YOR = 3.
      SF = SCF
      CALL CPLOT (Z(1),3)
      DO 20 L = 2,MM
   20 CALL CPLOT (Z(L),2)
C     LABEL THE PLOT
      SF = 1.
C     ****NON-ANSI - SEE WRITEUP AT END****
      ENCODE (60,30,A) EM,TC,CL,X,ALP
      CALL CSYMBL ((-.5,-1.0),A,60)
C     ****NON-ANSI - SEE WRITEUP AT END****
      ENCODE (60,40,A) M,N,NCY,EP
      CALL CSYMBL ((-.6,-1.5),A,60)
C     ****NON-ANSI - SEE WRITEUP AT END****
      ENCODE (20,50,A)
      SIZE = .07
      CALL CSYMBL ((1.1,-1.47),A,20)
      RETURN
   30 FORMAT (2HM=,F4.3,4X,4HT/C=,F4.3,4X,3HCL=,F5.3,4X,3HCD=,F5.3,4X,4H
     1ALP=,F5.2)
   40 FORMAT (13X,5HM N= ,2I3,5X,4HNCY=,I4,5X,3HEP=,F5.2)
   50 FORMAT (1HX,13X,1HX)
      END


      SUBROUTINE XYAXES (X,BOT,TOP,SCF)
C     X IS THE LOCATION OF THE ORIGIN ON THE AXIS
C     BOT IS THE LENGTH OF THE AXIS TO THE LEFT OF THE ORIGIN
C     TOP IS THE LENGTH TO THE RIGHT OF THE ORIGIN
      COMPLEX ZB,ZT,H,COR
      COMMON /D/ SF,SIZE,ANG,XMAX,YMAX,XOR,YOR,PGSIZ
      DIMENSION X(2), Y(2)
      ANGO = ANG
      SFO = SF
      SIZO = SIZE
      Y(1) = XOR
      Y(2) = YOR
      ANG = 0.
      SF = 1.
      SIZE = .14
      XOR = X(1)+XOR
      YOR = X(2)+YOR
      ZB = CMPLX(-BOT,0.)
      ZT = CMPLX(TOP,0.)
      COR = (-.25,-.3)
      NC = 16
      IF (ABS(ANGO).NE.90.) GO TO 10
C     VERTICAL Y-AXIS
      ZB = (0.,1.)*ZB
      ZT = (0.,1.)*ZT
      COR = (-.6,0.)
```

```
      NC = 15
C     DRAW LINE FOR THE AXIS
   10 CALL CPLOT (ZT,3)
      CALL CPLOT(ZB,2)
      K = BOT
      L = TOP
      N = 1+K+L
      S = -FLOAT(K)*SCF
      H = ZT/TOP
      ZB = -FLOAT(K)*H
      ZT = ZB+COR
      DO 20 I = 1,N
C     DRAW HATCH MARK
      CALL CSYMBL (ZB,NC,-1)
      B = S+FLOAT(I-1)*SCF
C     ****NON-ANSI - SEE WRITEUP AT END****
      ENCODE (10,30,A) B
C     LABEL AXIS
      CALL CSYMBL (ZT,A,4)
      ZB = ZB+H
   20 ZT = ZT+H
      SF = SFO
      SIZE = SIZO
      ANG = ANGO
      XOR = Y(1)
      YOR = Y(2)
      RETURN
   30 FORMAT (F4.1)
      END

      SUBROUTINE CSYMBL (X,N,L)
      COMMON /D/ SF,SIZE,ANG,XMAX,YMAX,XOR,YOR,PGSIZ
      DIMENSION X(2)
C     CHANGE RELATIVE MOVEMENTS TO ABSOLUTE INCHES
      XX = XOR+SF*X(1)
      YY = YOR+SF*X(2)
C     CHECK TO SEE IF WE ARE WITHIN THE PAGE
      IF ((XX.LT.0.).OR.(YY.LT.0.).OR.(XX.GT.XMAX).OR.(YY.GT.YMAX))
     1RETURN
      CALL SYMBOL (XX,YY,SIZE,N,ANG,L)
      RETURN
      END

      SUBROUTINE CPLOT (X,N)
      COMMON /D/ SF,SIZE,ANG,XMAX,YMAX,XOR,YOR,PGSIZ
      DIMENSION X(2)
C     CHANGE RELATIVE MOVEMENTS TO ABSOLUTE INCHES
      XX = XOR+SF*X(1)
      YY = YOR+SF*X(2)
C     CHECK TO SEE IF WE ARE WITHIN THE PAGE
      IF ((XX.LT.0.).OR.(YY.LT.0.).OR.(XX.GT.XMAX).OR.(YY.GT.YMAX))
     1 GO TO 20
   10 CALL PLOT (XX,YY,IABS(N))
      IF (N.GT.0) RETURN
      XOR = XX
      YOR = YY
      RETURN
   20 IF (N.LT.0) GO TO 30
      XX = AMAX1(0.,AMIN1(XX,XMAX))
```

```
      YY = AMAX1(0.,AMIN1(YY,YMAX))
      GO TO 10
C     GO TO NEXT PAGE
   30 XOR = 0.
      YOR = 0.
      CALL PLOT (PGSIZ,0.,N)
      RETURN
      END

      SUBROUTINE GOPLOT (N)
C     INITIATE PLOT
C     ***************************************************************
C     THIS SUBROUTINE SHOULD BE REPLACED BY ANY ROUTINE WHICH INSTRUCTS
C     THE SYSTEM TO INITIATE A PLOT
C     ***************************************************************
      DIMENSION ID(6), LTAB(8), NAME(16)
      DATA MS,NU/777777770000000B,16/
      DATA NAME/10HGARABEDIAN,7H 110204,10HDAVID KORN,7H 109201,10H F. B
     1AUER ,7H 110205,10HN. KASHDAN,7H 110208,10HGARABEDIAN,7H 146202,10
     2HDAVID KORN,7H 141201,9HF. BAUER ,7H 143207,10HN. KASHDAN,7H 14620
     31/
      DATA LTAB/34343337B,34334434B,34343340B,34343343B,34374135B,343734
     134B,34373642B,34374134B/
      ISHIFT(XXX,YYY) = SHIFT(XXX,YYY)
      CALL READCP (ID,21B,1)
      ID(1) = ISHIFT(ID(2).AND.MS,-18)
      DO 10 L = 1,NU,2
      J = L/2+1
      IF (LTAB(J)-ID(1)) 10,20,10
   10 CONTINUE
      L = NU+1
   20 ENCODE (60,30,ID) NAME(L),NAME(L+1),N
      CALL PLOTS (120,ID,30,1,10,,10,)
      RETURN
   30 FORMAT(A10,5H --- ,A7,11X,I3)
      END

      SUBROUTINE AIRFOL
C     READS IN DATA FOR AIRFOIL AND MAKES INITIAL GUESS FOR MAPPING
C     FUNCTION BY COMPUTING FOURIER COEFFICIENTS
C     IF ONLY X,Y COORDINATES ARE PRESCRIBED SMOOTHING IS DONE
      COMMON PHI(162,31),FP(162,31)
      COMMON /B/ AA(100),BB(100)
      COMMON /C/ M,MM,MP,N,NN,LL,LP,I,IM,IMM,IM3,II,JJ,IK,JK,IZ,IIYP,MXP
     1,NS,NCY,TE,PI,RAD,TP,TPI,DT,DR,DELTH,DELR,RA,RAS,RA2,RA3,RA4,RA5,E
     2M,QCRIT,C1,C2,C4,C5,C6,C7,BET,EPSIL,TC,CL,CHD,ALP,ALPO,DPHI,XPHI,C
     3N,SN,EP,C3,RA7,RA8,RA9,EL,XM,XS,FSYM,ST,X,Y,YM,XA,YA,AQ,BQ,KP,YR,E
     4MO,EE,IDIM,NFC,NMP,IS,N2,N3,N4,N5,M4,NRN
      COMPLEX Z
      COMMON /A/ A(40),B(40),C(40),D(40),E(40),RHO(40),RP(40),R(41),RS(4
     11),RI(41),SI(162),CO(162),Z(162),FM(162),PHIR(162)
      DIMENSION XX(1), YY(1), U(1), V(1), W(1), SP(1), CIRC(1), TH(1), T
     1 T(1),DS(1),SS(1),TITLE(15),CX(1),SX(1)
      EQUIVALENCE (SS(1),PHI(1,2)), (TH(1),PHI(82,5)), (U(1),PHI(1,9)),
     1(V(1),PHI(82,12)), (W(1),PHI(1,16)), (SP(1),PHI(82,19))
      EQUIVALENCE (XX(1),FP(1,2)), (YY(1),FP(1,5)), (CIRC(1),FP(1,9)), (
     1TT(1),FP(1,13)), (DS(1),FP(1,17)), (TITLE(1),FP(1,1)), (CX(1),FP(1
     2,21)), (SX(1),FP(1,25))
      SMOOTH(Q1,Q2,Q3,Q4,Q5) = .0625*(Q1+Q5+4.*(Q2+Q4)+6.*Q3)
```

```
      SMTH(Q1,Q2,Q3) = .25*(Q1+Q2+Q2+Q3)
      DIS(Q1) = (Q1-ERR)*((Q1-ERR)*(Q1-ERR)+CONST)
      DATA TOL,NT,ISYM,CONST,VAL/1.E-6,999,0,.2,4HRUN /
      XT = ABS(TE)
C     NMP IS THE NUMBER OF POINTS IN CIRCLE PLANE FOR FOURIER SERIES
      LC = NMP/2
      MC = NMP + 1
      PILC = PI/FLOAT(LC)
      WRITE (N4,470)
      REWIND N3
      READ (N3,410) TITLE
      IF (FSYM.GE.3.) GO TO 100
C     READ IN COORDINATES AS PRODUCED BY PROGRAMS D AND F
      EPSIL = 2.
      IF (NRN.LT.0) FSYM=2.
      XX(1) = 0.
      XMIN = 1.
      REWIND N3
      READ (N3,510) EM,CD,NRN
      IF(TE.LE.0.) XT = 1.+.3*CD
   10 READ (N3,500) U(2),V(2),XX(2),YY(2),FAC
      IF (XX(2).LT.XT) GO TO 20
C     SAVE AT MOST ONE POINT PAST XT
      U(1) = U(2)
      V(1) = V(2)
      XX(1) = XX(2)
      YY(1) = YY(2)
      GO TO 10
   20 DO 40 L = 3,NT
      READ (N3,500) U(L),V(L),XX(L),YY(L),FAC
C     ****CHECK FOR END OF FILE****
      IF (EOF(N3).NE.0) GO TO 50
      IF (XX(L).GE.XT) GO TO 60
      IF(XX(L).GE.XMIN) GO TO 40
      NL = L
      XMIN = XX(L)
   40 CONTINUE
   50 L = L-1
   60 IF (XX(L).GE.1.) GO TO 70
      L = L+1
      XX(L) = 1.
   70 NT = L
      IF ((NRN.GT.0).AND.(CD.EQ.0.)) GO TO 95
      NRN = IABS(NRN)
C     INTERPOLATE TO PUT THE TAIL AT X=XT
C     LOWER SURFACE INTERPOLATION
      I = 1
      L = 1
      IF (XX(1).EQ.0.) L = 2
C     DO NOT EXTEND TAIL SO THAT IT OVERLAPS
      R1 = (YY(L)-YY(L+1))/(XX(L)-XX(L+1))-(YY(NT-1)-YY(NT-2))/
     1 (XX(NT-1)-XX(NT-2))
      XT = AMIN1(XT,1.+(YY(NT-1)-YY(L))/AMAX1(.1E-20,R1))
   80 R1 = (XT-XX(L+1))/(XX(L)-XX(L+1))
      R2 = 1.-R1
      YY(I) = R1*YY(L)+R2*YY(L+1)
      U(I) = R1*U(L)+R2*U(L+1)
      V(I) = R1*V(L)+R2*V(L+1)
      XX(I) = XT
```

```
      IF (I.NE.NT) GO TO 90
      L = I
      IF (FSYM-1.) 170,170,150
C     UPPER SURFACE INTERPOLATION
   90 I = NT
      L = NT-1
      IF (XX(NT).EQ.1.) L = L-1
      GO TO 80
C     CUSPED TAIL
   95 XX(1) = 1.
      YY(1) = YY(NT)
      U(1) = U(NT)
      V(1) = V(NT)
      EPSIL = 0.
      IF (FSYM-1.) 170,170,150
C     READ IN AIRFOIL DATA FROM CARDS
  100 READ (N3,420) FNU,FNL,EPSIL
      READ (N3,470)
      NT = FNU+FNL-1.
      NL = FNL
      NP = NL+1
      DO 110 I = NL,NT
  110 READ (N3,420) U(I),V(I),XX(I),YY(I)
      READ (N3,470)
      DO 120 I = 1,NL
      J = NP-I
  120 READ (N3,420) U(J),V(J),XX(J),YY(J)
      XMIN = XX(NL)
      IF (FSYM-4.) 170,150,130
  130 DO 140 L = 1,NT
      TH(L) = XX(L)/RAD
      XX(L) = U(L)
  140 YY(L) = V(L)
      XMIN = XX(NL)
      GO TO 200
C     DEFINE SLOPES SO THAT ARC LENGTHS CAN BE COMPUTED TO FIRST ORDER
  150 DO 160 I = 1,NT
  160 TH(I) = 0.
      ISYM = 1
      GO TO 200
C     COMPUTE SLOPES FROM VELOCITIES
  170 TH(1) = ATAN2(V(1),U(1))
      FAC = 1.
      DO 190 I = 2,NT
      TH(I) = ATAN2(V(I),U(I))
C     CHOOSE NEAREST BRANCH FOR THE ARCTANGENT
  180 IF (ABS(TH(I)-TH(I-1)).LT.1.) GO TO 190
      TH(I) = TH(I)-PI*FAC
      IF (ABS(TH(I)).LT.6.) GO TO 180
      IF (FAC.LT.0.) CALL EXIT
      FAC = -1.
      GO TO 180
  190 CONTINUE
      IF (EPSIL.GT.1.) EPSIL = (TH(1)-(PI+TH(NT)))/PI
C     COMPUTE ARC LENGTH TO FOURTH ORDER ACCURACY
  200 SP(1) = 0.
      SUM = 0.
      DO 210 I = 2,NT
      DUM = AMAX1(.1E-20,.5*(TH(I)-TH(I-1)))
```

```
      UP = XX(I)-XX(I-1)
      VP = YY(I)-YY(I-1)
      SUM = SUM+SQRT(UP*UP+VP*VP)*DUM/SIN(DUM)
  210 SP(I) = SUM
      ARC = SP(NT)
      SN = 2./ARC
      SCALE = .25*ARC
      EE = .5*(1.-EPSIL)
      DO 220 L = 1,NT
  220 SS(L) = ACOS(1.-SN*SP(L))
      SS(NT) = PI
      IF (ISYM.NE.0) GO TO 350
      WRITE (N4,410) TITLE,VAL,NRN
      IF (N4.NE.N2) WRITE (N2,410) TITLE,VAL,NRN
      CALL SPLIF (NT,SS,TH,U,V,W,3,0.,3,0.)
C     PRINT OUT DATA ON THE AIRFOIL
      WRITE (N4,430)
      DO 230 L = 1,NT
      VAL = TH(L)*RAD
      SUM = SN*U(L)/AMAX1(.1E-5,SIN(SS(L)))
  230 WRITE (N4,480) XX(L),YY(L),SP(L),VAL,SUM,V(L),W(L)
      WRITE (N4,440)
C     MAKE INITIAL GUESS OF ARC LENGTH AS A FUNCTION OF CIRCLE ANGLE
      DO 240 I = 1,MC
      ANGL = FLOAT(I-1)*PILC
      CIRC(I) = ANGL
      CX(I) = COS(ANGL)
      SX(I) = SIN(ANGL)
      YY(I) = 1.
      IF (EE.NE.0.) YY(I) = (2.-2.*CX(I))**EE
      FAC = SIGN(1.+CX(I),FLOAT(LC-I))
      SP(I) = ACOS(.5*FAC)
  240 XX(I) = SCALE*(2.-FAC)
C     DO AT MOST 100 ITERATIONS TO FIND THE FOURIER COEFFICIENTS
      DO 320 KCY = 1,100
      CALL INTPL(NMP,SP,TT,SS,TH,U,V,W)
      DO 250 I = 1,NMP
  250 TT(I) = TT(I)-.5*(1.+EPSIL)*(PI-CIRC(I))+.5*PI
C     COMPUTE THE FIRST NFC FOURIER COEFFICIENTS
      DO 270 I = 1,NFC
      SUM = 0.
      FAC = 0.
      DO 260 L = 1,NMP
      LT = 1+MOD((L-1)*(I-1),NMP)
      SUM = SUM-TT(L)*CX(LT)
  260 FAC = FAC+TT(L)*SX(LT)
      BB(I) = SUM/FLOAT(LC)
  270 AA(I) = FAC/FLOAT(LC)
      BB(1) = .5*BB(1)
      BB(NFC) = .5*BB(NFC)
      DA = 1.-EPSIL-AA(2)
      AA(2) = 1.-EPSIL
C     ENSURE CLOSURE
C     COMPUTE THE CONJUGATE HARMONIC FUNCTION DS
      DO 290 I = 1,NMP
      SUM = (1.-EPSIL)*CX(I)
      DO 280 K = 3,NFC
      LT = 1+MOD((K-1)*(I-1),NMP)
  280 SUM = SUM+AA(K)*CX(LT)+BB(K)*SX(LT)
```

```
  290  DS(I) = YY(I)*EXP(SUM)
       DS(MC) = DS(1)
       TT(1) = 0.
       VAL = .5*PILC
C      INTEGRATE TO GET NEW ARC LENGTH
       DO 300 L = 2,MC
  300  TT(L) = TT(L-1)+VAL*(DS(L)+DS(L-1))
       SCALE = ARC/TT(MC)
       ERR = 0.
       DO 310 I = 1,NMP
       VAL = SCALE*TT(I)
       DUM = ABS(XX(I)-VAL)
       ERR = AMAX1(ERR,DUM/ARC)
       SP(I) = ACOS(1.-SN*VAL)
  310  XX(I) = VAL
       WRITE (N4,490) ERR,DA,BB(2)
       IF (ERR.LT.TOL) GO TO 330
  320  CONTINUE
       WRITE (N4,450)
  330  AA(1) = ARC
       WRITE (N4,460) EPSIL, NMP
       DO 340 L = 1,NFC
  340  WRITE (N4,490) AA(L),BB(L)
       BB(1) = ALOG(SCALE)
       RETURN
  350  CALL SPLIF (NT,SS,XX,U,SP,W,1,0.,1,0.)
       CALL SPLIF (NT,SS,YY,V,TT,DS,1,0.,1,0.)
       DT = PI/FLOAT(NMP)
       ERR = SS(NL)
       DUM = DIS(0.)
       FAC = PI/(DIS(PI)-DUM)
       DO 360 L = 1,MC
  360  CIRC(L) = FAC*(DIS(FLOAT(L-1)*DT)-DUM)
       CALL INTPL(NMP,CIRC,SX,SS,XX,U,SP,W)
       CALL INTPL(NMP,CIRC,CX,SS,YY,V,TT,DS)
       SX(MC) = XX(NT)
       CX(MC) = YY(NT)
       DO 370 L = 2,MC
       XX(L) = SX(L)
  370  YY(L) = CX(L)
       WRITE (N4,520) IS
       IF (N2.NE.N4) WRITE (N2,520) IS
       IF(IS.EQ.0) GO TO 395
C      DO  IS  SMOOTHING ITERATIONS
       DO 390 K = 1,IS
       XX(2) = SMTH(SX(1),SX(2),SX(3))
       YY(2) = SMTH(CX(1),CX(2),CX(3))
       XX(NMP) = SMTH(SX(MC),SX(NMP),SX(NMP-1))
       YY(NMP) = SMTH(CX(MC),CX(NMP),CX(NMP-1))
       DO 380 L = 4,NMP
       XX(L-1) = SMOOTH(SX(L-3),SX(L-2),SX(L-1),SX(L),SX(L+1))
  380  YY(L-1) = SMOOTH(CX(L-3),CX(L-2),CX(L-1),CX(L),CX(L+1))
       DO 390 L = 2,NMP
       SX(L) = XX(L)
  390  CX(L) = YY(L)
  395  NT = MC
       CALL SPLIF(NT,CIRC,XX,U,SP,W,1,0.,1,0.)
       CALL SPLIF(NT,CIRC,YY,V,TT,DS,1,0.,1,0.)
       U(1) = SP(1)
```

```
      V(1) = TT(1)
      U(NT) = SP(NT)
      V(NT) = TT(NT)
      ISYM = 0
      DO 400 L = 1,NT
      V(L) = -V(L)
  400 U(L) = -U(L)
      GO TO 170
  410 FORMAT (16A4,I3)
  420 FORMAT (5F10.7)
  430 FORMAT (35H0AIRFOIL COORDINATES AND CURVATURES/1H0,6X,1HX,14X1HY
     1 ,9X,10HARC LENGTH,6X5HTHETA,7X5HKAPPA,10X,2HKP,11X,3HKPP//)
  440 FORMAT (1H0,4X,3HERR,14X,2HDA,14X,2HDB//)
  450 FORMAT (32H FOURIER SERIES DID NOT CONVERGE)
  460 FORMAT (34H1MAPPING TO THE INSIDE OF A CIRCLE//3X11HDZ/DSIGMA =
     1 50H -(1/SIGMA**2)*(1-SIGMA)**(1-EPSIL)*(EXP(W(SIGMA))//3X,
     2 42HW(SIGMA) = SUM((A(N)+I*B(N))*SIGMA**(N-1))//3X,7HEPSIL =,
     3 F5.3,20X,I4,25H POINTS AROUND THE CIRCLE//7X4HA(N)10X4HB(N)//)
  470 FORMAT (1H1)
  480 FORMAT (F12.6,2F14.6,F14.3,F14.4,2E14.3)
  490 FORMAT (3E15.6)
C     ****CHANGE (4020) TO (20A4) ON IBM 360****
  500 FORMAT (4020)
  510 FORMAT (3X,F4.3,21X,F5.3,27X,I5)
  520 FORMAT (10H0THERE ARE,I4,26H SMOOTHING ITERATIONS USED /)
      END

      SUBROUTINE MAP
C     SUM UP FOURIER SERIES TO OBTAIN FIRST GUESS
      COMMON PHI(162,31),FP(162,31)
      COMMON /B/ AA(100),BB(100)
      COMMON /C/ M,MM,MP,N,NN,LL,LP,I,IM,IMM,IM3,II,JJ,IK,JK,IZ,ITYP,MXP
     1,NS,NCY,TE,PI,RAD,TP,TPI,DT,DR,DELTH,DELR,RA,RAS,RA2,RA3,RA4,RA5,E
     2M,QCRIT,C1,C2,C4,C5,C6,C7,BET,EPSIL,TC,CL,CHD,ALP,ALPO,DPHI,XPHI,C
     3N,SN,EP,C3,RA7,RA8,RA9,EL,XM,XS,FSYM,ST,X,Y,YM,XA,YA,AQ,BQ,KP,YR,E
     4MO,EE,IDIM,NFC,NMP,IS,N2,N3,N4,N5,M4,NRN
      COMPLEX Z
      COMMON /A/ A(40),B(40),C(40),D(40),E(40),RHO(40),RP(40),R(41),RS(4
     11),RI(41),SI(162),CO(162),Z(162),FM(162),PHIR(162)
C     ****CHANGE TO 1.E-6 FOR SINGLE PRECISION IBM 360****
      DATA TOL /1.E-12/
      DO 40 J = 1,N
      RN = R(J)
      DO 10 KK = 2,NFC
      A(KK) = AA(KK)*RN
      D(KK) = BB(KK)*RN
      IF (RN.LE.TOL) GO TO 15
   10 RN = R(J)*RN
      KK = NFC
   15 DO 30 L = 1,MM
      S = BB(1)
      DO 20 K = 2,KK
      LT = 1+MOD((K-1)*(L-1),M)
   20 S = S+A(K)*CO(LT)+D(K)*SI(LT)
   30 FP(L,J) = S
   40 FP(MP,J) = FP(2,J)
      DO 50 L = 1,MP
      Z(L) = (0.,0.)
   50 FP(L,NN) = 0.
```

```
      CALL MAP2
      RETURN
      END

      SUBROUTINE MAP2
      COMPLEX TMP,CEXP,TT,ZER,ONE
      COMMON PHI(162,31),FP(162,31)
      COMMON /B/ AA(100),BB(100)
      COMMON /C/ M,MM,MP,N,NN,LL,LP,I,IM,IMM,IM3,II,JJ,IK,JK,IZ,ITYP,MXP
     1,NS,NCY,TE,PI,RAD,TP,TPI,DT,DR,DELTH,DELR,RA,RAS,RA2,RA3,RA4,RA5,E
     2M,QCRIT,C1,C2,C4,C5,C6,C7,BET,EPSIL,TC,CL,CHD,ALP,ALPO,DPHI,XPHI,C
     3N,SN,EP,C3,RA7,RA8,RA9,EL,XM,XS,FSYM,ST,X,Y,YM,XA,YA,AQ,BQ,KP,YR,E
     4MO,EE,IDIM,NFC,NMP,IS,N2,N3,N4,N5,M4,NRN
      COMPLEX Z
      COMMON /A/ A(40),B(40),C(40),D(40),E(40),RHO(40),RP(40),R(41),RS(4
     11),RI(41),SI(162),CO(162),Z(162),FM(162),PHIR(162)
      DIMENSION SS(1), TH(1), U(1), V(1), W(1), SP(1), XY(2)
      EQUIVALENCE (SS(1),PHI(1,2)), (TH(1),PHI(82,5)), (U(1),PHI(1,9)),
     1(V(1),PHI(82,12)), (W(1),PHI(1,16)), (SP(1),PHI(82,19))
      EQUIVALENCE (XY(1),TMP)
      DATA ZER,ONE/(0.,0.),(1.,0.)/
C     DO MAPPING
      SN = 2./AA(1)
      IF (NS.NE.1) WRITE (N4,100)
      IF (N4.NE.N2) WRITE (N2,100)
      CALL MAP1
C     FIND SLOPES AT EQUALLY SPACED POINTS IN THE CIRCLE PLANE
      SP(MM) = PI
      CALL INTPL (MM,SP,FM,SS,TH,U,V,W)
C     COMPUTE ANGLE OF ZERO LIFT
      S = .5*(FM(1)+FM(MM))
      DO 60 L = 2,M
   60 S = S+FM(L)
      BB(1) = -(.5*PI+S/FLOAT(M))
      S = -BB(1)*RAD
      WRITE (N4,110) S,BQ
      IF (N4.NE.N2) WRITE (N2,110) S,BQ
C     COMPUTE DS
      DO 70 L = 1,MM
      FM(L) = FM(L)+PI
      Q = FP(L,1)
      Z(L) = Q*CEXP((0.,1.)*FM(L))
   70 FP(L,1) = Q*Q
      FP(MP,1) = FP(2,1)
      Z(MP) = Z(2)
      TMP = ZER
      S = 0.
      Q = 0.
      BQ = 0.
      DO 80 L = 1,MM
      TT = TMP+.5*DT*(Z(L+1)+Z(L))
      Z(L) = TMP
      TMP = TT
      S = AMIN1(S,XY(1))
      Q = AMIN1(Q,XY(2))
      BQ = AMAX1(BQ,XY(2))
   80 FP(L,NN) = 1.
      TC = (Q-BQ)/S
      CHD = -1./S
```

```
      DO 90 L = 1,MM
  90  Z(L) = ONE+CHD*Z(L)
      WRITE (N4,120) TC
      IF (N2.NE.N4) WRITE (N2,120) TC
      CN = COS(BB(1)+ALP)
      SN = SIN(BB(1)+ALP)
      RETURN
 100  FORMAT (1H1,5X,5HDEL S,8X,3HRES,9X,3HS/L,8X,4HW(0))
 110  FORMAT (21H0ANGLE OF ZERO LIFT =F9.5,7X22HOUTER MAPPING RADIUS =
     1 F9.5)
 120  FORMAT (32H THE THICKNESS TO CHORD RATIO IS ,F6.4/1H1)
      END

      SUBROUTINE MAP1
      COMMON PHI(162,31),FP(162,31)
      COMMON /B/ AA(100),BB(100)
      COMMON /C/ M,MM,MP,N,NN,LL,LP,I,IM,IMM,IM3,II,JJ,IK,JK,IZ,ITYP,MXP
     1,NS,NCY,TE,PI,RAD,TP,TPI,DT,DR,DELTH,DELR,RA,RAS,RA2,RA3,RA4,RA5,E
     2M,QCRIT,C1,C2,C4,C5,C6,C7,BET,EPSIL,TC,CL,CHD,ALP,ALPO,DPHI,XPHI,C
     3N,SN,EP,C3,RA7,RA8,RA9,EL,XM,XS,FSYM,ST,X,Y,YM,XA,YA,AQ,BQ,KP,YR,E
     4MO,EE,IDIM,NFC,NMP,IS,N2,N3,N4,N5,M4,NRN
      COMPLEX Z
      COMMON /A/ A(40),B(40),C(40),D(40),E(40),RHO(40),RP(40),R(41),RS(4
     11),RI(41),SI(162),CO(162),Z(162),FM(162),PHIR(162)
      DIMENSION SS(1), TH(1), U(1), V(1), W(1), SP(1), SPO(1)
      EQUIVALENCE (SS(1),PHI(1,2)), (TH(1),PHI(82,5)), (U(1),PHI(1,9)),
     1(V(1),PHI(82,12)), (W(1),PHI(1,16)), (SP(1),PHI(82,19))
      EQUIVALENCE (SPO(1),Z(82))
      EE = .5*(1.-EPSIL)
      AQ = 1.+EPSIL
      IM = N/2+1
C     COMPUTE ABS(1-SIGMA)**(1-EPSIL)
      DO 10 L = 1,M
      FM(L) = 1.
  10  PHIR(L) = (2.-2.*CO(L))**EE
      PHIR(MM) = 1.
C     DO AT MOST NS CYCLES
      DO 110 K = 1,NS
      XR = 0.
      YR = 0.
      X = 0.
C     COMPUTE DS AND FIND THE MEAN VALUE OF FP AT R=.5
      DO 20 L = 1,M
      XR = XR+FP(L,IM)
  20  SP(L) = EXP(FP(L,1))*PHIR(L)
      XR = XR/FLOAT(M)
      SP(MM) = SP(1)
      BQ = 0.
C     COMPUTE ARC LENGTH AT EQUALLY SPACED POINTS IN CIRCLE PLANE
      DO 30 L = 1,M
      AL = BQ+.5*DT*(SP(L+1)+SP(L))
      SP(L) = BQ
  30  BQ = AL
      SP(MM) = BQ
      BQ = AA(1)/AL
C     BQ IS THE RATIO OF ARC LENGTH BASED ON READ IN COORDINATES TO THE
C     ARC LENGTH COMPUTED IN THE CIRCLE PLANE
      IF (K.NE.1) GO TO 50
      DO 40 L = 1,MM
```

```
   40 SPO(L) = BQ*SP(L)
   50 DO 60 L = 1,MM
C     SET FP AT INFINITY TO MEAN VALUE TO ENSURE ANALYTICITY THERE
      FP(L,NN) = XR
C     SCALE ARC LENGTH TO TRUE ARC LENGTH
      SP(L) = BQ*SP(L)
C     COMPUTE MAXIMUM CHANGE IN ARC LENGTH AT EQUALLY SPACED POINTS
      AL = SP(L)-SPO(L)
      X = AMAX1(X,ABS(AL))
C     UPDATE ARC LENGTH AT EQUALLY SPACED POINTS IN THE CIRCLE PLANE
      SPO(L) = SPO(L)+XM*AL
C     COMPUTE T(S) SINCE SPLINE FIT USES T AS INDEPENDENT VARIABLE
   60 SP(L) = ACOS(1.-SN*SPO(L))
      IF (NS.EQ.1) GO TO 130
C     NORMALIZE X
      X = X/AA(1)
C     COMPUTE KAPPA AT THE POINTS CORRESPONDING TO SPO(L)
      CALL INTPL (M,SP,FM,SS,U,V,W,Z)
      DO 70 L = 2,M
      FM(L) = SN*FM(L)/SIN(SP(L))
   70 CONTINUE
C     COMPUTE KAPPA*ABS(1-SIGMA)**(1-EPSIL) AT THE TAIL
      FM(MM) = .5*(FM(2)*PHIR(2)+FM(M)*PHIR(M))
      I = 2
C     DO POINT RELAXATION
      CALL MAP3
      DO 80 J = 1,NN
   80 FP(MP,J) = FP(2,J)
      DO 90 I = 3,MM
   90 CALL MAP3
      DO 100 J = 1,N
  100 FP(1,J) = FP(MM,J)
      IF (MOD((K-1),KP).EQ.0) NTPE = N2
      WRITE (NTPE,170) YR,X,BQ,XR
      NTPE = N4
C     CHECK FOR CONVERGENCE
      IF (AMAX1(YR,X).LT.ST) GO TO 120
  110 CONTINUE
  120 NCY = K
C     SAVE THE RESULTS ON TAPE3 SO MAPPING MAY BE RESUMED
  130 REWIND N3
      CALL STORE
C     NOW COMPUTE MAP FUNCTION
      DO 150 L = 1,M
      DO 140 J = 2,N
      Q = EXP(FP(L,J)-XR)*(1.+RS(J)-2.*R(J)*CO(L))**EE
  140 FP(L,J) = Q*Q
      FP(L,1) = PHIR(L)*EXP(FP(L,1)-XR)
      FP(L,NN) = 1.
  150 CONTINUE
      DO 160 J = 1,NN
      FP(MM,J) = FP(1,J)
  160 FP(MP,J) = FP(2,J)
C     COMPUTE OUTER MAPPING RADIUS
      BQ = EXP(XR)
      RETURN
  170 FORMAT (2E12.3,2F12.5)
      END
```

```
      SUBROUTINE MAP3
C     DO POINT RELAXATION FOR LAPLACES EQUATION IN POLAR COORDINATES
C     ALONG LINE I FROM J=N TO J = 1
      COMMON PHI(162,31),FP(162,31)
      COMMON /B/ AA(100),BB(100)
      COMMON /C/ M,MM,MP,N,NN,LL,LP,I,IM,IMM,IM3,II,JJ,IK,JK,IZ,ITYP,MXP
     1,NS,NCY,TE,PI,RAD,TP,TPI,DT,DR,DELTH,DELR,RA,RAS,RA2,RA3,RA4,RA5,E
     2M,QCRIT,C1,C2,C4,C5,C6,C7,BET,EPSIL,TC,CL,CHD,ALP,ALPO,DPHI,XPHI,C
     3N,SN,EP,C3,RA7,RA8,RA9,EL,XM,XS,FSYM,ST,X,Y,YM,XA,YA,AQ,BQ,KP,YR,E
     4MO,EE,IDIM,NFC,NMP,IS,N2,N3,N4,N5,M4,NRN
      COMPLEX Z
      COMMON /A/ A(40),B(40),C(40),D(40),E(40),RHO(40),RP(40),R(41),RS(4
     11),RI(41),SI(162),CO(162),Z(162),FM(162),PHIR(162)
      J = N
   10 TA = RAS*RS(J)
      XX = (FP(I+1,J)+FP(I-1,J)+TA*(FP(I,J+1)+FP(I,J-1))+RA5*R(J)*(FP(I,
     1J+1)-FP(I,J-1)))/(2.+TA+TA)
      XX = XX-FP(I,J)
      YR = AMAX1(ABS(XX),YR)
      FP(I,J) = FP(I,J)+XX*XS
      J = J-1
      IF (J.GT.1) GO TO 10
C     USE REFLECTION ON THE BOUNDARY
      TA = FP(I,2)-DR*(AQ+FM(I)*PHIR(I)*2.*EXP(FP(I,1)))
      XX = (FP(I+1,1)+FP(I-1,1)+RAS*(FP(I,2)+TA)+RA5*(FP(I,2)-TA))/(2.+2
     1.*RAS)
      XX = XX-FP(I,1)
      YR = AMAX1(ABS(XX),YR)
      FP(I,1) = FP(I,1)+XX*XS
      RETURN
      END


      SUBROUTINE SPLIF (N,S,F,FP,FPP,FPPP,KM,VM,KN,VN)
C     SPLINE FIT - SUBROUTINE CONTRIBUTED BY ANTHONY JAMESON
C     GIVEN S AND F AT N CORRESPONDING POINTS,COMPUTE A CUBIC SPLINE
C     THROUGH THESE POINTS SATISFYING AN END CONDITION IMPOSED ON
C     EITHER END.  FP,FPP,FPPP WILL BE THE FIRST,SECOND AND THIRD
C     DERIVATIVE RESPECTIVELY AT EACH POINT ON THE SPLINE
C     KM IS THE DERIVATIVE IMPOSED AT THE START OF THE SPLINE
C     VM WILL BE THE VALUE OF THE DERIVATIVE THERE
C     KN IS THE DERIVATIVE IMPOSED AT THE END OF THE SPLINE
C     VN WILL BE THE VALUE OF THE DERIVATIVE THERE
C     KM,KN CAN TAKE VALUES 1,2, OR 3
C     S MUST BE MONOTONIC
      DIMENSION S(1), F(1), FP(1), FPP(1), FPPP(1)
      K = 1
      M = 1
      I = M
      J = M+K
      DS = S(J)-S(I)
      D = DS
      IF (DS.EQ.0.) GO TO 110
      DF = (F(J)-F(I))/DS
      IF (KM-2) 10,20,30
   10 U = .5
      V = 3.*(DF-VM)/DS
      GO TO 50
   20 U = 0.
      V = VM
```

```
      GO TO 50
   30 U = -1.
      V = -DS*VM
      GO TO 50
   40 I = J
      J = J+K
      DS = S(J)-S(I)
      IF (D*DS.LE.0.) GO TO 110
      DF = (F(J)-F(I))/DS
      B = 1./(DS+DS+U)
      U = B*DS
      V = B*(6.*DF-V)
   50 FP(I) = U
      FPP(I) = V
      U = (2.-U)*DS
      V = 6.*DF+DS*V
      IF (J.NE.N) GO TO 40
      IF (KN-2) 60,70,80
   60 V = (6.*VN-V)/U
      GO TO 90
   70 V = VN
      GO TO 90
   80 V = (DS*VN+FPP(I))/(1.+FP(I))
   90 B = V
      D = DS
  100 DS = S(J)-S(I)
      U = FPP(I)-FP(I)*V
      FPPP(I) = (V-U)/DS
      FPP(I) = U
      FP(I) = (F(J)-F(I))/DS-DS*(V+U+U)/6.
      V = U
      J = I
      I = I-K
      IF (J.NE.M) GO TO 100
      FPPP(N) = FPPP(N-1)
      FPP(N) = B
      FP(N) = DF+D*(FPP(N-1)+B+B)/6.
      RETURN
  110 STOP
      END

      SUBROUTINE INTPL (NX,SI,FI,S,F,FP,FPP,FPPP)
C     GIVEN S,F(S) AND THE FIRST THREE DERIVATIVES AT A SET OF POINTS
C     FIND FI(SI) AT THE NX VALUES OF SI BY EVALUATING THE TAYLOR SERIES
C     OBTAINED BY USING THE FIRST THREE DERIVATIVES
      DIMENSION SI(1), FI(1), S(1), F(1), FP(1), FPP(1), FPPP(1)
      DATA PT/.33333333333333/
      J = 0
      DO 30 I = 1,NX
      VAL = 0.
      SS = SI(I)
   10 J = J+1
      TT = S(J)-SS
      IF (FLOAT(J-1)*TT) 10,30,20
   20 J = J-1
      SS = SS-S(J)
      VAL = SS*(FP(J)+.5*SS*(FPP(J)+SS*PT*FPPP(J)))
   30 FI(I) = F(J)+VAL
      RETURN
```

```
      END

      BLOCK DATA
      COMMON PHI(162,31),FP(162,31)
      COMMON /B/ AA(100),BB(100)
      COMMON /C/ M,MM,MP,N,NN,LL,LP,I,IM,IMM,IM3,II,JJ,IK,JK,IZ,ITYP,MXP
     1,NS,NCY,TE,PI,RAD,TP,TPI,DT,DR,DELTH,DELR,RA,RAS,RA2,RA3,RA4,RA5,E
     2M,QCRIT,C1,C2,C4,C5,C6,C7,BET,EPSIL,TC,CL,CHD,ALP,ALPO,DPHI,XPHI,C
     3N,SN,EP,C3,RA7,RA8,RA9,EL,XM,XS,FSYM,ST,X,Y,YM,XA,YA,AQ,BQ,KP,YR,E
     4MO,EE,IDIM,NFC,NMP,IS,N2,N3,N4,N5,M4,NRN
      COMMON /D/ SF,SIZE,ANG,XMAX,YMAX,XOR,YOR,PGSIZ
      DATA SF,SIZE,ANG,XMAX,YMAX,XOR,YOR,PGSIZ/1.0,,14.0,,11.,11.,0.,0.,
     111.30/
C     ****IDIM MUST BE SET TO THE FIRST DIMENSION OF PHI****
      DATA EP,ALP,YR,YA,ST,AQ,BQ,EM,XS,TE,XM,XPHI,EMO,PI,RAD,ITYP,MXP,IK
     1 ,JK,NCY,KP,JJ,NRN,II,IZ,NFC,NMP,M,N,NS,IDIM,IS/7*0,,75,1.9,-1.
     2 ,3*1.,3.141592653898,57.295779513,5*0,3*1,130,70,16,300,160,30,
     3 400,162,10/
      END
```

```
C     *****WRITEUP FOR ENCODE-DECODE STATEMENTS*****
C
C     ENCODE/DECODE STATEMENTS
C
C     ENCODE IS SIMILAR TO A FORMATTED WRITE STATEMENT
C     DECODE IS SIMILAR TO A FORMATTED READ STATEMENT
C     NO TAPES ARE ACTUALLY INVOLVED SINCE THE TRANSFERS TAKE PLACE
C     WITHIN CORE
C
C     THE FIRST ARGUMENT IS THE NUMBER OF CHARACTERS TO BE READ OR
C     WRITTEN
C     THE SECOND ARGUMENT IS THE FORMAT NUMBER
C     THE THIRD ARGUMENT IS THE ADDRESS TO WHICH OR FROM WHICH THE
C     I/O LIST WILL BE WRITTEN OR READ
C
C     A MORE DETAILED DESCRIPTION CAN BE FOUND IN THE FOLLOWING MANUAL
C     CONTROL DATA 6400/6500/6600 COMPUTER SYSTEMS FORTRAN REFERENCE
C     MANUAL, SECTION 10.6(ENCODE/DECODE STATEMENTS), PAGES 13-17 (1969)
C
C     *****WRITEUP FOR CALCOMP ROUTINES*****
C
C     SYMBOL
C     SUBROUTINE TO WRITE MESSAGES AND SPECIAL CHARACTERS ON THE
C             GRAPHIC OUTPUT.
C
C     USAGE
C
C             CALL SYMBOL(X,Y,H,TEXT,ANGLE,NCHAR)
C
C             WHERE
C     X,Y     ARE THE COORDINATES ON THE GRAPH PAPER OF THE FIRST
C             CHARACTER OF THE MESSAGE.  IF NCHAR IS POSITIVE, THE
C             PEN STARTS AT THE LOWER LEFT CORNER OF THE FIRST
C             CHARACTER.  IF NCHAR IS NEGATIVE, THE PEN STARTS
C             AT THE CENTER OF THE FIRST CHARACTER.
C
C     H       IS THE HEIGHT OF A CHARACTER IN (REAL NUMBER) INCHES.
C
C             CHARACTERS FROM THE BI-OCTAL EQUIVALENCE TABLE
```

```
C              ARE 4/7 AS WIDE AS THEY ARE HIGH.  THE SPACE
C              BETWEEN CHARACTERS IS 2/7 THAT OF THEIR HEIGHT.
C              THUS, THE TOTAL SPACE REQUIRED FOR N CHARACTERS
C              EQUALS (6/7)*(H)*(N).
C              AS THE CHARACTERS ARE STORED IN A 7 BY 4 MATRIX,
C              AN INTEGER MULTIPLE OF .07 INCHES GIVES THE BEST
C              RESOLUTION.
C
C    TEXT      IS THE MESSAGE USED IF NCHAR IS POSITIVE OR ZERO
C              (A HOLLERITH CONSTANT -- NH MESSAGE).  OR
C              IS ONE SYMBOL TAKEN FROM THE INTEGER EQUIVALENCE
C              TABLE IF NCHAR IS NEGATIVE. (SEE BELOW)
C
C    ANGLE     IS THE ANGLE AT WHICH THE LINE OF CHARACTERS IS DRAWN
C              IN DEGREES
C
C    NCHAR>0 GIVES THE INTEGER NUMBER OF CHARACTERS IN TEXT TO BE
C              WRITTEN
C        =0  WRITES CHARACTERS IN TEXT UNTIL A 0 CHARACTER IS
C              ENCOUNTERED
C        <0  ONLY ONE CHARACTER IS PRINTED, THE CHARACTER BEING
C              TAKEN FROM THE INTEGER EQUIVALENCE SYMBOL TABLE.
C
C    THE FOLLOWING INTEGER EQUIVALENCES ARE USED
C              INTEGER  3 DRAWS A +
C              INTEGER 10 DRAWS A *
C              INTEGER 15 DRAWS A -
C              INTEGER 16 DRAWS A VERTICAL LINE
C              INTEGER 20 DRAWS AN ARROW POINTING TO THE RIGHT
C              INTEGER 26 DRAWS AN O
C
C    PLOT
C    SUBROUTINE TO MOVE PEN ON PLOTTER.
C
C    PURPOSE
C
C    A) CREATE AN ORIGIN
C    B) POSITION THE PEN AND DO THE DRAWING
C    C) TERMINATE THE USE OF THE PLOT PACKAGE.
C    PLOT IS CALLED BY ALL ROUTINES THAT DO GRAPHIC WRITING.
C
C    USAGE
C
C    CALL PLOT(X,Y,IPEN)
C
C    X,Y       THE PEN IS MOVED FROM ITS PRESENT COORDINATES TO
C              THE COORDINATES (X,Y) RELATIVE TO THE CURRENT
C              ORIGIN.  X AND Y ARE REAL NUMBERS MEASURED IN INCHES.
C
C    IPEN=1  WHILE MOVING TO (X,Y) THE PEN REMAINS ON OR OFF THE
C              PAPER, AS BEFORE BEING CALLED.
C        =2  THE PEN MARKS THE PAPER WHILE MOVING FROM ITS
C              PRESENT POSITION TO (X,Y)
C        =3  THE PEN DOES NOT MARK THE PAPER WHILE MOVING FROM
C              ITS PRESENT POSITION TO (X,Y)
C    =-1,-2,-3 THE PEN IS MOVED RESPECTIVELY AS FOR +1,+2, OR +3
C              MOREOVER, THE FINAL POSITION OF THE PEN (X,Y)
C              BECOMES THE NEW ORIGIN (0.,0.).
C        =999  TERMINATES THE PLOT FILE.  THE USER MUST CALL THIS
```

```
C          AT THE END OF THE PROGRAM IF THE GRAPHIC OUTPUT
C          IS NOT TO BE DESTROYED.


EOF
```

Lecture Notes in Economics and Mathematical Systems